Praise for *108 Mystics*

"Carl McColman offers an inspiring introduction to a broad range of 108 Western Christian mystics, helpfully divided into nine different kinds of mystics. The book is written in lucid, nonacademic language that allows it to be accessible to a wide range of people."

—Tilden Edwards, author of *Living in the Presence*

"I used to carry around Evelyn Underhill's classic, *Mysticism*. My copy of Bernard McGinn's anthology is marked on every page. But now, Carl McColman's *108 Mystics* will be my go-to guide."

—Jon M. Sweeney, author of *The Enthusiast: How the Best Friend of Francis of Assisi Almost Destroyed What He Started*

"How blessed we are to have this book! I have begun my morning sit lately by reading here from another ancestor in the ways of faith, hope, and love. Carl McColman not only broadens our notion of mysticism, but in rather simple format, also deepens it, and thus invites every Christian on the same beloved path."

—Fr. Richard Rohr, OFM, Center for Action and Contemplation

"This useful and engaging book is, as the author says, a kind of "speed-dating" introduction to the world of Christian mystics. It's of real value both for beginners and for more experienced readers, who may have overlooked some of the great mystics of the past."

—Richard Smoley, author of *Inner Christianity: A Guide to the Esoteric Tradition*

"A treasure trove of the Christian mystics—seers, saints and sages—presented in all their rich diversity and offered as mentors to guide the contemporary Christian toward an encounter with the presence of God."

—Dana Greene, author of *Evelyn Underhill: Artist of the Infinite Life* and *Denise Levertov: A Poet's Life*

"A great gift of a distillation of 108 wise and worthy guides on the mystical way, each entry offering a spark for further exploration."

—Christine Valters Paintner, PhD, author of nine books on the spiritual life including *Illuminating the Way: Embracing the Wisdom of Monks and Mystics*

"We live to feel alive. We need to know love and joy. And I feel this book could help safeguard—and encourage—many tender, precious unfurling wings."

—Daniel Ladinsky, bestselling author of *The Gift* and *Love Poems from God*

"*108 Mystics* is a delightful spiritual banquet, a real feast, giving us a taste of the many mystics throughout time who can serve as our teachers and companions."

—Colette Lafia, author of *Seeking Surrender: How my Friendship with a Trappist Monk Taught me to Trust and Embrace Life*

"Carl McColman's wise and gentle primer has introduced me to many mystics I've never heard of, as well as renewed my acquaintance with some favorites like Julian of Norwich, Meister Eckhart, and Richard Rohr. This book brings mystics down to earth even while bringing readers that much closer to heaven. I will be turning to it many times in the coming years."

—Jana Riess, author of *Flunking Sainthood*

"Drawing together an array of colorful visionaries and sublime poets, this book is an elegant guide to the essence of those awakened souls who transcend religiosity while simultaneously opening our hearts to the love of their Master, Christ."

—Mirabai Starr, translator of *The Showings of Julian of Norwich* and author of *God of Love: A Guide to the Heart of Judaism, Christianity and Islam* and *Caravan of No Despair: A Memoir of Loss and Transformation*

"The genius of this book lies in its ability to introduce the reader to the heart of the mystics through tiny, sparkling jewels of their writings."

—Margaret Benefiel, author of *Soul at Work* and *The Soul of a Leader*

"With exceptional clarity Carl McColman snaps together words which lead us into the breadth, diversity, and depth of the Christian contemplative tradition. This book makes clear the fundamental distinction between mysticism and extraordinary phenomena. For this, I, for one, offer a deep bow of gratitude."

—Brother Elias Marechal, OCSO, Trappist monk and author of *Tears of an Innocent God*

"Christianity is a vast sea of wisdom, and yet most of us are content only to skim the surface. Carl McColman's introduction to the Christian mystics invites us to dive deep and discover a Christianity most of us have never even imagined."

—Rabbi Rami Shapiro, author of *Perennial Wisdom for the Spiritually Independent*

108 MYSTICS
THE ESSENTIAL GUIDE TO SEERS, SAINTS AND SAGES

Carl McColman

HAY HOUSE

Carlsbad, California • New York City • London
Sydney • Johannesburg • Vancouver • New Delhi

First published and distributed in the United Kingdom by:
Hay House UK Ltd, Astley House, 33 Notting Hill Gate, London W11 3JQ
Tel: +44 (0)20 3675 2450; Fax: +44 (0)20 3675 2451; www.hayhouse.co.uk

First published and distributed in the United States of America by:
Hampton Roads Publishing Company, Inc., Charlottesville, VA 22906
Published in the United States of America under the title *Christian Mystics: 108 Seers, Saints, and Sages*

Published and distributed in Australia by:
Hay House Australia Ltd, 18/36 Ralph St, Alexandria NSW 2015
Tel: (61) 2 9669 4299; Fax: (61) 2 9669 4144; www.hayhouse.com.au

Published and distributed in the Republic of South Africa by:
Hay House SA (Pty) Ltd, PO Box 990, Witkoppen 2068
info@hayhouse.co.za; www.hayhouse.co.za

Published and distributed in India by:
Hay House Publishers India, Muskaan Complex, Plot No.3, B-2,
Vasant Kunj, New Delhi 110 070
Tel: (91) 11 4176 1620; Fax: (91) 11 4176 1630; www.hayhouse.co.in

Copyright © 2016 by Carl McColman

The moral rights of the author have been asserted.

Interior by Howie Severson; Typeset in Warnock Pro

The information given in this book should not be treated as a substitute for professional medical advice; always consult a medical practitioner. Any use of information in this book is at the reader's discretion and risk. Neither the author nor the publisher can be held responsible for any loss, claim or damage arising out of the use, or misuse, of the suggestions made, the failure to take medical advice or for any material on third party websites.

A catalogue record for this book is available from the British Library.

ISBN: 978-1-78180-841-2

Printed and bound by CPI Group (UK) Ltd, Croydon, CR0 4YY

For all the mystics,

and for all who have been inspired

by their silence and their words.

Contents

Introduction

One day, I spoke with a teacher, for just a minute. It changed my life.

Mrs. Smith taught eighth grade English. I, being an introvert, rarely spoke up in her (or any other) class. One day, after returning a writing assignment to students, Mrs. Smith asked me to stay after class for a moment. It made me anxious, because in my mind the only reason a teacher would detain me was because I had done something so terribly wrong that the punishment had to be meted out in utmost secrecy.

Mrs. Smith did not ask me to linger after the bell to scold me, though, but to praise me.

"Carl, do you like to write?"

"Well, yes, ma'am," I said nervously, not bearing to look her in the eye.

"Because you write very well," she said. "And if you enjoy it, then I think it's something you should pursue."

"Yes, ma'am," I replied, and if I were paying attention to my Southern manners, I probably added, "Thank you, ma'am."

"That's all, Carl," she said. "I just want to encourage you."

That's all indeed—a brief word of inspiration. But for an introverted, socially awkward geek like me, it proved momentous. To have my teacher pull me aside, praise me, and encourage me—that made all the difference in the world.

Four decades have passed, and now I'm the teacher—I teach writing to adult learners. And I'm a full-time professional writer with a blog and numerous books to my credit. And I still talk about Mrs. Smith because of that one little conversation forty years ago that helped me find the initial burst of confidence to follow this particular dream.

I suspect I'm not the only person to have been inspired by a teacher this way. You may have your own Mrs. Smith in your background, too. Teachers matter, more than we give them credit for. A word of insight, a moment of praise, a challenge, a suggestion for further study—these kinds of encounters form the heart of teaching and can make a life-changing world of difference for the student who is ready to receive such guidance. A teacher is not ultimately *responsible* for the successes (or failures) that any one student may achieve. But how the teacher may shape, or guide, or inspire, or encourage the student—such an impact can be huge and needs to be celebrated.

Sadly, we don't celebrate teachers in our society. We say disparaging things like "Those who can't do, teach," implying that teachers are somehow the also-rans in life, second-tier wannabes who can't quite measure up to the real stars of business, politics, sports, or the arts. We blame teachers for how undisciplined our children may be, or for their falling test scores. And perhaps most damning of all, we celebrate the high school dropouts and never-went-to-college types who become wildly successful in their fields, assuming that this somehow proves that teachers (and education) are really not very necessary at all. "I'll never let schooling get in the way of my education," as one smart aleck once told me.

Nowhere is our societal rejection of teachers more evident than in terms of spirituality. "No guru, no method, no teacher!" proclaimed the musician Van Morrison. "Don't tell me what to believe" is the rallying cry for today's spiritually independent seeker, who goes on to say, "I don't need anyone to teach me, or anyone to guide me, no priest to absolve me or to bless me." We live in a culture that idolizes individualism and freedom—so who needs a teacher that might get in the way of our do-it-yourself spirituality?

But let's think this through. If a middle school language arts teacher just doing her job can make such an impact on a teenager's life, then maybe teachers—even *spiritual* teachers—matter more than we care to admit.

If the IRS accused you of fraud, would you hire an attorney who never bothered to go to law school or take the bar exam? Or if you needed to have your appendix removed, would you seek out just anyone who claimed to be a surgeon, with no concern for whether he or she was a medical school graduate and a licensed physician? Of course not. To be a professional requires years of training and study, and a mastery of knowledge and skill that is required for accreditation.

Here's my question: We understand that solving the mundane problems of life requires the assistance of someone with the knowledge and expertise to guide and help us. Doesn't it make sense that our hearts and souls, likewise, deserve the care and support of *spiritual* masters?

"No man is an island," pointed out John Donne. Even though we live in a Lone Ranger society where the individual is king (or queen), in reality we all need and depend on one another. This is just as true when it comes to spirituality as to any other aspect of life.

My point is very simple: we need good spiritual teachers. We all do. This is true even if you consider yourself to be spiritual but not religious, or spiritually independent. If we are serious about nurturing our interior lives to our fullest potential, we need companions to show us the way as surely as a mountain climber making a first attempt to scale Mount Everest needs a skilled Sherpa to lead the expedition.

This is where the great mystics come in.

The mystics are our masters, our teachers, our guides. Granted, we remain responsible for our own spiritual lives. But their insight, guidance, inspiration, and encouragement can help us go farther than we ever dreamed possible.

Mystic, *mystical*, and *mysticism* are difficult and challenging words, with vague, abstract, and sometimes directly contradictory meanings. Evelyn Underhill, the renowned British scholar of Christian spirituality, wrote about this a century ago in her classic book *Practical Mysticism*:

> *The genuine inquirer will find before long a number of self-appointed apostles who are eager to answer his question in many strange and inconsistent ways . . . He will learn that mysticism is a philosophy, an illusion, a kind of religion, a disease; that it means having visions, performing conjuring tricks, leading an idle, dreamy, and selfish life, neglecting*

one's business, wallowing in vague spiritual emotions, and
being "in tune with the infinite." He will discover that it eman-
cipates him from all dogmas—sometimes from all morality—
and at the same time that it is very superstitious . . . At the end
of a prolonged course of lectures, sermons, tea-parties, and
talks with earnest persons, the inquirer is still heard saying—
too often in tones of exasperation—"What is mysticism?"[1]

At the risk of being just one more "self-appointed apostle,"
here's my understanding of what makes someone a mystic. The
Greek root for *mystic* and *mysticism* is *mueo*, which means to
shut or to close, as in shutting one's mouth or closing one's eyes.
It comes from the pagan mystery religions and originally suggested an initiate—someone who had been initiated into the
spiritual mysteries, who had ritually received the secret knowledge or power of whichever god or goddess the particular religion revered. Once a person was initiated, he or she made a
solemn promise never to divulge the secrets to outsiders. So
the "shutting" or "closing" quality of *mueo* implied keeping the
secrets or mysteries hidden, locked away in the heart or mind.

The writers of the New Testament adapted this language for
Christian purposes. Some historians believe Christianity itself
qualified as a type of mystery religion—after all, only baptized
Christians could take communion or even participate in the
communion liturgy. To this day, what Catholics and Protestants
call sacraments are referred to as *mysteries* by the Eastern
Orthodox Church—so baptism, communion, confirmation, and
so forth are "mysteries" by which new Christians are initiated
into the Body of Christ.

But even if Christianity originally maintained a veil of secrecy over its mystical rites, by the fourth century, when Christianity became a legal, accepted religion in the Roman Empire, this notion of holding secret knowledge or power was no longer part of its culture. Among Christians, the idea of *mystery* referred not so much to what is *secret* as to what is *hidden*. And topping the list of hidden things is God himself: as the prophet Isaiah wrote, "Truly, you are a God who hides himself" (Isaiah 45:15). Meanwhile, Jesus, the Son of God, represented the hidden things of God made manifest—and not only in Christ himself, but also in his followers, who were said to be part of his "body." So *mystery* in Christianity involves the hidden things of God made manifest, or revealed, in the hearts and minds and spirituality of those who love God and follow Christ.

In every generation, in every century of the Christian era, men and women have existed who have exemplified this spirituality of manifesting the presence of God, the wisdom and power of God, the love and mercy of God, in their own lives, in their hearts and minds. On an external level, such people became renowned as saints—from the Latin word *sanctus*, meaning holy or consecrated. In the Western church especially, holiness came to be understood primarily in a moralistic sense: a holy person, or a saint, was someone who embodied extraordinary sanctity or virtue (qualities such as faith, hope, love, courage, justice, temperance, and prudence). So a saint is essentially an awesomely *good* person. And Christianity, especially in terms of the Catholic and Orthodox churches, developed a process for officially recognizing (canonizing) the saints.

There is no similar process for canonizing or officially recognizing a mystic. While the idea of sainthood came to be associated with almost supernatural levels of goodness, mystics encountered and embodied the presence of God in profound and life-changing ways. And the mystics (at least the ones we know about) shared their encounters with God through poetry, confessional or autobiographical writing, philosophy, theology, and spiritual teaching. The language of the mystics is often deeply beautiful, expressing love of God, communion with God, even union with God (which sometimes got some mystics in trouble with the less spiritually inclined authorities in the Church).

Of course, many mystics have also been recognized as saints, and some authors suggest that it is impossible to be a saint without also being a mystic.[2] But the two words have distinct meanings, at least in popular usage: a saint is someone who is good and holy, while a mystic is someone who knows God, who embodies the presence of God, and whose life has been transfigured by this divine presence. Put even more briefly, saints embody *goodness* while mystics embody *love*.

There's plenty of overlap here. But this is one way to understand the distinction.

What makes someone a mystic is less about a top-down kind of approval and more about an organic, broad-based recognition on the part of the people whose lives have been touched. In other words (and this brings us back to Mrs. Smith), mystics *teach* us how to find God, and a great mystic is someone who has been recognized as doing this particularly well.

The first Christian mystics appear in the Bible, figures like John the Evangelist and Paul of Tarsus. But mysticism didn't end when the Bible was written. Great mystics appear in every century of Christian history. By the fourth and fifth centuries, when Christianity became socially acceptable in the cities of the Roman Empire, remote wilderness locations like the deserts of Egypt and Palestine or the forests of Ireland became home to many saints and mystics. Out of the deserts came the first monasteries, intentional communities of Christians who sought to give their entire lives to God. As this movement caught on throughout the Christian world, it became a natural home for great mystics and visionaries; and, indeed, nearly all of the great mystics between the fifth and the fifteenth centuries lived as monks or nuns. But with the dawn of the modern era—and the social changes such as the Renaissance and the Reformation in particular—monasteries became less central to Catholic Christianity and were largely rejected by the Protestant churches, so in recent centuries more mystics have emerged who did not live in a cloister. By the twentieth century, several important figures, such as Evelyn Underhill and Karl Rahner, began to insist that mysticism was not just a special quality for the "elite" Christians found in abbeys or convents, but rather everyone is meant to be a mystic. Indeed, Rahner, widely recognized as one of the greatest of twentieth-century theologians, famously remarked that "the Christian of the future will be a mystic or . . . will not exist at all."[3]

Those are challenging words, especially for Christians who may not think of themselves as mystics at all—which is probably most Christians. But here is a more inspirational perspective from the Carmelite friar William McNamara: "the mystic is not a special kind of person; each person is a special kind of mystic."[4]

Rahner's point is important, but it needs to be framed this way: in order for Christianity to survive, all Christians need to discover the mystical heartbeat that is already alive in the center of our tradition—and our souls. Put another way, mysticism is not something we achieve; it is something we receive.

But how do we discover the mystical heartbeat hidden deep within us? How do we find out what "special kind of mystic" we are called to be? Certainly, the ultimate guide to union with God can only be God himself. But God is assisted in this task by the wisdom and the writings of the great mystics throughout history.

Not all mystics are writers, of course. But the ones who made the effort to record their life stories, their insights, their wisdom, their poetry and teachings, are the ones who have left behind "lessons," so to speak, in the school for the love of God. Saint Benedict, who wrote a holy rule for monks, describes a monastery as a "school of the Lord's service." Later generations of monks, especially Cistercian monks,[5] expanded on this idea and saw the spiritual life as a "school of charity" or school of love.

This brings us back to talking about teachers. We who seek to grow spiritually are like children ushered off to school for their education and personal growth. God is the principal or headmaster, and the saints and mystics are the various teachers and coaches who will interact with us on a day-to-day basis. Our goal, therefore, is to learn: to learn the curriculum of a truly spiritual life, a curriculum grounded in love, mercy, tenderness, compassion, forgiveness, hope, trust, simplicity, silence, peace, and joy. To embody union with God is to discover these beautiful characteristics emerging from within and slowly transfiguring us to remake us in the very image and likeness of God himself.

One of the interesting qualities of the mystics is that they are hardly uniform. Mystics come in a variety of shapes and sizes. Some of them are profound seers who behold supernatural visions or perhaps just profound intuitive insights, with such heavenly graces changing them in profound and loving ways. Others are natural-born storytellers whose autobiographical writings are filled with lessons and principles that can help anyone who seeks to grow closer to God. Many mystics are poets, masters of their language who create with words stirring and enlightening windows into divine grace. Others are lovers who relate to God primarily through passion and intimacy, or wisdom keepers who plumb the mysteries of their minds to find philosophical and theological truths about God. Some are saints, as we have already said, but others are "heretics"—holy mischief-makers who break the rules and color outside the lines, inviting their readers to find entirely new ways of relating to God. Others are what I call "soul friends" from an old Irish word that means just that: loving companions who gently share their knowledge and care with anyone who seeks to follow in their spiritual footsteps. And finally, some mystics are truly "unitives" who embody non-dual union with God in such a mind-blowing and life-altering way that their consciousness is expanded—to the point where the lines separating God from creation seem to fall away.

Some mystics are passionate, fiery, and dramatic. Others are measured, thoughtful, and subtle. Some encounter God's presence in vivid ways; others find in God a profound mystery, infused with darkness, absence, and unknowing. Some are profoundly sorry for their sins, while others rejoice in God's overwhelming mercy. William McNamara is right: every mystic is a unique expression of what it means to touch the presence of God, and it's nearly impossible to make any kind of categorical statement that could apply to them all. So it's best not even to bother trying.

Just because someone is a mystic (or a saint) does not therefore mean that everything they wrote or taught will necessarily be helpful to you. If everyone is a different kind of mystic (which I believe to be true), then it follows that not every mystic will have something useful to say to every other kind of mystic (or aspiring mystic). Many of the most renowned mystics can come across as dualistic, judgmental, hostile to the human body or sexuality, sexist, chauvinistic, anti-Semitic, homophobic, or otherwise rigid or narrow in their thinking. Which only stands to reason, since they lived in eras where such limiting ways of seeing the world were the norm.

Why, then, would we even bother to read such persons, let alone revere them as spiritual teachers? One way to answer this question comes from a living contemplative, Richard Rohr, writing about the challenges of reading the writings of some of the earliest Christian spiritual masters, the desert fathers and mothers:

> *You might pick up one of the collections of their "sayings" and, after reading the first few pages, throw it out as unreal, dualistic, naive, and pre-rational—all of which, I think, would be largely true. The desert mystics represent a level of human consciousness and historical development that we*

have collectively moved far beyond. And yet we, or at least I, still admire and even need them! . . . You can be a high level thinker and be quite astute about psychology, theology, history, or philosophy . . . but you do it all from a perspective of individualism and arrogance . . . Conversely, you could be quite unified within and with others, in a high state of loving consciousness, but be poorly informed, lacking in exposure and education to helpful and informative knowledge.[6]

In other words: reading the mystics, like reading the Bible, means recognizing that they may be bound by cultural, social, or historical limitations *even while they speak about extraordinary or supernatural encounters with God.* Someone writing four hundred or a thousand years ago will naturally display limitations based on their time and place in history. (In a similar way, those who live centuries in the future will find today's writing limited and rigid as well!) When we read the mystics, we need to read with discernment, good judgment, and common sense, looking for the jewels of wisdom embedded in their words and forgiving them for the natural limitations in their thought and awareness due to the time in which they wrote.

In introducing you to the mystics, I am approaching them not chronologically but thematically. Other writers, such as Evelyn Underhill, Hilda Graef, and Ursula King,[7] have done a wonderful job telling the story of the Christian mystics chronologically. While that makes good history, it's not necessarily the most spiritually helpful way to approach our topic. The mystics represent such a wide variety of perspectives, theologies, and approaches to intimacy with God that it's important to recognize this diversity up front, if for no other reason than to remember that they will not all speak to us in the same way. Just as different people have different personalities, so too do the mystics have their own "personality types," meaning that some will appeal to us more than others. Perhaps you are more drawn to the philosophers and wisdom keepers, mystics whose writings are erudite and intellectual, but your best friend prefers the lovers, who tend to approach God in a more intuitive, fiery, heart-centered way. As Pete the Cat would say, "It's all good!" It *is* all good, and it's also to be expected that everyone will more naturally bond with some mystics, but not all. And every one of us will have our own favorites.

You can read this book straight through to get an overview of the great mystics and their various ways of encountering God. Or, if you already have a favorite mystic or two, you can look them up and see who else embodies a similar approach to the ultimate mystery. Or you can simply dive in wherever, letting chance introduce you to someone new, whether from the twelfth century or the twentieth, who stands in our great tradition of humble men and women who've given all to God. Mysticism is an adventure, and the mystics are our guides.

The Nine Categories

Visionaries • Confessors • Lovers • Poets • Saints
Heretics • Wisdom Keepers • Soul Friends • Unitives

Visionaries

1. Adrienne von Speyr
2. Birgitta of Sweden
3. Elisabeth of Schönau
4. Gemma Galgani
5. George MacDonald
6. Hildegard of Bingen
7. Julian of Norwich
8. Maria Maddalena de' Pazzi
9. Marie of the Incarnation
10. Mechtilde of Hackeborn
11. Paul of Tarsus
12. Teresa of Ávila

7. John Wesley
8. Margery Kempe
9. Maximus the Confessor
10. Phoebe Palmer
11. Thérèse of Lisieux
12. The author of *The Way of a Pilgrim*

Confessors

1. Angela of Foligno
2. Augustine of Hippo
3. Dag Hammarskjöld
4. George Fox
5. Henry Suso
6. Ignatius of Loyola

Lovers

1. Beatrice of Nazareth
2. Bernard of Clairvaux
3. Blaise Pascal
4. Catherine of Siena
5. Elizabeth of the Trinity
6. Gertrude the Great
7. Hadewijch
8. John the Evangelist
9. Maria Faustina Kowalska
10. Mechthild of Magdeburg
11. Symeon the New Theologian
12. William of St.-Thierry

Poets

1. Angelus Silesius
2. C. S. Lewis
3. Caryll Houselander
4. Coventry Patmore
5. Ephrem the Syrian
6. Evelyn Underhill
7. George Herbert
8. Jacopone da Todi
9. John Donne
10. John of the Cross
11. Ramon Llull
12. Thomas Traherne

Heretics

1. Clement of Alexandria
2. Evagrius Ponticus
3. François Fénelon
4. Jakob Boehme
5. Jeanne Guyon
6. John Scotus Eriugena
7. Marguerite Porete
8. Meister Eckhart
9. Origen
10. Pierre Teilhard de Chardin
11. Simone Weil
12. Thomas Merton

Saints

1. Saint Benedict of Nursia
2. Saint Catherine of Genoa
3. Saint Edith Stein
4. Saint Francis de Sales
5. Saint Francis of Assisi
6. Saint Gregory of Narek
7. Saint Gregory of Nyssa
8. Saint Isaac the Syrian
9. Saint John Climacus
10. Saint Nicodemus of the Holy Mountain
11. Saint Thomas Aquinas
12. Saint Teresa of Calcutta

Wisdom Keepers

1. Albertus Magnus
2. Bernard Lonergan
3. Bonaventure
4. Francisco de Osuna
5. Gregory Palamas
6. Johannes Tauler
7. Karl Rahner
8. Nicholas of Cusa
9. Pseudo-Dionysius
10. Raimon Panikkar
11. Richard of St. Victor
12. William Law

Soul Friends

1. Aelred of Rievaulx
2. Brother Lawrence
3. Friedrich von Hügel
4. Howard Thurman
5. Jean-Pierre de Caussade
6. John Cassian
7. Kenneth Leech
8. Rufus Jones
9. Thomas R. Kelly
10. Walter Hilton
11. The author of *The Cloud of Unknowing*
12. The author of *Theologia Germanica*

Unitives

1. Abhishiktananda
2. Anthony de Mello
3. Bede Griffiths
4. Bruno Barnhart
5. Gerald G. May
6. John O'Donohue
7. John Ruusbroec
8. Richard Rohr
9. Sara Grant
10. Thomas Keating
11. Wayne Teasdale
12. Willigis Jäger

Chapter 1

Visionaries

"Visions and voices are such frequent accompaniments of the mystic life, that they cannot be ignored,"[1] wrote Evelyn Underhill in 1911. Writing a book in which she was attempting to defend mysticism from its skeptical or rationalist critics, she makes this admission rather begrudgingly. And yet, she's right. Visionary phenomena may be on the fringe of religion as a whole, but it is much more common in the lives of at least some mystics.

Not all mystics, Christian or otherwise, are visionaries, and I suppose one could also say that not all visionaries truly are mystics. One could have visions simply as a result of mental illness or an overactive imagination. For that matter, many mystics would say that visions could just as easily come from the devil as from an angel or God. In other words, having a vision in itself means very little. To discern that a vision is truly mystical (i.e., it comes from God) requires careful and prayerful consideration. Teresa of Ávila (whom you will meet shortly) believed that visions or other extraordinary phenomena mattered far less than the humble matter of loving and serving one's neighbors—that was the mark of truly being touched by God.

Visions, like the mystics who have them, come in many different forms. For some, like Julian of Norwich, a visionary encounter is truly singular and extraordinary: Julian had sixteen visions in a single twenty-four-hour period, and if she ever had another one, she doesn't say. On the other hand, Hildegard of Bingen began to have visions while still a young girl, and she proceeded to fill several books with accounts of her many visions that she continued to receive throughout her long life (she lived to be eighty-one, a remarkable feat in the twelfth century).

Visions can be spiritual, intellectual, or bodily in nature, meaning that they might come in the midst of a dream, an imaginal encounter with heaven, or a can-you-believe-it encounter with non-ordinary reality. Visions also have a wide variety of content: most are filled with typical spiritual imagery (God, Jesus, Mary, angels), but others seem to be surprisingly creative or original (Hildegard saw *viriditas*, a kind of spiritual energy flowing through all creation that seems very much like the Force from *Star Wars*).

What are we to make of mystical visions? Like Jesus walking on water, such phenomena may seem hard to swallow—it's too easy in our skeptical age to dismiss such incidents as little more than psychological drama. Evelyn Underhill, following a long tradition of Christian mystics, felt that visions themselves should not be taken too seriously; what matters is the spirituality of the visionary. I think this is a helpful rule of thumb.

A Trappist monk read an early draft of this book and suggested that I not put visionaries at the beginning. He was concerned that it could give the impression that supernatural phenomena are more important to mysticism than they truly are. I see it the other way around: I'm leading off with visionaries precisely because, of all the characteristics of mysticism—beholding God's presence, cultivating a compassionate heart, maintaining a daily practice of prayer or meditation, and so forth—having visions is actually the *least* important. Even though some visionaries (like Teresa of Ávila) are among the greatest of mystics, when it comes to all the various qualities of the mystics, well, we're starting at the bottom and working our way up.

Enjoy the stories of the visionaries in the pages to come, but remember the wisdom of Julian of Norwich, who insisted that the point behind extraordinary graces is only to grow in the love of God. Someone who has never had a vision but who loved God better than Julian was, to her, further along the path.

Adrienne von Speyr (1902–1967)

Adrienne von Speyr, a mystic in the most skeptical of ages, the twentieth century, is remarkable not only for her spiritual genius but also because she was a renowned physician. Furthermore, she is noteworthy for her close friendship with one of the great theologians of her time, the Swiss priest Hans Urs von Balthasar. Like many visionaries, her extraordinary encounters with angels or saints began in childhood. She had a vision of Saint Ignatius of Loyola when she was six years old; nine years later she saw the Virgin Mary, surrounded by angels and saints.

After becoming the first woman in Switzerland licensed to practice medicine, she met von Balthasar in 1940 and shortly thereafter entered the Catholic Church. Although she struggled with health issues, she continued to work as a doctor until 1954. At this time she also began dictating her prolific, visionary mystical writings to von Balthasar, eventually completing over twenty-five books, including devotional commentaries on scripture, meditations on Mary and the saints, and reflections on topics such as prayer and contemplation. Even her writing has a "visionary" quality to it, since she dictated from a state of deep contemplative absorption into the presence of God. Von Balthasar once noted that "a veritable cataract of mystical graces poured over Adrienne in a seemingly chaotic storm that whirled her in all directions at once. Graces in prayer above all: she was transported beyond all vocal prayer or self-directed meditation in order to be set down somewhere after an indeterminate time with new understanding, new love and new resolutions."[2]

"God relates to the world, not just in speech, but also in silence,"[3] writes von Speyr in her book *The Boundless God*, setting forth a theme we will see again and again: that the heart of mysticism and contemplation is silence; not just human silence, but indeed a heavenly silence: the silence of God.

Recommended Reading

The Boundless God by Adrienne von Speyr, translated by Helena M. Tomko (San Francisco: Ignatius Press, 2004).

Birgitta of Sweden (ca. 1303–1373)

Birgitta of Sweden was widely renowned as a visionary during her lifetime and shortly after; she was canonized as a saint in

1391, less than twenty years after her death. Born of a wealthy Swedish family, she married young and gave birth to eight children—one of whom, Catherine, became friends with another great mystic, Catherine of Siena. After Birgitta's husband died, she founded a religious order and moved to Rome.

A visionary since childhood, her "celestial revelations" included scenes from the life of Christ, including the nativity and the crucifixion. She became associated with a popular medieval devotional practice of saying certain prayers for each wound that Christ suffered during his passion; in a vision, Christ told Birgitta that he'd received a total of 5,480 such wounds. Her visions are rich with detail, including many questions posed to Christ or Mary about religious or philosophical matters, each answered patiently. For example, when asked why spiritual people still commit sins, Christ replied, "I, God, am charity; and where I am, there is freedom. Therefore he who accepts my Spirit has the ability to sin if he wishes, because every human being has free will."[4]

Recommended Reading

Birgitta of Sweden: Life and Selected Revelations, edited by Marguerite Tjader Harris, translated by Albert Ryle Kezel (New York: Paulist Press, 1990).

Elisabeth of Schönau (1129–1164)

Elisabeth of Schönau made her profession as a Benedictine nun in 1147 and began to receive visions in 1152, when she was only twenty-three years old. Over the remaining years of her short life (she died in her mid-thirties), she received enough visions to fill six books, along with instructions to write letters of admonition to various religious leaders of her day. Elisabeth corresponded with one of the great visionaries of her time, Hildegard of Bingen, and sent letters to many other religious figures, including the abbots of monasteries and bishops. Most of her visions consist of ordinary religious symbolism, including apparitions of the Virgin Mary, angels, the devil, and various biblical figures. She also saw scenes from biblical history. Such visions usually included some sort of exhortation, admonitions, instruction, or consolation, such as the time she saw Mary standing in "a wheel of great light." The Blessed Mother marked Elisabeth with the sign of the cross and silently communicated to her, "Do not fear, because these things [her visions, which must certainly have been awe-inspiring] will not harm you at all."[5]

Recommended Reading

Elisabeth of Schönau: The Complete Works, translated by Anne L. Clark (New York: Paulist Press, 2000).

Maria Gemma Umberta Pia Galgani (1878–1903)

Maria Gemma Umberta Pia Galgani became renowned in her day as a visionary, ecstatic, and stigmatist. An intelligent child, she contracted spinal meningitis as a young adult, only to be miraculously healed shortly before her twenty-first birthday. About this time her mystical visions began, leading to the night before the Feast of the Sacred Heart, 1899, when she went into a rapture and saw the Virgin Mary (who covered her with her cloak) and Christ—from whom flames of fire emerged, striking Gemma's hands, feet, and heart and leaving her with the stigmata. During another rapturous vision, Jesus took his crown of thorns and placed it on Gemma's head, causing her to suffer along with him.

She shared her visions with her confessor, who at first didn't believe her but eventually instructed her to keep a diary and to write her autobiography, in which she recorded numerous extraordinary events. Despite healing from meningitis, her ill health returned. She was diagnosed with tuberculosis in the fall of 1902, leading to her death on Holy Saturday the following spring, just a few weeks after her twenty-fifth birthday.

While the Catholic hierarchy was initially hesitant to accept her story (skeptics dismissed her as suffering from a mental illness), by 1940 the Church declared her a saint.

Gemma Galgani insisted that she spoke to her guardian angel, Jesus, Mary, and various saints. Her writings seem very simple and perhaps even naive, especially when compared to the philosophical masterworks of other, more educated mystics. But what shines through is a profound love for God, sorrow for her sins, and a tremendous desire to be worthy of the unconditional love that she encountered through her visions and ecstasies.

Recommended Reading

The Saint Gemma Galgani Collection by Gemma Galgani (London: Catholic Way Publishing, 2013).

George MacDonald (1824–1905)

George MacDonald, a minister of the Church of Scotland, found a higher calling as a writer of fiction, nonfiction, and poetry. Much of his fiction is imbued with fantasy and wonder, visionary literature that inspired some of the great writers of the twentieth century, including J. R. R. Tolkien, Madeleine L'Engle, and especially C. S. Lewis, who called MacDonald his "master." Lewis edited an anthology of excerpts from MacDonald's works and paid homage to this Scottish mystic by having him appear as a character in Lewis's dream-novel about hell and heaven, *The Great Divorce.*

MacDonald is not a visionary in the traditional sense of someone who receives extraordinary, ecstatic encounters with the Divine. Rather, his visionary genius manifested in creativity—through his ability to write stories about magical worlds filled with a sense of numinous mystery. Even MacDonald's sermons and other nonfiction writing shimmers with mystical insight. Take, for example, this excerpt from MacDonald's *Unspoken Sermons,* "The New Name":

> *Each of us is a distinct flower or tree in the spiritual garden of God,—precious, each for his own sake, in the eyes of him who is even now making us,—each of us watered and shone upon and filled with life, for the sake of his flower, his completed being, which will blossom out of him at last to the glory and pleasure of the great gardener. For each has within him a secret of the Divinity; each is growing towards the revelation of that secret to himself, and so to the full reception, according to his measure, of the divine. Every moment that he is*

*true to his true self, some new shine of the white stone breaks
on his inward eye, some fresh channel is opened upward for
the coming glory of the flower, the conscious offering of his
whole being in beauty to the Maker . . .*

*Life and action, thought and intent, are sacred. And what
an end lies before us! To have a consciousness of our own
ideal being flashed into us from the thought of God! Surely
for this may well give way all our paltry self-consciousnesses,
our self-admirations and self-worships! Surely to know what
he thinks about us will pale out of our souls all our thoughts
about ourselves! and we may well hold them loosely now, and
be ready to let them go.*[6]

In *Listening for the Heartbeat of God*, J. Philip Newell writes
about the Celtic wisdom at the heart of MacDonald's visionary
writing:

*MacDonald was reared on the old Celtic stories and legends
of the West and in time allowed these to shape the spirituality that he was to express through his fictional works. Many
of his stories have been read particularly by the young, but
he claimed to write for the "childlike," both young and old,
that is, for those who see with the eyes of a child. His works
of the imagination strove to recover the inner faculty of sight
whereby God may be seen within us, among us and in all the
things of creation.*[7]

Is there a relationship between the imagination (such as
inspired writers like MacDonald or, for that matter, C. S. Lewis)
and mystical vision (such as fueled the mystical wisdom of a

Birgitta of Sweden or Elizabeth of Schönau)? I believe so—not to reduce mystical visions to mere imagination, but to recognize that at its most exalted, the human imagination might usher us to the very threshold of the divine mysteries.

Recommended Reading

Unspoken Sermons, Series I, II and III by George MacDonald (public domain Kindle edition).

Hildegard of Bingen (1098–1179)

Hildegard of Bingen stands as one of the most colorful and remarkable of mystics of any age. A Benedictine abbess, Hildegard was a Renaissance woman who lived several centuries before the Renaissance. More than just a mystic and visionary, she was also an accomplished musician, an artist (or, at least, an art director), a preacher, an herbalist, a prophet, and a respected leader in the church of her day. She lived at a time when women had no channels open to them to influence public opinion or assert their own will, and yet she managed to form the right relationships with the right people in order to ensure that her voice would be heard. As the first major woman mystic in Western Christianity, she paved the way for others who are now regarded as some of the greatest of Christian spiritual teachers: Catherine of Siena, Julian of Norwich, Teresa of Ávila, and Maria Faustina Kowalska all stand on the shoulders of this spiritual giant.

By her own admission, Hildegard was a lifelong visionary. She first encountered the *lux vivens*, or "living light," when only three years old and went on to write three books about her extraordinary revelations, the last one completed only a few years before she died. At first she made no effort to publicize her mystical visions, but in her forty-second year she received instructions to commit her story to writing. Recognizing that women did not routinely write about their spirituality, she shrewdly appealed to Bernard of Clairvaux for advice, and he in turn appealed to the Pope, who issued a written statement approving of Hildegard's work.

The visions themselves range from the luminously beautiful to the starkly terrifying. In her writings, she combines vivid descriptions of what she saw with detailed reflections on their meaning. Part of what makes Hildegard so remarkable a figure—and appealing to us today—is that she created (or instructed one of her sister nuns to create) illuminations to illustrate many of the visions. While much of the content of her seeing is predictably religious in nature, filled with the glory of God and the depiction of biblical stories, plenty of meaningful insight characterized her experiences. By providing both literary and visual records of her visions, Hildegard often made subtle contributions to an alternative way of seeing even the dogmas of the Church.

For example, one of her most remarkable visions was of the Holy Trinity: the Christian understanding of God as consisting of three persons, the Father, the Son, and the Holy Spirit. Many efforts to depict the Trinity rely on abstract symbolism, such as a triangle imposed upon a circle. The circle represents the "unity" of the Oneness of God, while the triangle with its three points symbolizes each of the distinct "persons" of the Trinity.

In contrast, Hildegard's vision of the Trinity is both strikingly original and profoundly organic. Christ stands at the center of this image, hands held up in a position of prayer or blessing, his entire figure colored a lovely sapphire blue. Surrounding Christ are concentric circles of what appear to be shimmering energy in gold and silver or white. In Hildegard's own words,

> I saw a bright light, and in this light the figure of a man the color of a sapphire, which was all blazing with a gentle glowing fire. And that bright light bathed the whole of the glowing fire, and the glowing fire bathed the bright light; and the bright light and the glowing fire poured over the whole human figure, so that the three were one light in one power of potential.[8]

The spheres of light and gold energy surrounding the Christ-figure represent the fire of the Holy Spirit and the light of the Father, embracing and upholding the Body of Christ, the Son of God incarnate in human form. With its emphasis on energy, the body, and embracing, Hildegard's vision seems strikingly feminine, in contrast to the usually strictly masculine ways in which God has been depicted in Christianity.

Hildegard also describes the Trinity using the concept of the Word (following the classic idea that Jesus is the Word of God made flesh). A spoken word consists of three elements: the meaning of the word, the breath of the person who is speaking, and the physical sound of the word as it is spoken. To Hildegard, the sound represents the Father, the meaning represents the Son, and the breath represents the Holy Spirit.[9]

Even more striking is Hildegard's perception of *viriditas*, an almost untranslatable Latin word that basically means "green power" or "life force." In traditional Christian terms, *viriditas* could be equated to the Holy Spirit, but it could just as easily be thought of as the energy of nature—the greening that emerges through plants and, by extension, all living things. Hildegard issued warnings that God would allow humans to be punished if they misused creation—a prophecy that seems particularly apt today.

Writing in the twelfth century, Hildegard's theology and values are steeped in the worldview of the medieval mind, which makes her writing somewhat challenging for the casual reader. Therefore, many people find their deepest connection to Hildegard through her music. In recent years, many of Hildegard's chants and hymns have been recorded; her compositions are strikingly melodic for medieval music and make for ethereally beautiful listening.

As a graduate student in the early 1980s, I remember browsing in a large book and music store in Georgetown when suddenly it seemed as if the entire shop was filled with an angel's song. I went to the desk and discovered that the clerk was playing a record (this was before CDs were widely available) called *A Feather on the Breath of God* by Abbess Hildegard of Bingen. The soprano, Emma Kirkby, had a voice as pure and beautiful as a fine wine. That album won the Gramophone Award in 1982 and launched an explosion of interest in the music of Hildegard. The German early music ensemble Sequentia recorded all of Hildegard's compositions, most of which were designed for use during the nuns' worship, released in a box set of eight

CDs. Other artists have taken Hildegard's compositions and set them to arrangements of electronic or new age music, giving this ancient body of mystical music a new interpretation for our time.

Unlike many other mystics, Hildegard did not write instructions on the practice of prayer or meditation. Thus, her music may be her richest contribution to spiritual seekers of our age: listening to a recording like *A Feather on the Breath of God*, it is easy to sense just how clearly Hildegard could gaze into what she called "the living light" of heaven.

Although it was a long time coming, Hildegard of Bingen's spiritual genius was finally recognized by the Catholic Church; during the pontificate of Pope Benedict XVI, she was canonized a saint and declared a Doctor (teacher) of the Church—in the year 2012, a mere 833 years after her death.

Recommended Reading

Selected Writings by Hildegard of Bingen, translated and edited by Mark Atherton (London: Penguin Books, 2001).

Recommended Listening

A Feather on the Breath of God: Sequences and Hymns by Saint Hildegard of Bingen by Gothic Voices with Emma Kirkby (London: Hyperion Records, 1982).

Julian of Norwich (1342–ca. 1412)

Julian of Norwich wrote a beautiful book about her visions, but it reveals very few details about her life; in fact, we have no idea what her real name is. The name by which she is known comes from her association with the Church of Saint Julian in the English town of Norwich, where at some point in her life she became an anchoress—a vowed solitary who lived her days devoted to prayer and meditation, confined to a cell adjoining the church.

Virtually nothing is known about her aside from what she writes in her remarkable book, but even there she reveals little about herself, preferring instead to talk about her "courteous" God. In her work, Julian recounts an amazing series of visions she had while suffering from a life-threatening illness; as she reflects on the meaning of her visions, she reveals a profound level of mystical wisdom and insight that, over six hundred years later, remains on the cutting edge of Christian theology.

Julian wrote very little—just a short treatise recounting a series of visions she had during a dramatic twenty-four-hour period in May 1373, which she probably wrote shortly after the fact, only to expand into a full-length book some twenty years later. This makes Julian the first woman to have written a book in the English language, and that fact alone gets her included in college literature anthologies.

When Julian was "thirty and one-half years old," she became sick enough that a priest was summoned to issue her last rites. While on her apparent deathbed, he held a crucifix before her face and instructed her to gaze upon Christ for comfort. When she did so, she entered a visionary, altered state of consciousness, seeing actual flowing blood on the corpus. This was the beginning of a series of vivid, profound visions or "showings"—sixteen different revelations in which Christ, Mary, heaven, and even hell and the devil were revealed to the sick woman. Shortly after this visionary episode, she recovered from her illness and subsequently wrote about her showings with poetic and vividly rendered reflections on the theological meaning of what had happened to her, centered on the lavish nature of divine love. For centuries, her writings were obscure, found only in a few convent libraries in northern Europe; the first printed edition was published in 1670, and with the revival of interest in Christian mysticism in the early twentieth century, new editions of her book were published and her popularity has steadily increased.

Her writing is earthy and lyrical and therefore a delight to read. Her visions cover a variety of vivid images: some are fairly traditionally religious, including a graphic depiction of Christ being crucified as well as the joyful celebration of the banquet in heaven. But some of her showings are more creative, such as when she saw the entire cosmos in a tiny object that could fit in the palm of her hand. Nature imagery dances throughout her writing, as she draws inspiration from herrings and hazelnuts, from raindrops to the ocean. But the heart of her showings is always the love of God, of Christ, of Mary. In describing the love she encounters, she subtly challenges the theology of her time, which tended to stress punishment for sin and God's wrath as central to the Christian faith. While Julian insists she does not want to challenge church teaching, she makes it clear that love, not anger, is at the heart of her encounter with God.

As vivid as Julian's visions were, what matters most for us today are the spiritual lessons conveyed through them. Julian's message is one of spiritual optimism and of love. She is most often quoted for saying, "All shall be well, and all shall be well, and all manner of things shall be well" (which was Christ's response to her when she wondered about why sin had to exist).

A lesser-known but equally lovely quote: "The fullness of joy is to behold God in all." Julian is also celebrated for naming both God and Christ as "mother." And while she is not the only Christian mystic who saw God as Mother as well as Father, her poetic description of God-as-Mother knows no equal. More than a cute theological ploy, she articulates a fully formed spirituality of the motherhood of God, yet always within the parameters of an orthodox appreciation of the Christian faith. In this way, Julian anticipates (by six centuries!) the best and most creative expressions of feminist Christian theology as has emerged in our time.

One of the loveliest stories from Julian's series of visions centers on her holding a tiny object no bigger than a hazelnut. When she asks God what this is, she is told, "It is everything that is made." She marvels that this thing could even continue to exist, so small and delicate it appears. She then comes to understand that this little thing exists—and continues to do so—because God loves it. "In this little thing, I saw three properties. The first is that God made it. The second is that God loves it. The third is that God keeps it." Note the Trinitarian nature of Julian's insight; indeed, Trinitarian imagery abounds throughout her writing.

Her words ring true for anyone today who intuitively grasps that God is love, and that to be intimate with God means being intimate with Love in its purest and most exalted form. God made it, God loves it, and God keeps it. This sums up Julian's optimistic, visionary theology—a theology where the love of God is expressed not in terms of law and duty, but in terms of joy and heartfelt compassion.

Recommended Reading

The Showings of Julian of Norwich: A New Translation, translated by Mirabai Starr (Charlottesville, VA: Hampton Roads, 2013).

Maria Maddalena de' Pazzi (1566–1607)

Maria Maddalena de' Pazzi as a young girl received ecstasies, raptures, and mystical revelations. Born into a noble family, she received early instruction from Jesuits, including learning how to meditate as a child. Her first mystical ecstasy occurred when she was only twelve; two years later she entered convent school and became a Carmelite nun shortly after that. She is a remarkable mystic in that her books were not written by her so much as recorded by her sisters, who attended to Maria Maddalena during her ecstasies and raptures and wrote down the mystic's oral utterances—even going so far as to document the silent pauses between her words. Maria Maddalena did not see the importance of writing down her story, and she became involved in editing her books only because her confessor insisted that she do so. Her mystical experiences ranging over a six-year period, from 1584 to 1590, fill several books.

Here's an example of one of her ecstasies—"a great transport of love"—that occurred when she was eighteen years old:

> *Then she had a marvelous vision of pure love. She saw God all pure in himself loving himself and loving the creature with a similar pure and infinite love. All of a sudden . . . she was forced to scream out loud, externally, so that she was heard by all those who were present: "Love love, oh God, you*

love the creature with a pure love, oh God of love, oh God of love."[10]

Maria Maddalena died at age forty-one. She was canonized a saint in 1669 and remains a popular saint in Italy; however, critics have also accused her of suffering from mental illness, eating disorders, and even masochism.

Recommended Reading

Maria Maddalena de' Pazzi: Selected Revelations, translated by Armando Maggi (New York: Paulist Press, 2000).

Marie of the Incarnation (1599–1672)

Marie of the Incarnation, after being widowed at age nineteen, entered the Ursuline Order of nuns in France. As an Ursuline, she received a vision calling her to emigrate to Quebec (what she knew as "New France") to help establish the Ursuline nuns in the New World. In 1639, she founded the Ursuline Monastery of Quebec, the first European-based school for girls and women in North America. She remained in Quebec for the rest of her life. Her visionary spirituality is recounted in her autobiographical book *The Relations*. "At the very moment when I recalled the divine perfections, I found myself in a state of infinity where there were neither boundaries nor limits," wrote Marie. "In this infinity, all thought was forgotten except that this immense infinity in which I am lost is my love, that he is in me and I in him, and that he alone is my riches and my treasure."[11]

Recommended Reading

Marie of the Incarnation: Selected Writings, edited by Irene Mahoney (New York: Paulist Press, 1989).

Mechtilde of Hackeborn (ca. 1241–1298)

Mechtilde of Hackeborn, one of the lesser-known women vision-aries of the Middle Ages, came from a noble family of Saxony (modern day Germany); her elder sister was the abbess of the great women's monastery of Helfta, which produced several notable mystics. Mechtilde was so drawn to monastic life that she entered a convent school at age seven and joined her sister's community a decade later. At Helfta, Mechtilde ran the convent school; among her students was Gertrude the Great.

Mechtilde's first mystical vision occurred during Communion. Christ appeared to her, took her hands, and made an imprint in her heart, like a seal in wax. He also presented his heart to her, making Mechtilde one of the first mystics to cul-tivate a devotion to the Sacred Heart. Like many other mystics, Mechtilde held great devotion for Christ's humanity, and in one vision she saw that "the smallest details of creation are reflected in the Holy Trinity by means of the humanity of Christ, because it is from the same earth that produced them that Christ drew his humanity."[12]

At age fifty, Mechtilde learned that Gertrude along with two other nuns was documenting her visions in writing; troubled by this, Mechtilde turned to Christ in prayer, who told her that he had inspired them to write down her revelations. He also instructed her that her book should be called *The Book of Spiritual Grace* since it would bring grace to so many people. Reassured by this vision, Mechtilde began to work with the other nuns on the manuscript, which was then circulated among other religious communities after her death.

Mechtilde of Hackeborn is sometimes confused with her better-known contemporary, Mechthild of Magdeburg, who is profiled in Chapter 3: Lovers.

Recommended Reading

Select Revelations of S. Mechtild, Virgin, Taken from the Five Books of Her Spiritual Grace, and Translated from the Latin by a Secular Priest (London: Thomas Richardson and Sons, 1875).

Paul of Tarsus (ca. 5–ca. 66)

Paul of Tarsus, also known as Saint Paul the Apostle, is the most dramatic figure in the New Testament besides Christ himself. He first appears in the Acts of the Apostles as a zealous Pharisee dedicated to persecuting the young Christian church in its vulnerable first few years after the ascension of Christ. To Paul, the Christians were heretics and troublemakers, liable to create difficulty between the Jewish community and its Roman overlords, so Paul arranged to travel from Jerusalem to Damascus with appropriate credentials authorizing him to find and arrest those terrible Christians.

But something happened on the road to Damascus. Best to let Paul recount it in his own words. (Saul was his Jewish name; Paul his Latin equivalent.)

On that journey as I drew near to Damascus, about noon a
great light from the sky suddenly shone around me. I fell to
the ground and heard a voice saying to me, "Saul, Saul, why
are you persecuting me?" I replied, "Who are you, sir?" And
he said to me, "I am Jesus the Nazorean whom you are per-
secuting." My companions saw the light but did not hear the
voice of the one who spoke to me. I asked, "What shall I do,
sir?" The Lord answered me, "Get up and go into Damascus,
and there you will be told about everything appointed for you
to do." Since I could see nothing because of the brightness of
that light, I was led by hand by my companions and entered
Damascus.[13]

Blinded after this encounter, Paul turned to the Christians—
the people he had previously been persecuting—for help.
Fortunately for him, a believer named Ananias in Damascus
had received a word from God to trust Paul, pray for the restoration of his sight, and then help him. (Because Paul had become
a believer, he himself was now a target for persecution.)

Within a few years, Paul had gone from being a sworn enemy
of the Christians to one of the most energized evangelists. He
preached the Gospel throughout much of the Roman Empire,
and his teaching is preserved for us in a series of letters now
found in the Bible. While much of the New Testament writings attributed to Paul concern mundane matters (refereeing
conflicts or chastising churches that have abandoned Christian
teaching), various points throughout his letters shimmer with
mystical insight (see Philippians 2, Ephesians 3, and Colossians
1 for a few examples). Incidentally, some scholars question

whether all of the letters in the New Testament traditionally attributed to Paul were in fact written by him—some may have been written by his students or admirers.

Toward the end of his second letter to the Corinthians, Paul recounts the story of someone who had an ecstatic vision of heaven. Most scholars believe he was speaking about himself but out of humility did not identify himself as the visionary. He notes that "this person" was "caught up into paradise and heard ineffable things, which no one may utter."[14]

This tantalizing hint at Paul's visionary ecstasy leaves us with more questions than answers. But one thing is for sure: by the strength of his mystical relationship with God, Paul literally changed the world. Perhaps we who seek to behold the face of God will be asked to do the same.

Recommended Reading
The Letters of Saint Paul (from the New Testament).

Teresa of Ávila (1515–1582)

Teresa of Ávila, also known as Teresa of Jesus, is one of the most colorful and beloved mystics of all time. Born in the medieval walled city of Ávila just a few years before the Protestant Reformation, she lived during a time when Spain was a dominant political and military power in Europe. (The Spanish Armada's defeat would not occur until several years after Teresa's death.) It was a time of great religious anxiety, however, thanks to the religious upheaval that swept across northern Europe beginning when Teresa was only two years old. Hers was the time of the

Spanish Inquisition, of persecution particularly against Jews and suspected heretics, and of suspicion against anything that could be viewed as flouting church authority. It hardly seems a congenial time to be a mystic—and yet sixteenth-century Spain was a virtual petri dish of contemplative activity, for not only did Teresa thrive during this time, but also Ignatius of Loyola (1495–1556), founder of the Jesuits, and Teresa's own protégé, the sublime poet and mystical theologian John of the Cross (1542–1591).

Teresa exerted a profound influence not only on the inner life (as a spiritual director and teacher of prayer, particularly to the nuns in her order) but also as a reformer of her religious order, the Carmelites. Born of a venerable Spanish family, she entered the convent in 1535 but for most of her youth led what she later criticized as a spiritually lax life. However, a vivid conversion experience at age forty propelled her toward a life of devout prayer and devotion, leading to a succession of ecstatic and mystical experiences that kept the fires of her zeal alive. By 1562 she was chafing against the lukewarm culture of her order and so endeavored to establish a new convent where the sisters would lead a more rigorous and devoted life of prayer. Although she faced opposition within the Carmelite order as well as the church at large, the Convent of St. Joseph was founded in Ávila; it was the first of fourteen convents founded by Teresa over the final twenty years of her life.

Teresa never saw herself as a writer; indeed, she thought writing was a frivolous activity when she could be doing more practical things, such as spinning wool. But her spiritual mentors recognized her mystical genius and also saw in her a gifted ability to teach others about the life of prayer. They directed her to write, and so she did so, as an act of religious obedience. Her collected writings fill three large volumes, but three of her works are generally regarded as contemplative classics: her autobiography *The Book of My Life* and two manuals of instruction, *The Way of Perfection* and *The Interior Castle*. All are written in her colorful, conversational style, full of digressions and opinionated pronouncements on various aspects of the cloistered life. Readers in the third millennium may find her work difficult for two reasons: her adamant insistence on complete and unquestioning submission to the authority of the church, and her near-constant self-denigration. I think both of these qualities have to be understood in context; Teresa lived at a time when failure to obey the church could have truly dire consequences, and laypersons—particularly women—asserting their own spiritual voice by virtue of their mystical experience would have been met with considerable suspicion. By continually putting herself down and insisting on obedience, Teresa was effectively shielding herself from potential criticism—while ensuring that her insights into mystical truth were being recorded for generations to come.

But the point behind reading Teresa today is not so much about understanding church politics of sixteenth-century Spain as about accessing the majesty of her wisdom as a contemplative. Although her writing is anything but systematic, Teresa provides a remarkably complete overview of the contours of spiritual development, emphasizing virtues such as humility and self-forgetfulness, the necessity of balancing outward religious forms (such as reciting memorized prayers like the Our Father) with inner heartfelt devotion, and perhaps most important of all, a clear understanding that the life of prayer involves growth and maturity, and that the more advanced forms of prayer require increasing willingness to let God take the lead in the deepening of the prayer. Teresa recognizes that prayer is about relationship, and that we are never alone, nor "in charge" when we pray.

Although Teresa struggled with opposition to her monastic reforms during her lifetime, recognition from the church followed after her death: she was canonized a saint of the Catholic Church in 1622 (a mere forty years after her death), and in 1970 Pope Paul VI declared her a Doctor of the Church, meaning that her writings are considered exemplary in their sanctity and exposition of Christian theology. Teresa is one of only four women to receive this honor.

Recommended Reading

The Book of My Life by Teresa of Ávila, translated by Mirabai Starr (Boston: New Seeds, 2007).

Chapter 2

Confessors

"I love to tell the story . . . of Jesus and this love." So goes a nineteenth-century hymn—and it speaks to a universal truth not only about Christian mysticism or Christianity in particular but indeed about human nature in general. To be human is to be a storyteller (or, at least, a "story enjoyer"). Movies, plays, great novels, folktales, even television shows: all are, at their heart, stories. The classic ones tell a moving or entertaining story, filled with memorable characters, exciting or intriguing plots, and some sort of meaningful transformation on the part of at least one hero or heroine. For that matter, even something as mundane as business marketing involves telling a story. To sell a product, promote a candidate for public office, or support a cause of some sort all require being able to tell a story that connects with potential buyers, voters, or donors in a meaningful way.

Spirituality is all about great stories—whether they are mythical or allegorical in nature, or grounded in real history. Few Christians today believe literally in Adam and Eve or Noah's flood, yet those stories continue to inspire people with the spiritual truths encoded within them. Likewise, the Gospels proclaim stories about Jesus, who himself told stories masterfully. His parables are all wonderfully compact stories filled with a significant spiritual or moral message.

Given how human and how spiritual it is to communicate with stories, is it any surprise that many of the great mystics were masters of the art? Some were poets, others teachers, others lovers (all categories we will examine). But for now, we'll look at the mystical storyteller as *confessor*—one who tells his or her own story, reflecting on its spiritual meaning.

We've come to associate "confession" with admitting to one's sins, as in "going to confession." But owning up to our wrongdoing is only one part of confession in the broader sense of the word. When Augustine of Hippo (whom we'll meet shortly) wrote his *Confessions*, he admitted to a variety of sins, including some juicy ones (such as having a mistress for many years and fathering a child out of wedlock). But the main point of the book is to tell his overall life story, including his conversion to Christianity—and his encounter with mystical truth. George Fox in the seventeenth century and Dag Hammarskjöld in the twentieth kept journals, and their personal reflections have become doorways into their deep relationships with God. Again and again, mystics recognized that a powerful way to convey their intimacy with God was to simply recount the details of their own lives.

As you learn about these confessors of mystical truth, consider how God has touched your life, even if only in very small or humble ways (that's God's usual *modus operandi*). Perhaps you will be inspired to start or continue a personal journal, so you can love to tell *your* story, even if it's for your eyes only.

Angela of Foligno (1248–1309)

Angela of Foligno received mystical visions of Christ, which she dictated to a scribe and which were widely circulated in the Middle Ages as *The Book of Angela of Foligno* under two parts, "The Memorial" and "The Instructions." Her book recounts the story of her spiritual conversion; in a way, Angela can be thought of as a female equivalent to the prodigal son. Born of a wealthy Italian family (not far from Assisi, the home of Saint Francis), in her youth she lived an ordinary and rather worldly life, marrying and bearing children and enjoying the luxuries of her class. But when she was in her late thirties, she underwent a conversion of heart, weeping and fearing the loss of her soul to hell.

She sought out a priest for confession but was so ashamed of her sins that she couldn't bear to confess them all at first. She prayed to Saint Francis for a confessor she could trust; he appeared to her in a dream and told her he would grant her request, and the next day she met a Franciscan friar named Arnaldo, to whom she made a complete confession. Following this conversion, Angela became a visionary, receiving a series of mystical encounters with Christ, particularly seeing him in his passion (crucifixion) and feeling great sorrow for her sins. The trajectory of her spiritual path reached a powerful turning point when, in the Basilica of St. Francis of Assisi, she received such a powerful sense of divine presence that it left her shrieking and sobbing in the church, much to Brother Arnaldo's dismay.

Eventually, though, her confessor also became her scribe, writing down the story of Angela's extraordinary life and spiritual journey. After the death of Angela's entire family—her mother, her husband, and her children—she became a Third Order Franciscan and devoted the last two decades of her life to prayer, penance, and documenting her extraordinary life of faith.

The "Instructions" section of Angela's book provides practical guidance to those who sought her spiritual wisdom. Among other things, she emphasized the primacy of prayer: "If you want faith, pray. If you want hope, pray. If you want charity, pray. If you want poverty, pray. If you want humility, pray."[1] Furthermore, she equated prayer with reading the Gospel, which echoes the ancient monastic practice of *lectio divina* (sacred, meditative/prayerful reading, usually of the Bible).

In 2013, Pope Francis declared Angela of Foligno a saint.

Recommended Reading

Angela of Foligno: Complete Works, translated by Paul Lachance (New York: Paulist Press, 1993).

Augustine of Hippo (354–430)

Augustine of Hippo is like Paul of Tarsus: he has a bad reputation in our time that is not entirely fair. In Augustine's case, he is blamed for much of Christianity's historical discomfort with the human body and sexuality. While it is true that this kind of dualism does appear in Augustine's writings, it's important to remember that this was a typical prejudice of his age, when many spiritual seekers felt that the only way to ascend to an untainted realm of spiritual purity would involve rejecting the transitory, suffering-prone, mortal quality of human nature, including the body, with its appetites and desires.

But Augustine is far more than an ancient killjoy. Born in the middle of the fourth century, as a youth he had no faith, although he was a seeker, exploring several of the trendy philosophies of his day, including Manichaeism and Neoplatonism. His mother, Monica, was a follower of Christ, and she patiently prayed for her son as he pursued both worldly ambitions and worldly pleasures (including having a mistress who bore him a son).

Augustine's search led eventually to his conversion to Christianity in 387. He lived another forty-three years, eventually being ordained as a priest and consecrated as bishop of the town of Hippo in Northern Africa (modern day Algeria). He had a keen mind and is respected as much as a philosopher as a theologian. He was a prolific writer and left numerous sermons, treatises, and Bible studies.

Perhaps his most famous single work is his *Confessions*. Written toward the end of the fourth century, it has been called the first autobiography, for the purpose of the text is simply to recount the author's own life story, including his conversion from paganism to Christianity. Because it is Augustine, the text is densely philosophical, but it is also filled with luminous passages describing his vivid inner life, including an extraordinary encounter with God, remarkable because it was a "shared" encounter involving both Augustine and his mother. This took place shortly after his conversion—and shortly before her death. The two were staying at a villa in the Roman port town of Ostia, and one evening the mother and son began to speculate on what life must be like for the saints in heaven. As their conversation fired their imagination, both felt a light touch of the presence of God, leading to a sense of ecstasy—of being carried into the consciousness of heaven.

Reading Augustine today, I am struck by the passion and fervor of his search and the devotion he held for Christ once he embraced the Christian Mystery. "You have made us for yourself, and our heart is restless until it rests in you,"[2] confessed Augustine, speaking not only of his own heart, but of all our hearts. Perhaps his confession can inspire those with a restless heart in our day.

Recommended Reading

Saint Augustine: Confessions, translated by Henry Chadwick (Oxford: Oxford University Press, 2008).

Dag Hammarskjöld (1905–1961)

Dag Hammarskjöld hailed from a prominent Swedish family (his father was the prime minister during World War I) and served as the United Nations' second secretary-general. After he died in a plane crash while on a UN mission in Northern Rhodesia (Zambia), his book of confessional writings, *Markings*, was published. *Markings* features poetry, meditations, and musings on Hammarskjöld's rich inner life, covering the author's entire adulthood. (The first entry is dated 1925, and the last entry is a poem composed shortly before his fateful trip to Africa.) *Markings* is remarkable in that it is silent on Hammarskjöld's public life, unlike the memoirs of most statesmen; rather, it focuses entirely on his spiritual growth and inner questioning.

Hammarskjöld's sympathy with mysticism appears on the first page of the book, where he quotes Meister Eckhart. His writing covers a variety of topics, including duty, courage, integrity, and morality; because of the humility in the author's voice, he never attempts to show off the depth of his spiritual insight. But glimmers of his vision certainly shine through: "I am the vessel. The draught is God's. And God is the thirsty one"[3]; "In our era, the road to holiness necessarily passes through the world of action"[4]; "To have humility is to experience reality, not *in relation to ourselves*, but in its sacred independence"[5]; and my personal favorite, "Suddenly I saw that I was more real to himself than I am to myself, and that what was required of me was to experience this reality of his not as an object but as a subject—and *more* real than mine."[6]

Hammarskjöld never talks about visions, or locutions, or experiencing union with God. His mysticism is not one of signs and wonders, but rather of a life filled with quiet integrity and inner humility even while he was a global leader who literally changed the world.

Recommended Reading

Markings by Dag Hammarskjöld, translated by Leif Sjöberg and W. H. Auden (New York: Alfred A. Knopf, 1964).

George Fox (1624–1691)

George Fox is known as the founder of the Religious Society of Friends—the Quakers. Quakerism itself is a profoundly mystical sect of Christianity, with its emphasis on communal silence, nonviolence, government by consensus, and a theology that recognizes the presence of God in every person: what the twentieth-century Quaker theologian Rufus Jones called "the doctrine of the inner light."

As a writer, Fox's masterpiece is his journal, in which he confesses his own deeply devout faith in Christ and his willingness to endure public conflict and even legal trouble in his efforts to establish the Society of Friends. Fox began preaching publicly while in his twenties, and he devoted the rest of his life to supporting the burgeoning Quaker movement. Yet, like Teresa of Ávila a century before him, Fox's skill as a religious leader was grounded in a deep personal relationship with God. *The Journal of George Fox* reveals him as a man of prayer and someone willing to flout the religious establishment of his time in order to help people discover their own innate connection with the Divine. "The Lord showed me clearly that He did not dwell in these temples which men had commanded and set up, but in people's hearts" wrote Fox. "He did not dwell in temples made with hands . . . but that His people were His temple, and He dwelt in them."[7]

Later in his journal, Fox details his commitment to nonviolence, mentioning a letter he wrote to Oliver Cromwell: "I was sent of God to stand a witness against all violence, and against the works of darkness; and to turn people from darkness to light; and to bring them from the causes of war and fighting, to the peaceable gospel."[8] In the more than three centuries since Fox's death, the Quakers continue to stand for peace, nonviolence, silence, and a mystical spirituality that is available to everyone.

Recommended Reading

The Journal of George Fox, edited by Rufus Matthew Jones (Richmond, IN: Friends United Press, 1983).

Henry Suso (ca. 1295–1366)

Henry Suso entered the Dominican order as a boy, and as a young man he studied under the great (and controversial) mystic Meister Eckhart. Suso experienced a deeper conversion after living in the Dominican monastery for several years and pursued a promising career as a theologian. This ended abruptly in the early 1330s, however, perhaps due to Suso's admiration of and defense of Eckhart, who by this time had been condemned as a heretic. Suso spent the remainder of his life providing spiritual direction for nuns and writing his life story and a variety of mystical meditations, which were collected and published as a single work, *The Exemplar*. His writings were popular in the late Middle Ages, and hundreds of copies of manuscripts from that time are still in existence.

Unlike his master, Eckhart, whose writings were more philosophical than personal, Suso's work is deeply confessional, recounting his mystical experience as well as detailing how he matured in his relationship with God. According to scholar Bernard McGinn, Suso was one of the first male mystics to write about "his pious practices, visions and mystical experiences as exemplary of profound theological truths."[9] But his writings are more than just a catalog of supernatural events. He shows a deep contemplative spirit—he talks about having "an urge in his interior life to attain real peace of heart, and it seemed to him that silence might be useful to him."[10]

Perhaps most challenging for modern readers is Suso's mortifications—the ways in which he disciplines his body in the interest of spiritual growth. He fasted excessively and wore a hair shirt with nails and even a barbed cross on his back, all in the interest of "mortifying" his flesh. Today, many people would see this kind of behavior as masochistic, not mystical. Yet it was not unusual for medieval monks to engage in this kind of self-punishing discipline, so convinced were they that the body was depraved and needed to be chastised.

What makes Suso important is his eventual recognition that these kinds of bodily penances were harmful. He eventually realized that self-chastising, taken to its logical end, would result in death (in other words, suicide). In a vision, God told him to stop punishing his body, and Suso threw all of his implements of self-torture into a river. While he never abandoned his medieval belief that God demanded severe discipline from his followers, Suso's eventual coming to his senses is a reminder to us today that, while spirituality may involve an aspect of sacrifice and self-denial, it is never about self-harm or self-hatred.

Recommended Reading

Henry Suso: The Exemplar, with Two German Sermons, translated and edited by Frank Tobin (New York: Paulist Press, 1989).

Ignatius of Loyola (ca. 1491–1556)

Ignatius of Loyola founded the Society of Jesus (the Jesuits) and is generally considered one of the three great Spanish mystics of his age, alongside Teresa of Ávila and John of the Cross. A nobleman from the Basque Country in the north of Spain, Ignatius pursued military glory as a knight in the service of a Duke, but a severe leg injury suffered in battle forced him into a lengthy convalescence. After reading religious texts about the lives of Jesus and the saints, Ignatius decided to become a soldier for Christ; he visited an altar devoted to Mary in a Benedictine monastery, where he gave up his sword and exchanged his clothes with those of a beggar. He then walked fifteen miles to the village of Manresa, where he lived for a year in solitude, experiencing visions and devoting himself to prayer and asceticism. It is likely that Ignatius began his masterpiece, *Spiritual Exercises*, while in Manresa. In this work, Ignatius provides instruction for a four-week retreat, featuring daily imaginative exercises based on events from the life of Christ, to help retreatants more fully discern God's will for their lives—and to embrace the freedom necessary to embody that divine will wholeheartedly.

After a pilgrimage to the Holy Land, Ignatius returned to Spain, where twice he ran afoul of the Inquisition, which accused him of spreading dangerous teachings. He was imprisoned on more than one occasion, although ultimately he was deemed innocent. He went to Paris to study, where he led a number of companions through the Spiritual Exercises. Eventually, Ignatius and six others founded a new religious congregation that in time became known as the Society of Jesus. Several members of the community traveled to Rome, where they placed themselves in service to the Pope. One day, while praying in Rome, Ignatius received an apparition of Christ, who offered words of blessing for him and his young community. Ignatius devoted the rest of his life to organizing and fostering the society.

Although he is best known for his *Spiritual Exercises*, Ignatius also dictated his autobiography to one of his companions, detailing his life story from his injury to his arrival in Rome. Written in the third person, it offers insight into his conversion and spiritual growth, including matter-of-fact descriptions of his mystical experiences. For example, he writes, "One day, a few miles before reaching Rome, he was at prayer in a church and experienced such a change in his soul and saw so clearly that God the Father placed him with Christ his Son that he would not dare doubt it . . ."[11] Ignatius saw himself as a servant to Christ and the Trinity, a sinner who nevertheless has been called by God to be a companion to Jesus. The heart of his spirituality entailed a sense of being loved by God and being liberated by that love to follow Jesus and to give his life in service to God and others. His Spiritual Exercises were designed to help others find a similar path to devotion and service.

Recommended Reading

Ignatius of Loyola: Spiritual Exercises and Selected Works, edited by George E. Ganss (New York: Paulist Press, 1991).

John Wesley (1703–1791)

John Wesley, a priest of the Church of England, founded the Methodist movement, which after his death became the Methodist Church. While he spent most of his life in his native England, he did make a two-year missionary trip to Savannah,

Georgia, which at the time was one of the thirteen British colonies in North America. In his youth, Wesley and several friends formed an association for intentionally living their faith as Christians; with a commitment to regular daily prayer, weekly reception of Holy Communion, and reading the Bible (including the New Testament in Greek), this group became known as the Holy Club, although Wesley himself referred to them as Methodists, presumably since their commitment to their faith was expressed in a methodical way.

A major turning point for Wesley came in 1738 when he attended a meeting of Moravian Christians and received an interior sense of God's presence. He wrote in his journal, "I felt my heart strangely warmed. I felt I did trust in Christ, Christ alone for my salvation; and an assurance was given me that he had taken away *my* sins, even *mine*, and saved *me* from the law of sin and death . . . But it was not long before the enemy suggested, 'This cannot be faith, for where is your joy?' Then was I taught that 'peace and victory over sin are essential to faith in the Captain of our salvation but that, as to the transports of joy—that usually attend the beginning of it especially in those who have mourned deeply—God sometimes giveth, sometimes withholdest them, according to the counsels of his own will.'"[12]

Living during the so-called Age of Reason, Wesley's legacy of pious religion and writing that sometimes seems stern may strike readers in the twenty-first century as hardly "mystical" or "contemplative." But Wesley, who studied many of the writings of great Christian mystics, including the desert fathers and mothers (especially the sermons of Macarius of Egypt), Thomas à Kempis, Jeremy Taylor, and William Law, understood that

Christian faith meant more than simply obeying the letter of the law. Perhaps his most eloquent statement of his profound spirituality was *A Plain Account of Christian Perfection* (1777), in which he equates "perfection" with Christ consciousness (Wesley's definition of a perfect Christian is someone "in whom *is the mind which was in Christ*"[13]) and with having "a heart so all-flaming with the love of God."[14] This, of course, recalls the "heart strangely warmed" that Wesley himself confessed—a heart mystically transfigured by the presence of God.

Recommended Reading

John and Charles Wesley: Selected Prayers, Hymns, Journal Notes, Sermons, Letters and Treatises edited by Frank Whaling (New York: Paulist Press, 1981).

Margery Kempe (ca. 1373–1438)

Margery Kempe comes at the end of what is called the golden age of English mysticism—the age of Julian of Norwich (whom she knew), Walter Hilton, and *The Cloud of Unknowing*. Margery is not as well known as her older contemporaries, but what she lacks in renown she more than makes up for in character. Many Christian mystics are colorful figures, but Kempe may well have been one of the craziest of them all—in almost every sense of the word. You can find selections of her autobiography, *The Book of Margery Kempe*, in anthologies devoted to the history of mental illness; but she has also won the respect of historians of Christian spirituality such as Anglican author Martin Thornton, who insisted that her remarkable book "contains the solid core of . . . spirituality vividly alive."[15] Like Julian of Norwich, Margery has a place not only in the history of spirituality but in the history of literature as well, since her book is the first autobiography by a woman in English. Apparently, she was illiterate, but she found a sympathetic cleric who worked as her secretary while she dictated her remarkable life to him.

Margery was not a nun but rather a wife and mother, the daughter of a member of Parliament who married a public official in her hometown of King's Lynn, in the east of England. She bore fourteen children—after which she talked her husband into abstaining from further sexual relations! After the birth of her first child, she experienced frightening visions of demons. (Some modern interpreters speculate that she may have suffered from postpartum depression.) She tried her hand as a businesswoman, operating a brewery, but it was unsuccessful and she gave it up. Eventually, she simply adopted the life of a pious Christian woman, going on pilgrimages (including trips to Jerusalem, Venice, and Assisi) and doing works of mercy, but she also annoyed priests and bishops with her tendency to sob and wail uncontrollably during Mass—crying tears of love and sorrow, expressing her profound devotion for Christ. As a mystic, she carried on conversations with Christ, Mary, and God and experienced visions and supernatural phenomena.

One remarkable facet of Kempe's story is her visit with Julian of Norwich toward the end of that mystic's life (probably in the early fifteenth century). Margery recounts the advice Julian gave her, words of wisdom that are remarkably consistent with Julian's own writing. "The Holy Spirit can never urge us to do anything against charity," counseled Julian, "for if he did so, he would be acting against his own self, for he is the sum of all charity."[16] In other words, for Margery to discern if she was following God's will, she needed to reflect on if she was being led into greater love, charity, and compassion—for God, who is Love, can only lead us to love.

Margery's simplicity and effusive emotionalism may not be for everyone. But she represents an unusual figure for the Middle Ages: a full-blown mystic who was neither a nun nor a hermit. As a representative of someone who embraced a fully contemplative life in the context of ordinary family life, she is an inspiration for us today.

Recommended Reading

The Book of Margery Kempe: A New Translation, translated by John Skinner (New York: Image Books, 1998).

Maximus the Confessor (ca. 580–662)

Maximus the Confessor was said to have been in Constantinople and abandoned an appointment in the court of the Byzantine emperor in order to become a monk. He eventually settled in North Africa, where he became a leading figure in African Christianity, and participated in the Lateran Council in Rome in 649. But by 655 he was back in Constantinople, tried for heresy, and punished by mutilation. According to tradition, his hand and his tongue were cut off (to keep him from writing and speaking, thus spreading his "heretical" ideas). Exiled to the shore of the Black Sea, he died shortly thereafter—but within twenty years of his passing his views were vindicated, which led to Maximus being venerated as a saint.

His title "the Confessor" refers to the fact that he was not directly killed for his faith in Christ—only mutilated—so it would be inaccurate to call him "Maximus the Martyr." But since he did suffer for his faith, he is acknowledged as one who truly confessed belief in Christ.

Maximus has been described as a "theologian of the transfigured cosmos."[17] He recognized that a crucial distinction exists between *thinking about God* and *knowing God directly* through immediate perception or engagement "which surpasses all reason."[18] Much of Maximus's writing explores the question of just who this God is that we seek to know directly; for Maximus, the "Cosmic Mystery of Jesus Christ" points to the mystical union of divinity and humanity that Christ embodies. But this union has a larger, more cosmological significance:

> *This union has been manifested in Christ at the end of time, and in itself brings God's foreknowledge to fulfillment, in order that natural mobile creatures might secure themselves around God's total and essential immobility, desisting altogether from their movement toward themselves and toward each other. The union has been manifested so that they might also acquire, by experience, an active knowledge of him in whom they were made worthy to find their stability and to have abiding unchangeably in them the enjoyment of this knowledge.*[19]

In other words, the mystical life begins in Christ, who manifests the union of humanity and divinity, but we who are mortal creations are invited into this unity (by "experience") so that we may find stability, abiding, and joy in our participatory relationship with him.

While, unlike other "confessors," Maximus did not leave an autobiographical mystical statement, the breadth of his writings as well as the testimony of his own suffering reveal a man whose deep love for Christ and understanding of mystical truth shaped his work and his identity.

Recommended Reading

Maximus the Confessor: Selected Writings, translated and edited by George C. Berthold (New York: Paulist Press, 1985).

Phoebe Palmer (1807–1874)

Phoebe Palmer was a nineteenth-century evangelist whose writings reveal a profound spirituality grounded in John Wesley's ideal of "Christian perfection." Born into a devout Methodist family, Palmer and her husband became itinerant preachers, spreading a message of holiness and sanctification while leading revivals and missions at churches and camp meetings. Along with her husband, she also was involved in humanitarian work and efforts on behalf of the poor.

Her most famous writing, *The Way of Holiness*, is subtitled "A Narrative of Religious Experience," but her profound encounter with God shows up in her letters as well, such as in this passage from a letter in 1837:

> *I felt that the Spirit was leading into a solemn, most sacred, and inviolable compact between God and the soul that came forth from Him, by which, in the sight of God, angels and men,*

I was to be united in oneness with the Lord my Redeemer,
requiring unquestioning allegiance on my part, and infinite
love and everlasting salvation, guidance and protection, on
the part of Him who had loved and redeemed me, so that
from henceforth He might say to me, "I will betroth thee unto
Me forever."[20]

Similar to other Protestant mystics (for example, C. S. Lewis), Phoebe Palmer was uncomfortable with the idea of mysticism and would not have called herself a mystic. But her intense devotion, her sense of divine union, and her tireless work spreading the message of holiness mark her as a mystic of her time.

Recommended Reading

Phoebe Palmer: Selected Writings, edited by Thomas C. Oden (New York: Paulist Press, 1988).

Thérèse of Lisieux (1873–1897)

Thérèse of Lisieux, popularly known as "the Little Flower," became world renowned shortly after her death at age twenty-four thanks to the publication of her autobiography, *Story of a Soul*. Born Marie Françoise-Thérèse Martin to a pious Catholic family in Normandy, France, she followed her four older sisters into consecrated religious life, becoming a Carmelite nun at age fifteen, receiving special permission to enter the convent at such a young age. Full of youthful enthusiasm, she saw being a nun as her means to become a saint, but as she grew in humility she came to see herself (and her sanctity) as very small and insignificant. But rather than feel defeated by this insight, Thérèse saw herself as following a "little way"—in her words, "the way of spiritual childhood, the way of trust and absolute surrender."[21] This little way implies the beauty of a humble, simple, even childlike spirituality, where the emphasis is not on achieving great things but rather on trusting that even the smallest sacrifice, the smallest act of mercy or forgiveness, is beautiful in the eyes of God. Along these lines, Thérèse took on the identity of "a little flower of Jesus," growing out of her own personal love of wildflowers and her sense that even the simplest and most ordinary of flowers can give glory to God. "It seems to me that if a little flower could speak, it would tell simply what God has done for it without trying to hide its blessings."[22]

Her autobiography tells the story of her faith, her vocation as a nun, and her eventual suffering and untimely death from tuberculosis. It is not "mystical" in the sense of profound philosophy or remarkable descriptions of supernatural visions, but it is beautiful in its celebration of divine love and earthly humility. Thérèse has been called "a saint of the people" whose "simple self-sacrifice gave the average believer a hope for perfection."[23]

Recommended Reading

Story of a Soul: The Autobiography of St. Thérèse of Lisieux, translated by John Clarke (Washington, DC: ICS Publications, 1996).

The Way of a Pilgrim (1884)

The Way of a Pilgrim is an anonymously written story of a Russian Orthodox peasant who found spiritual enlightenment through the recitation of the Jesus Prayer: "Lord Jesus Christ,

Son of God, have mercy on me." This uniquely Orthodox form of spiritual practice has its roots in the teachings of the desert fathers and mothers, with Evagrius Ponticus and John Cassian recommending using scripture verses as prayers to facilitate contemplation. The Jesus Prayer is cobbled together from several different verses in the New Testament, but it became the gold standard for Eastern Christian contemplative practice.

The pilgrim's story begins with him searching to find a way to pray without ceasing, following the mandate from Saint Paul in I Thessalonians 5:17. Eventually, he meets an Eastern Orthodox monk who introduces him to the classic of Eastern Christian spirituality, *The Philokalia*. This book, an anthology of writings by Orthodox masters from between the fourth and fifteenth centuries, included the following passage from Symeon the New Theologian:

> Sit alone and in silence; bow your head and close your eyes; relax your breathing and with your imagination look into your heart; direct your thoughts from your head into your heart. And while inhaling say, "Lord Jesus Christ, have mercy on me," either softly with your lips or in your mind. Endeavor to fight distractions but be patient and peaceful and repeat this process frequently.[24]

Like the instructions found in *The Cloud of Unknowing*, this is one of the most succinct descriptions of the practice of contemplative prayer found in the Christian tradition.

The book goes on to suggest that this prayer could be entrained to the beating of one's heart.

Imagine your heart; direct your eyes as though you were look-
ing at it through your breast, see the heart as vividly as you
can, and listen attentively to its rhythmic beat . . . then begin
to say the words of the Prayer, while looking into your heart,
to the rhythm of your heartbeat. . . direct the flow of the Jesus
Prayer in the heart in harmony with your breathing; that is,
while inhaling say, "Lord Jesus Christ," and while exhaling
say, "have mercy on me."[25]

Much more wisdom is to be found in this deceptively simple book, including instruction on the importance of spiritual guidance (and what to do when a spiritual mentor is not available) and words of caution against focusing too much on visions or other supernatural phenomena.

Although *The Way of a Pilgrim* never names its author (or, for that matter, the pilgrim who is its protagonist), the book has a confessional feel. Even if the author were, as scholars believe, a monk instead of a wandering pilgrim, its detailed description of spiritual guidance and practical instruction in the life of prayer must surely be indicative of the author's own experience.

Recommended Reading

The Way of a Pilgrim and The Pilgrim Continues His Way, translated by Helen Bacovcin (New York: Image Books, 2003).

CHAPTER 3

Lovers

"God is love" (I John 4:16) may be the single most important verse in the entire Bible. Many things have been said about God, both in scripture and beyond: God is omnipotent, God is almighty, God is jealous, God is wrathful, God is forgiving, God is merciful, God is just, and so forth. But *God is love* always seems to win out as the single most essential piece of information about the Divine. Maybe "the fear of the Lord is the *beginning* of wisdom" (Proverbs 1:7, emphasis added), but the *end* of wisdom is surely the love of God, which is both given to us and received from us in turn.

With all this in mind, is it any wonder that many of the great Christian mystics are renowned as lovers of God? This can take a variety of forms: for some, being God's lover is very ethereal and philosophically abstract; but for others, an embodied, physical, even erotic quality characterizes their mysticism of love. There is even a term—"bridal mysticism"—for the many mystics (both female and male) whose experience of profound love of

God was so deep and all-encompassing that it led to a spiritual sense of being "married" to God—or at least loving God with the same all-pervasive devotion that a bride and groom have for one another.

Before you decide that this kind of mysticism is just plain creepy, consider that this derives from the Bible itself. One of the loveliest books in the Hebrew Bible (the Old Testament) is the Song of Solomon, also called the Song of Songs or the Canticle of Canticles. It's a short book, only about three thousand words; but it is filled with lovely, poetic language about (what else?) love. It is the story of a bride and bridegroom, their passion for one another, their devotion to one another, and their (strongly hinted at) passion as physical lovers.

Historically, the Song of Songs has been read as a kind of allegory: the two lovers symbolize the caring relationship between God and Israel, or Christ and the Church, or Christ and the individual believer. This is where the mysticism of love comes in: for the mystics, the power and splendor of their intimacy with God are so great that the only earthly love that even comes close to describing it is the love between a husband and wife.

In thinking about your encounter with God's love, erotic or marital imagery may or may not work for you. But even if this analogy leaves you cold, try to imagine the power of God's love and how it can set a mystic's heart aflame with passion, longing, and desire. This will give you some insight into the earthy devotion that infused the mystics of love.

Beatrice of Nazareth (ca. 1200–1268)

Beatrice of Nazareth was the youngest child of a devout Flemish family; her father may have been a mason involved in the construction of three different monasteries. After her mother's death when she was seven, Beatrice lived for a year with Beguines (Christian lay women who lived communally). Afterward she went to live with nuns, and even as a child she began to engage in severe ascetic practices, including fasting and self-denial.

As a teen, her superiors sent her to a neighboring convent to learn the art of manuscript writing. At this time she met Ida of Nivelles, who was only a year older than Beatrice but already renowned as a mystic. Forming a close bond with Ida, soon Beatrice, at age sixteen, received her own ecstatic vision—of the Trinity, the heavenly Jerusalem, and choirs of angels. After the vision, Beatrice reacted with profound emotion: she sobbed when she realized her ecstasy had ended, but she also felt such immense gratitude that she laughed out loud. After a short period of happiness, she fell into a state of fatigue and inertia; Beatrice's religious observance became slack for several months. After receiving a letter from Ida in which she encouraged her friend to take communion, Beatrice began to reintegrate herself into the religious observance of convent life. From here, the youth began to understand that the spiritual life was not about making demands of God; and that extreme acts of asceticism or self-denial could be harmful rather than sanctifying.

As a young adult, Beatrice immersed herself in the ordinary life of a nun, studying scripture, striving to grow in virtue, and participating in the spiritual exercises of her religious community. She struggled to cleanse herself of her sins but came to see that penance or asceticism did more harm than good. She also tried to motivate her quest for holiness through willfully forcing herself to be more grateful and loving—but she naturally discovered that such headstrong actions could not achieve the sanctity she desired. Distraught, Beatrice prayed to God for help—and in response realized that God wanted her to affirm her soul's innate beauty. She realized that God gives all people natural virtues, in different measures to each soul. Seeing that her soul contained its own beauty, and that furthermore each person is unique, liberated Beatrice to follow the path of sanctity given to her alone by God—which is to say, to become holy by being true to her own unique gifts and virtues.

But this insight did not mark the culmination of Beatrice's journey. After several years of relative peace and stability in her life as a nun, another long season of depression and inner turmoil returned. She was beset by fear that she might lose her faith or succumb to sinful thoughts and temptations. Yet she also received the insight that even her struggles could be a gift—a way God could train her for greater holiness.

Her depressed state lasted for a number of years but was punctuated by occasional visions or ecstasies. One time she heard God tell her that they would never be separated; another time she received a momentary vision of the Sacred Heart. She also suffered physical torments in addition to her spiritual struggle, including fevers and physical pain. Her ecstasies continued, along with insight into how impossible it was to retain the intensity or beauty of her visions.

In 1231, Ida of Nivelles died, causing Beatrice much grief. Meanwhile, Beatrice had developed her own reputation as a mystic and holy woman, but she tried to ignore the adulation she received from others.

Eventually Beatrice was appointed the prioress of the Nazareth convent in Belgium. Little is known about this period of her life, but before her death at age sixty-eight she composed her one written work, which has survived to the present day—a brief mystical treatise, *The Seven Manners of Holy Love*. This meditation on the dynamics of how mortals respond to God in love offers a poetic exploration of how love for God evolves over time.

Here are Beatrice's seven manners of mystical loving:

1. Active longing for restoring the image and likeness of God, which proceeds out of love;

2. Offering oneself to God;

3. Suffering for God;

4. Enjoying the splendor of God's love;

5. Accepting that love includes both ecstasy and agony;

6. Resting confidently in God's love; and

7. Contemplating the divine mystery of love, which paradoxically brings us back to an ever-deeper longing.

In this brief treatise (the English translation is only about 3,700 words long), Beatrice has beautifully unpacked the rich dynamics of the process by which mortal humans may respond to God through love. Of course, God *is* love, so the love we offer to God is merely a return of the gift of love God has given to us. Over the course of the seven manners, the lover of God experiences successive stages of enjoying God's presence and suffering God's apparent absence; of enjoying the beauty of love while also suffering the inevitable pain of love; but after reaching a place of acceptance, the process culminates with a non-dual encounter with love, through an ordinary sense of rest, leading to a rich contemplation of love that bridges the gap between "earthly" and "heavenly"—even while it continues to inspire a sense of longing (it reminds me of Bernard of Clairvaux, who suggested that the more we receive divine love, the greater our longing for it grows).

It would be a mistake to assume that Beatrice's map of the seven manners of loving is universally applicable—in other words, just because this is how the dance between divine and human love took place in her life doesn't mean that everyone will necessarily embody these seven manners in this precise sequence. As a general rule, it's wise not to universalize the teachings of the mystics and assume that our journey into the heart of God must look just like theirs (which is a good thing, since the mystics often contradict each other). Nevertheless, Beatrice's map of love is quite compelling, and perhaps most people who long for God's love (which, after all, is manner number one) might recognize many or even all of these seven dimensions of love in their lives. At the very least, this is great material for meditation.

Recommended Reading

The Life of Beatrice of Nazareth (includes the Seven Manners of Holy Love), translated by Roger DeGanck (Kalamazoo, MI: Cistercian Publications, 1991).[1]

Bernard of Clairvaux (1090–1153)

Bernard of Clairvaux, one of the most respected church leaders of his day, counseled popes, advised kings and commoners, promoted noble causes (his monastic order) and ignoble ones (the Second Crusade), and left behind a literary legacy of beautiful writing and an almost incandescent understanding of God as love. Born into a noble French family, he entered monastic life as a young man and was so charismatic and persuasive that he convinced thirty of his brothers, relatives, and fellow noblemen to enter the cloister with him. After only two years as a monk, Bernard was appointed the abbot of a new monastery in Clairvaux, France. He would hold that position for the rest of his life, inspiring not only the monks under his care but the church at large with his eloquent preaching and writing.

Bernard was not the first Christian contemplative to recognize the heart of mysticism as the union of lovers (divine and human), but he expressed this insight so poetically and beautifully that it is a concept perennially associated with him. His masterpiece is generally considered to be his eighty-six *Sermons on the Song of Songs*, in which he reflects on the great love poem in the Hebrew Bible, the Song of Songs, as a metaphor for the mystical love that flows between God and humanity. He also wrote a philosophical treatise, *On Loving God*, which reflects on the relationship between self-love (in healthy and unhealthy ways) and love for God.

In Sermon 3 of the *Sermons on the Song of Songs*, Bernard uses a metaphor of "three kisses" to describe the journey of ever-increasing intimacy with God. When we first turn away from worldly concerns, we are like Mary Magdalene, kissing Christ's feet. As we grow in grace, we are like a grateful servant, kissing the hand of the Lord—a metaphor for our attempts to live a graceful, holy life. But finally, the one who truly enjoys mystical union is like the lover who kisses the beloved on the mouth.

In Sermon 74, Bernard offers a detailed description of a mystical encounter with Christ. It's an encounter filled with mystery, one that the saint struggles to put into words: "He did not enter by the eyes, for he has no color; nor by the ears, for he made no sound; nor by the nostrils, for he is not mingled with the air, but the mind. He did not blend into the air; he created it. His coming was not tasted by the mouth, for he was not eaten nor drunk; nor could he be touched, for he is impalpable."[2] Bernard goes on to note that "only by the warmth of my heart . . . did I know he was there"[3]—a statement that we find echoed in John Wesley's famous encounter with Christ, where his heart felt "strangely warmed."[4]

Steeped as he is in the language and the worldview of the Middle Ages, Bernard's writings may not be immediately accessible to us here in the third millennium. But the sensuality and honest love that shaped Bernard's faith and spirituality shine through, especially in his sermons. Many later mystics, such as Julian of Norwich, Teresa of Ávila, and Thérèse of Lisieux, stand on the shoulders of this medieval troubadour of God's infinite love.

Recommended Reading

Bernard of Clairvaux: Selected Works, translated by G. R. Evans (New York: Paulist Press, 1987).

Blaise Pascal (1623–1662)

Blaise Pascal, best known as a French philosopher, scientist, and mathematician, was also an amateur theologian and a mystic who had at least one passionate, fiery encounter with the love of God for two hours on a Monday night. When he died shortly after his thirty-ninth birthday, he left unfinished a work called *Pensées* (*Thoughts*), which apparently was intended to be a defense of the Christian religion. Beautifully written, it reveals the author's keen understanding of the paradoxes and mysteries of faith, suggesting that spirituality ultimately must be grounded in humility.

The loving heart of Pascal's mystical faith was recorded on a single sheet of paper called his "Memorial," which he carried with him in the lining of his coat. Dated Monday, November 23, 1654, the memorial records in poetic, ecstatic, almost incoherent language an encounter with "Fire. God of Abraham, God of Isaac, God of Jacob. Not of philosophers and scholars. Certainty, joy, certainty, emotion, sight, joy . . . Oblivious to the world and to everything except God. He can only be found in the ways taught in the Gospel . . . Joy, Joy, Joy and tears of joy."[5]

What exactly happened to Pascal that evening, for two hours starting about ten thirty? As cryptic as the "Memorial" is, we can only speculate; but it reads like nothing so much as a love poem, apparently signifying such a meaningful encounter that its author kept it near his heart for the remainder of his short life.

Recommended Reading

Pensées and Other Writings by Blaise Pascal, translated by Honor Levi (Oxford: Oxford University Press, 1995).

Catherine of Siena (1347–1380)

Catherine of Siena is one of the most remarkable women of her age. In addition to being a renowned mystic and a popular saint, she was active in church politics, helping to bring the papacy back to Rome from Avignon, France, where popes had resided for almost seventy years, and then attempting to resolve a schism that occurred two years before her death (which would not be resolved until 1417). Rejecting her mother's plans for her to marry, Catherine became a Third Order Dominican, which meant she continued to live in her family home but observed a life of prayer and silence. A visionary since childhood, at age twenty-one Catherine underwent her "mystical marriage" to Jesus, consecrating her life and her virginity to him. She wrote a mystical treatise called *The Dialogue* a few years before her early death at age thirty-three.

One of her most renowned visions consists of a bridge from earth to heaven, symbolizing Christ. This bridge represented the love of God, through Christ, flowing to the earth. As Catherine writes in *The Dialogue*, reporting the words that God had spoken to her,

> *I said that, having been raised up, [Christ] would draw everything to himself... the human heart is drawn by love, as I said, and with all its powers: memory, understanding, and will. If these three powers are harmoniously united in*

my name, everything else you do, in fact or in intention, will be drawn to union with me in peace through the movement of love, because all will be lifted up in the pursuit of crucified love.[6]

Recommended Reading

Catherine of Siena: The Dialogue, translated by Suzanne Noffke (New York: Paulist Press, 1980).

Elizabeth of the Trinity (1880–1906)

Elizabeth of the Trinity serves as a wonderful modern example of a bridal mystic. She entered the Carmelite order at age twenty-one and died only a fear years later, but her legacy of letters and other writings reveals a deep sense of God's presence in her life, a presence luminous with love. As she wrote in one of her letters, "I feel so much love on my soul; it's like an ocean into which I plunge and lose myself. That is my vision here on earth, while I await the vision face to face in light. He is in me, and I am in him. I have only to love him, to let myself be loved, and to do that always and in everything."[7]

Elizabeth prayed that God would make her soul his heaven. In doing so, she recognized the heart of the mystery: that heaven is not just a place we go after we die, it is a state into which we are invited now.

Recommended Reading

Always Believe in Love: Selected Spiritual Writings of Elizabeth of the Trinity, edited by Marian T. Murphy (Hyde Park, NY: New City Press, 2009).

Gertrude the Great (1256–ca. 1302)

Gertrude the Great was the youngest of three remarkable contemplatives associated with the women's monastery of Helfta in Germany. Like her older contemporaries Mechtilde of Hackeborn and Mechthild of Magdeburg, Gertrude was renowned as a visionary and a devotee of mystical love; indeed, her most significant book is called *The Herald of Divine Love*, a five-volume compendium of her revelations and wisdom. Like Hildegard of Bingen, Gertrude lived in the cloister from a very early age, having entered Helfta when she was five. She underwent a conversion experience in her twenties, which led to her mystical awakening.

Gertrude was one of the earliest devotees to the Sacred Heart of Christ. For her, the Sacred Heart marked the point of union between God and humanity, and the source of all heavenly joy and virtues. In one vision Christ tells her, "I stretch out my heart to draw you to myself and again, when, your inmost thoughts in harmony with mine, you recollect yourself and again attend to me, then I draw back my heart again, and you with it, into myself, and from it I offer you the pleasure of all its many virtues."[8] Of course, like any lover, she is concerned that her heart offers a worthy response. "No words of mine, O Dayspring from on high, can express the affectionate way in which you visited

me, in the warmth and sweetness of your love. Give me, therefore, Giver of gifts, the grace to offer in gratitude a joyful sacrifice on the altar of my heart; so that I may obtain the grace I
ardently desire for myself . . . to experience frequently the union
which is sweetness, the sweetness which is union with you."[9]

In addition to the passionate writing that courses throughout
The Herald of Divine Love, Gertrude also composed *Spiritual
Exercises*, which has been described as "both traditionally
monastic and authentically, but unself-consciously, feminine."[10]
One of these exercises, called "Mystical Union," reflects on the
liturgy of monastic prayer as a setting for beautiful expressions
of love for Christ: "O dulcet face, when will you satisfy me with
yourself? Then I will go into the place of the wonderful taber-
nacle even to the very aspect of God; at its threshold my heart
is made to groan because I am delayed by my sojourn there. Oh,
when will you fill me with gladness by your mellifluous face?
Then I will contemplate and warmly kiss the true spouse of my
soul, my Jesus, to whom it has already clung in thirst and to
whom, at the same time, all my heart goes out."[11]

Recommended Reading

The Herald of Divine Love by Gertrude of Helfta, translated and edited
by Margaret Winkworth (New York: Paulist Press, 1993).

Hadewijch (Thirteenth Century)

Hadewijch is an obscure mystic whose dates of birth and death
are unknown but who flourished probably in the early thirteenth century; she was admired by the great Flemish mystic

John Ruusbroec, who lived a century after her. In our time, the Jesuit scholar Harvey Egan says she "stands out as one of the most sublime exponents of love mysticism in the Western mystical tradition."[12] Like her younger contemporary Mechthild of Magdeburg, Hadewijch was a Beguine; the Beguines were a semireligious Christian order of women who lived a common life devoted to prayer and community service.

While we know precious little about Hadewijch, her writings, intended primarily for younger Beguines, encompass both poetry and prose detailing her passionate and visionary relationship with Christ. In one vision, a voice issuing from "the Countenance of the Holy Spirit" declared to Hadewijch, "See and receive my Spirit! With regard to all things, know what I, Love, am in them! And when you fully bring me yourself, as pure humanity in myself, through all the ways of perfect Love, you shall love what I, Love, am. And then you will be love, as I am Love . . . In my unity, you have received me and I have received you. Go forth, and live what I am; and return bringing me full divinity, and have fruition of me as who I am."[13]

"When by fruition man is united to Love, he becomes God,"[14] stated Hadewijch in one of her letters. And if her gendered language feels antiquated in our time, keep in mind that for Hadewijch, Love is feminine, suggesting she clearly understood God, as Love, in a feminine way.

Recommended Reading

Hadewijch: The Complete Works, translated by Mother Columba Hart (New York: Paulist Press, 1980).

John the Evangelist (ca. 15–ca. 100)

John the Evangelist, or Saint John the Apostle, is traditionally regarded as the author of some of the most mystical texts in the New Testament, including the Gospel that bears his name, and three short letters, also identified simply by their reputed author. Biblical scholarship being what it is, we must acknowledge that we really do not know if these texts were written by the same person, or if any of them actually were written by the young man who was Jesus's "beloved disciple." Perhaps at this point in time such questions are largely irrelevant. What matters are the writings themselves, which shimmer not only with spiritual wisdom and mystical insight but also a clear recognition that God is love.

The Gospel of John was the last of the four biblical Gospels written; it probably was written (or completed) near the end of the first century. It may be the work of one author or possibly an edited text, drawing material from several sources. It is markedly different in its structure, tone, and content from the other three Gospels. John emphasizes a series of signs that Jesus performs, including changing water into wine, feeding the multitude, walking on water, healing various people, and raising Lazarus from the dead. But it is also filled with "discourses," lengthy passages in which Jesus offers detailed spiritual instruction to his listeners. Some of the teachings found in these discourses have a clearly mystical nature. Jesus proclaims his unity with God the Father (John 10:30), saying that he is "in the Father" and the Father is in him (John 14:11) and in turn promises his followers that they will "abide" in him, suggesting that they share in his mystical union with God (John 15:4). The key to this mystical abiding is love: Jesus says that he and God will dwell with those who love him and keep his commandment (John 14:15–23), and that commandment is to love one another (John 15:9–12). This teaching of Jesus, that he is one with God and we are invited into union with him in God through love that we share not only with him but with one another, is the foundation not only of Christian spirituality in general, but of Christian mystical theology.

In the first letter of John, the essential unity between God and love is further unpacked. "God is love," the author states, more than once (I John 4:8, 16), echoing Jesus's promise that in love we abide in God, and God abides in us. While the language is at times stern in its insistence that only by loving one another can we hope to abide in God, John also insists that "there is no fear in love"—that the heart of mystical spirituality lies in a bold confidence, grounded in the divine love that casts out all fear.

According to legend, John lived to old age—the only one of the twelve apostles to do so. It is said that he brought the Virgin Mary to live with him in Ephesus. While there is no solid historical evidence for this, it has been a traditional belief among Christians for many centuries.

Recommended Reading
The Gospel of John, The Letters of John (in the New Testament).

Maria Faustina Kowalska (1905–1938)

Maria Faustina Kowalska, popularly known as Saint Faustina, was a Polish nun, visionary, and the Apostle of Divine Mercy. An image based on one of her visions—of Jesus standing with one hand over his heart and the other extended in blessing, with rays of white and red light emerging from his Sacred Heart, featuring the motto "Jesus, I trust in you" at the bottom—has become a popular work of devotional art among Roman Catholics. Faustina kept a diary detailing both her simple piety and her loving relationship with Christ, who encouraged her in her devotion to mercy and instructed her to promote such a devotion. She says, "I understood that the greatest attribute of God is love and mercy. It unites the creature with the Creator."[15]

Recommended Reading

Diary of Saint Maria Faustina Kowalska: Divine Mercy in My Soul (Stockbridge, MA: Marian Press, 2005).

Mechthild of Magdeburg (ca. 1212–1282)

Mechthild of Magdeburg was a visionary, a poet, and a theologian, in addition to being a lover of God. But it is the passion and ecstasy found in her spiritual masterpiece, *The Flowing Light of the Godhead*, that sets her apart. "You should ask that God love you passionately, often, and long; then you shall become pure, beautiful, and holy"[16] she instructs her readers.

Born into a noble German family, as a young woman Mechthild entered the Beguines. When she began reporting visions to her confessor, he instructed her to commit them to writing. Later in life she became a Cistercian nun, joining the same convent where Mechtilde of Hackeborn and Gertrude the Great lived, and she continued to add material to *The Flowing Light of the Godhead* even after entering cloistered life. The book itself is considered a classic of German religious literature and deeply influenced later generations of mystics.

Reminiscent of the love poetry of the Song of Songs, the poetry in *The Flowing Light* shimmers with yearning and desire for love given and received. Likewise, the visionary narratives in Mechthild's writing convey a similar highly charged energy of love and devotion. Writing about herself in the third person, she reports a visionary encounter with the Lord whom she so deeply loves.

> *She stood there, her heart melting, looked upon her Lover and said: "O Lord, when I look upon you, I have to praise you for your astonishing wisdom. Where have I come to? Am I now lost in you? I cannot even remember earth or any of my interior sufferings . . . Now, Lord, the sight of you has struck me down. You have elevated me utterly beyond my worth."*[17]

For Mechthild, a mystical relationship with God meant more than simply receiving visions and knowledge; it meant being immersed in the flow of a love that cannot be put into words, that renders the mystic speechless with ecstatic joy, her "heart melting," her soul ablaze with heavenly fire. To be a mystic means to become the Bride of Christ. To be a mystic means to encounter Love, to love Love, to be purified to Love, to be loved by Love, and finally, to become one with Love.

Recommended Reading

Mechthild of Magdeburg: The Flowing Light of the Godhead, translated by Frank Tobin (New York: Paulist Press, 1998).

Symeon the New Theologian (949–1022)

Symeon the New Theologian was one of the most important mystics of his age, a charismatic and passionate lover of God who is unfortunately not well known among Western Christians since he lived on the eve of the great schism between Eastern Orthodoxy and Roman Catholicism. He has been called "the greatest of Byzantine mystical writers"[18] and "a mystic of fire and light."[19] After a period of service to the emperor in Constantinople, Symeon became a monk, eventually leaving Constantinople for Asia Minor after some of his ideas became controversial. He is called "the new theologian" because in Orthodoxy the fourth-century saint Gregory of Nazianzus is known as "Gregory the Theologian," so therefore Symeon, living six centuries later, is by comparison the "new" theologian.

So filled with love are Symeon's writings that his hymns have been published under the title *Divine Eros*.[20] In his discourses, love is a constant theme, both in terms of God's perfect love for humankind but also the necessity of loving God in return, as well as loving our neighbors as ourselves.

Symeon speaks of one mystical encounter with God like this: "The ineffable beauty of that which appeared to me wounded my heart and attracted me to infinite love."[21] He insists that a person cannot be a true child of God "unless we even in this life through zeal become partakers of the Holy Spirit."[22] Such a partaking means to participate in the very heart of love itself. Keeping the commandments of divine love causes to "grow up within us, like succulent fruits, love, mercy, compassion for our neighbor, gentleness, humility, endurance of trials, chastity, and purity of heart through which we shall be found worthy to see God, and in which the presence and the enlightenment of the Holy Spirit are granted."[23] Such presence and enlightenment "even here and now causes us to be conscious partakers of eternal life."[24]

Recommended Reading

Symeon the New Theologian: The Discourses, translated by C. J. deCatanzaro (New York: Paulist Press, 1980).

William of St.-Thierry (ca. 1085–1148)

William of St.-Thierry is the most significant Cistercian mystic from the Middle Ages after his friend Bernard of Clairvaux. For the first twenty years of his monastic life, he was a Benedictine monk and abbot before joining a small Cistercian community in the north of France in 1135. An accomplished theologian and a prolific writer, William wrote a variety of treatises and commentaries. His recognition of love as the heart of the mystical life shone through works like *On the Nature and Dignity of Love* and *The Exposition on the Song of Songs*.

"Love in us, Lord, ascends to you on high, because love in you descended here to us," wrote William. "You loved us, therefore you came down to us; by loving you we shall climb where you are."[25] He also understood that, mystically speaking, the love that flows between God and humanity is the same love we are called to give to our neighbors as ourselves: "It is, therefore, that there may be no defect in charity that we are told to love our neighbor, according to the law of perfect love. Just as God loves only himself in us, and we have learned to love in ourselves only God, so we are to begin now to love our neighbor 'as' ourselves. For in our neighbor we love God alone, even as we love him in ourselves."[26]

Recommended Reading

On Contemplating God, Prayer, Meditations by William of St. Thierry (Kalamazoo, MI: Cistercian Publications, 1977).

Chapter 4

Poets

We have seen how mystics convey their deep encounter with God through storytelling, whether in a fictionalized way (*The Way of a Pilgrim*) or by sharing the truth of their own life experience (Augustine's *Confessions*). Part of telling a good story is the ability to use language in a creative, narrative way. Gifted storytellers know how to use words to paint vivid pictures of memorable characters, dramatic conflicts, colorful scenery, and lifelike dialogue. It's amazing how language—which is, after all, just a finite number of sounds (when spoken) or characters (when written)—can evoke such a deeply embodied sense of the knowledge of, or encounter with, God in the minds and hearts of those who hear or read a well-crafted mystical narrative.

While many mystics are world-class journal-keepers and memoirists, others have literary skills that go beyond just the ability to recount their own life adventure. More than a few mystics made names for themselves as poets. Some, such as John Donne or John of the Cross, wrote world-class poetry that to this day students read in literature courses, even when taught from an entirely secular viewpoint. Other mystical wordsmiths, such as Ephrem the Syrian or Charles Wesley, wrote lyrics to hymns, some of which are still sung in Christian worship today. Meanwhile, writers like C. S. Lewis or Evelyn Underhill not only composed poetry but also wrote classic works of fiction and literary nonfiction.

So when I say many mystics were great poets, I'm referring to poetry in a broad sense, although all the mystics presented in this chapter did compose verse in some form. Jacopone da Todi and George Herbert are known almost exclusively as poets, while others, like Underhill and Caryll Houselander, are perhaps remembered now more for their prose—yet even when a poet writes prose, often it shines precisely because the paragraphs shimmer with a lyrical beauty that only a true poet can convey.

Perhaps when you explore the mystic poets featured here, you'll be inspired to explore their poetry and allow their creative use of language to enlighten your own search for the love of God. Or perhaps you will try your own hand at poetry, playing with words as you seek to give voice to God's ineffable love.

Angelus Silesius (1624–1677)

Angelus Silesius was a German Lutheran who converted to Catholicism as an adult, eventually becoming a priest. His contribution to mystical literature consisted of two volumes of epigrammatic poetry, *The Soul's Holy Desire* and *The Cherubinic Wanderer.* He has been described by one of his English translators as a "European Zen poet," but that is merely a romanticized description; still, his gnomic verse is not unlike what one might expect from an Eastern sage. Most of the poems in *The*

Cherubinic Wanderer are short (two to four lines), pithy, and evocative of a dreamlike state of mind.

Considered a classic of German literature, *The Cherubinic Wanderer* epitomizes the power of poetry to convey mystical truth: through vivid imagery and insightful, sometimes playful language, Silesius manages to express what is fundamentally inexpressible with immediacy and clarity. By turns philosophical, deeply contemplative, conventionally pious, and down to earth, Silesius's poetry captures the breadth of mystical spirituality in an astonishing economy of language.

Some of Angelus Silesius's poetry has also been set to music as hymns, such as this example, called "A Song at Daybreak":

Morning Star in darksome night,
Who the sad earth makest bright,
> *I am Thine!*
> *In me shine,*
Fill me with Thy light divine!

Lo, Thy heaven is in me here,
Longs to see its Star appear;
> *Break of Day,*
> *No more delay,*
Come and chase these mists away!

For Thy brightness, O my Star,
Earth's poor sun surpasseth far;
> *From Thy sight,*
> *Lovely Light,*
Other suns must hide in night.

All things stand revealed by Thee,
Past and Present and To-Be,
    And Thy smile
    Can erewhile
Night itself of gloom beguile.

Where Thy joyous splendours dart
Faith soon follows in the heart,
    Star most clear,
    Far and near
Thou as Lord art worshipped here!

Come then, Golden Light of souls,
Ere fresh darkness o'er me rolls,
    Be Thou mine,
    In me shine,
Fill me with Thy Light divine![1]

Recommended Reading

Angelus Silesius: The Cherubinic Wanderer, translated by Maria Shrady, edited by Josef Schmidt (New York: Paulist Press, 1986).

C. S. Lewis (1898–1963)

C. S. Lewis was one of the most popular Christian writers of the twentieth century, even though he was not a minister or a priest, nor a theologian—for his day job he taught and wrote about English literature at Oxford (and later, Cambridge). Converting to Christianity as an adult after a secular childhood, he went on to write a number of books that continue to appeal to the ordinary (non-specialist) reader on topics as diverse as pain and suffering, miracles, education, and grief. He is responsible for the term "mere Christianity," referring to a faith that is not situated in a particular church or denomination (like Catholicism or Lewis's own Church of England), but rather that seeks to affirm the mere basics of belief that all mainstream Christians might affirm. Today, however, Lewis is probably best known for his fiction, including satire (*The Screwtape Letters*), science fiction (*Out of the Silent Planet*), and the popular young-adult fantasy series *The Chronicles of Narnia*.

C. S. Lewis insisted he was not a mystic. In one of his last books, *Letters to Malcolm*, he writes, "You and I are people of the foothills. In the happy days when I was still a walker, I loved the hills, and even mountain walks, but I was no climber. I hadn't the head. So now, I do not attempt the precipices of mysticism."[2] He goes on to suggest that for him to adopt the role of a teacher in prayer would be "impudence" and then offers a fairly insightful argument as to why he believed Christian mysticism was essentially different from the mysticisms of other faiths. In doing so, he makes this statement, which reveals the nature of his bias: "One thing common to all mysticisms is the temporary shattering of our ordinary spatial and temporal consciousness and of our discursive intellect. The value of this negative experience must depend on the nature of that positive, whatever it is, for which it makes room."[3]

In other words, C. S. Lewis saw mysticism as an extraordinary expansion of consciousness, which had value only insofar as it was accompanied by truly holy beliefs or practices. The expansion of consciousness itself is neutral; there can be "good" or "bad" variations of it, depending on the philosophical and religious worldview that any given mystic might espouse.

Do you catch the irony here? Lewis is like an accomplished, talented guitarist who insists that you only get to call yourself a guitarist if you are as good as Eric Clapton, Jimmy Page, or Andrés Segovia. On the surface, his viewpoint seems to be a paragon of humility. But if you really think about it, it just seems to be a copout that enables him to avoid taking responsibility for his own God-given gift.

For the fact of the matter is that C. S. Lewis's fiction and poetry (if not his nonfiction) reveal an artist with a profoundly nuanced eye for mystical splendor. Books like *The Voyage of the Dawn Treader, The Last Battle, Perelandra,* and *Till We Have Faces* all shine with language that lyrically evokes God's glory, beauty, and love and suggests that intimacy with God is both our birthright and our destiny should we accept the gift that is freely offered.

Consider this passage from *Till We Have Faces*:

> *Joy silenced me. And I thought I had now come to the highest, and to the utmost fullness of being which the human soul can contain . . . The air was growing brighter and brighter about us; as if something had set it on fire. Each breath I drew let into me new terror, joy, overpowering sweetness. I was pierced through and through with the arrows of it. I was being unmade. I was no one.*[4]

Or this, from *The Voyage of the Dawn Treader*:

What they saw—eastward, beyond the sun—was a range of mountains . . . warm and green and full of forests and waterfalls however high you looked. And suddenly there came a breeze from the east, tossing the top of the wave into foamy shapes and ruffling the smooth water all round them. It lasted only a second or so but what it brought them in that second none of those three children will ever forget. It brought both a smell and a sound, a musical sound. Edmund and Eustace would never talk about it afterward. Lucy could only say, "It would break your heart." "Why," said I, "was it so sad?" "Sad!! No," said Lucy. No one in that boat doubted that they were seeing beyond the End of the World into Aslan's country.[5]

The fact that C. S. Lewis wrote mystical fiction does not, in itself, prove that Lewis was a mystic; but if we accept William McNamara's idea that "the mystic is not a special kind of person; each person is a special kind of mystic,"[6] then it's obvious that Lewis was a "special kind of mystic" indeed: one who knew how to convey a sense of wonder and mystery and awe through the humble means of a children's story or a science fiction novel. And while Lewis left us only one slender volume of poetry, it contains works like "An Expostulation" or "As the Ruin Falls," which reveal not only a masterful command of the English language but also a clear insight into the rich dynamics of the human quest for (and resistance to) intimacy with God.

Recommended Reading

The Voyage of the Dawn Treader by C. S. Lewis (New York: Macmillan, 1952).

Caryll Houselander (1901–1954)

Caryll Houselander wrote one of the loveliest devotional books for the season of Advent, *The Reed of God*. This English poet, artist, writer, and mystic was not a particularly pious woman (she smoked cigarettes and was known to swear), and she suffered from panic attacks and poor health, eventually losing her life to breast cancer. Baptized at age six (she called herself a "Rocking Horse Catholic" rather than a "Cradle Catholic"), she made the faith her own as a young adult and became a popular spiritual writer in her lifetime. But she was also a mystic, having had several visions of Christ, including one where she saw Christ like he might be depicted on a Russian Orthodox icon, spread across the sky and watching over the world. Another time, in a vision reminiscent of Thomas Merton's epiphany on a street corner in Louisville, she was riding the London Underground when she saw Christ within everyone on the train. From this, Houselander developed a truly mystical ability to see Christ in all persons, even in "sinners"—those who, on the surface, may seem to be the most alienated from Christ or from spirituality. "We should never come to a sinner without the reverence that we would take to the Holy Sepulchre," she writes, referring to the tomb in Jerusalem where Christ's body was interred after the crucifixion. "Pilgrims have travelled on foot for years to kiss the Holy Sepulchre, which is empty. In sinners, we can kneel at the tomb in which the dead Christ lies."[7]

The author of over a dozen books, her output included poetry and prose, and even her prose writings have a decidedly poetic voice. But no work is as enduring as *The Reed of God*, her meditation on Mary, emphasizing how real, how human, how down to earth the Mother of God was. The book shimmers with contemplative insight. She calls Advent (the season of preparation before Christmas, symbolically linked to Mary's season of pregnancy) "the season of the secret, the secret of the growth of Christ, of Divine Love growing in silence. It is the season of humility, silence, and growth."[8] She speaks of the importance of praying in silence, of waiting, and of seeking Christ, "because in the search we become aware of the wonder and mystery that contentment blinds us to."[9]

Houselander's poetry was collected in a book called *The Flowering Tree*, now out of print. But some of her poems are anthologized in *Caryll Houselander: Essential Writings*, edited by Wendy M. Wright (Orbis Books, 2005), which also includes samples of her artwork.

Recommended Reading

The Reed of God by Caryll Houselander (Notre Dame, IN: Christian Classics, 2006).

Coventry Patmore (1823–1896)

Coventry Patmore is remembered as a minor poet of the Victorian era, but his poetry as well as a remarkable book of aphorisms and meditations called *The Rod, the Root, and the Flower* reveal a rich contemplative sensibility as well. Evelyn Underhill quotes him repeatedly in her book *Mysticism*, leading off with an epigram quoting Patmore's definition of mysticism: "the science of ultimates . . . of self-evident Reality, which cannot be 'reasoned about,' because it is the object of pure reason or perception."[10] She also quotes in full one of Patmore's epigrams that I consider one of the finest brief statements of mystical spirituality composed in any tongue:

> *Lovers put out the candles and draw the curtains when they wish to see the god and the goddess; and in the higher communion the night of thought is the light of perception.*[11]

Patmore's spirituality stood in the long tradition of so-called "bridal mysticism"—interpreting the Song of Songs as a sign of God's love for the human soul, symbolized in the passionate embrace of husband and wife.

As a poet of his age—Victorian England—Patmore's writing often sounds sentimental or sexist. As a midlife convert to Roman Catholicism, he at times comes across as chauvinistic in his religious identity. But at its best, his work weaves together a romantic appreciation of nature with a recognition that the love that flows between two earthly lovers is the same love lavishly bestowed upon creation by God.

> *So she repeated soft her Poet's line,*
> *"By grace divine,*
> *Not otherwise, O Nature, are we thine!"*
> *And I, up the bright steep she led me, trod,*
> *And the like thought pursued*
> *With, "What is gladness without gratitude,*
> *And where is gratitude without a God?"*[12]

Recommended Reading

The Rod, the Root, and the Flower by Coventry Patmore (Freeport, NY: Books for Libraries Press, 1968).

Ephrem the Syrian (ca. 306–373)

Ephrem the Syrian, one of the fathers and a Doctor of the Church, was a deacon and prolific writer, with most of his work in verse form. His writings include biblical commentaries, meditations, and letters, but he is renowned primarily for his verse. Ephrem's poetry and hymns cover a variety of topics, from devotion to the saints, to the exposition of biblical themes, to denunciations of the heresies that were popular in the fourth century. He wrote exclusively in his native Syriac, a language related to Aramaic, which was the language Jesus spoke. In the days of the Roman Empire, Syriac was the third most-used language behind Latin and Greek.

Ephrem saw the world as filled with "mysteries"—signs and symbols that point to the hidden reality of God's presence in all things. His poetry and hymns celebrate the glorious presence of God throughout all creation—even God's presence within humanity, imprinted upon our souls the way an emperor's image is minted on a coin.

> *Quite despised is gold to our king,*
> *Who does not stamp his image in money;*
> *In a human being, the one greater than all,*
> *Our savior stamps his beauty.*
> *Who[ever] has believed in the name of God*
> *Receives the stamp of God.*[13]

"It is amazing how much the clay is able to be imprinted with the beauty of its sculptor,"[14] remarked Ephrem. This ability to see the splendor of God in God's creation marked the heart of Ephrem's symbolic poetry and anticipates a long tradition found among later mystics that the heart of spirituality is the ability to see with the eyes of love, and in so doing to (in the words of Julian of Norwich) "behold God in all."

Recommended Reading

Ephrem the Syrian: Hymns, translated by Kathleen E. McVey (New York: Paulist Press, 1989).

Evelyn Underhill (1875–1941)

Evelyn Underhill never claimed to be a mystic, never wrote about having visionary or ecstatic experiences, and her work was aimed more at introducing her readers to the history and teachings of the mystics than in asserting any spiritual authority of her own. In other words, Underhill was a great popularizer of mysticism, similar to how Alan Watts was a popularizer of Zen or Michael Harner a popularizer of shamanism. But her knowledge of the subject was so vast, her work so thorough and wide ranging, and her interest in the spiritual welfare of those who corresponded with her or who participated in the retreats she led was so genuine and so wise that she deserves to be included in the roster of Western mystics as much as theologians like Bernard of Clairvaux or philosophers like Saint Thomas Aquinas, who are widely regarded as mystics even though their writings do not recount their own spiritual experiences.

Truly a mystic of the twentieth century, Underhill's spirituality is more democratic than aristocratic in its focus: she champions not so much extraordinary moments of divine union as experienced by an elite few, but rather a more down-to-earth but no less life-transforming encounter with divine grace that is available to, as she put it, "normal people"—in other words, average people who may or may not be an ordained minister, a consecrated monk or nun, or an erudite scholar. Underhill introduced her ordinary readers to extraordinary spirituality, and in doing so, celebrated the idea that anybody—regardless of pedigree, background, education, or religious vocation—just might be able to scale those visionary heights.

She lived from 1875 to 1941, which makes her a contemporary of Thérèse of Lisieux and Pierre Teilhard de Chardin. Born into a middle-class British family, she married a barrister with whom she bore no children, leaving her free to write and pursue her lifelong commitment to spirituality. In her youth, she wrote three novels, as many volumes of poetry, a collection of medieval tales about the Virgin Mary, and over twenty specifically religious books, including collections of essays and transcripts of radio talks she did on the spiritual life. She also edited and wrote introductions for a variety of mystical classics, including *The Cloud of Unknowing*, Walter Hilton's *The Scale of Perfection*, and an anthology of writings by John Ruysbroeck (Ruusbroec), her personal favorite of the great mystics. Her masterpiece, *Mysticism*, was published in 1911, when she was only in her mid-thirties; other key works include *Practical Mysticism*, *The Mystics of the Church*, and *Worship*. Although her later works tend to emphasize a down-to-earth Christian spirituality rather than "mysticism" per se, all of her writing is imbued with a deep sense of the glory and possibility of a spiritual life wholly given to the love of God and the desire for divine union.

She came from a family of non-practicing members of the Church of England, but as a young woman Underhill felt drawn to the Catholic Church. But when an encyclical by Pope Pius X criticized modern intellectualism, and her husband expressed reservations about his wife entering Catholicism, she eventually found her spiritual home in the Anglican Communion. She became a pioneering lay minister in her church, where in addition to writing numerous books and essays she also delivered lectures (she was the first woman to lecture on religion at Oxford University), led retreats, and engaged in works of mercy, devoting time each week to charitable work among the London poor.

In addition to being a scholar, a retreat leader, a spiritual director, and an accomplished author of spiritual writing, Underhill also was a poet, though only two volumes of spiritual poetry were published in her lifetime: *Immanence* (1912) and *Theophanies* (1916). While not as renowned for her poetry as for her prose, some of Underhill's work is delightful, and all of it conveys her keen sense of mystical insight. The title poem of the first book is especially lovely.

> *I COME in the little things,*
> *Saith the Lord:*
> *Not borne on morning wings*
> *Of majesty, but I have set My Feet*
> *Amidst the delicate and bladed wheat*
> *That springs triumphant in the furrowed sod.*

There do I dwell, in weakness and in power;
Not broken or divided, saith our God!
In your strait garden plot I come to flower:
About your porch My Vine
Meek, fruitful, doth entwine;
Waits, at the threshold, Love's appointed hour.[15]

Although Underhill is not renowned for her poetry, clearly she was a poet at heart, for even her prose is characterized by a literary elegance and obvious love of language that arises from her poetic sensibility. One of her biographers, Dana Greene, has called Underhill an "artist of the infinite life," and indeed she felt strongly that being an artist—a lover and cultivator of beauty— was the nearest and next best thing to being a mystic. Clearly, for Underhill, her artistry was expressed through language.

Underhill died in 1941, shortly after suffering a stroke; her final writings during the early days of World War II revealed a strong commitment to pacifism, seeing peace as a natural mandate for a mature spiritual life. After her passing, her work remained influential, with C. S. Lewis and Thomas Merton among the more popular Christian writers who were students of her wisdom.

Recommended Reading

Practical Mysticism by Evelyn Underhill (New York: E. P. Dutton, 1915).

George Herbert (1593–1633)

George Herbert, an Anglican priest, on his deathbed gave a collection of poems to a friend, who published them shortly thereafter. Today, Herbert is considered one of the greatest metaphysical poets of the seventeenth century; several of his poems were used by composers like John Wesley and remain popular hymns, and five of his poems, including *Love (III)*, were set to music by the twentieth-century composer Ralph Vaughan Williams, who called them "Five Mystical Songs."

Herbert's poetry is at times playful and allegorical, filled with ecstatic utterances and heartfelt prayer. "Thou hast giv'n so much to me, / Give one thing more, a grateful heart." Peace, sorrow, gratitude, even giddiness dance through Herbert's verse. But always he returns to love. His gentle and optimistic understanding of the mystical life as constituting a love relationship with Love itself is no better expressed than in his quietly ecstatic poem, *Love (III)*:

> *Love bade me welcome: yet my soul drew back,*
>   *Guiltie of dust and sinne.*
> *But quick-ey'd Love, observing me grow slack*
>   *From my first entrance in,*
> *Drew nearer to me, sweetly questioning,*
>   *If I lack'd any thing.*
> *A guest, I answer'd, worthy to be here:*
>   *Love said, You shall be he.*
> *I the unkinde, ungratefull? Ah my deare,*
>   *I cannot look on thee.*
> *Love took my hand, and smiling did reply,*
>   *Who made the eyes but I?*
> *Truth Lord, but I have marr'd them: let my shame*
>   *Go where it doth deserve.*

And know you not, sayes Love, who bore the blame?

  My deare, then I will serve.

You must sit down, sayes Love, and taste my meat:

  So I did sit and eat.[16]

More than three centuries after it was written, this poem became much loved by the French mystic Simone Weil, who wrote about having a mystical experience while reciting it; in her words, "Christ came down and took possession of me."[17]

Recommended Reading

George Herbert: The Country Parson—The Temple, edited by John N. Wall Jr. (New York: Paulist Press, 1981).

Jacopone da Todi (ca. 1230–1306)

Jacopone da Todi was a Franciscan lay brother and poet born of a noble family and whose early life followed a normal worldly path—a successful lawyer, married to a noblewoman, but everything changed with his wife's early death in 1268. Jacopone apparently went off the deep end after this, becoming what we would now call a "holy fool." He wandered around aimlessly, once showing up at a wedding having tarred and feathered himself. Another time, he was seen wearing a saddle like a jackass and crawling around the public square. This is probably when he earned the name "Jacopone," which can roughly be translated as "Crazy Jim."

Eventually, his erratic behavior calmed down and Jacopone entered the Franciscan order. He became renowned for his poetry written both in Latin and in the local dialect of his time. He is possibly the author of the *Stabat Mater*, a hymn about Mary standing at the foot of the cross while Jesus was crucified. A classic of Marian devotion, it has been set to music by many great composers, including Giovanni Pierluigi da Palestrina, Arvo Pärt, Antonio Vivaldi, and Giuseppe Verdi. But his most lasting contribution to the literature of mysticism is his *Lauds*, a collection of over ninety poems remarkable for their vivid emotionality and profound devotion but also containing an edge of satire, even attacking the pope, whose views on Franciscan spirituality clashed with Jacopone's.

> *Gazing on Thee, Thou Bright and Morning Star,*
> *I am led far, I know not where I be;*
> *My heart is melted like a waxen bar,*
> *That moulded in Christ's likeness it may be;*
> *Christ, Thy barters keen and wondrous are!*
> *I am stript naked, to be drest in Thee:*
> *My heart transformed in me,*
> *My mind lies dumb,*
> *To see Thee come,*
> *In sweetness and in Love.*

—Laud 90[18]

Recommended Reading

Jacopone da Todi: The Lauds, translated by Serge Hughes and Elizabeth Hughes (New York: Paulist Press, 1982).

John Donne (ca. 1571–1631)

John Donne achieved renown as one of the great metaphysical poets of the seventeenth century, but he was also a prominent priest of the Church of England, serving as dean of St. Paul's Cathedral in London the last decade of his life. As a youth, Donne wrote secular poetry that is considered great English literature, but by midlife his poetry began to adopt a more markedly religious tone. Ordained to the priesthood in 1615, the most significant writing of his final years was his sermons, but also his *Devotions upon Emergent Occasions*, written in 1623 during a period of illness. *The Oxford Dictionary of the Christian Church* draws an interesting connection between his secular love poetry and his later thinking as a homilist: "His great theme as a love-poet was the bliss of union; his great theme as a preacher was God's mercy. Both themes are given singular force coming from one who wrote so often of a love that was 'rage' and not 'peace'; and knew in experience the meaning of working out one's salvation with fear and trembling."[19]

Donne has a clear understanding of the spirituality of prayer. "God is replenishingly everywhere; but most contractually and workingly in the temple. Since then every rectified man is the temple of the Holy Ghost, when he prays; it is the Holy Ghost itself that prays; and what can be denied where the asker gives?"[20]

Yet perhaps his most sublime statements of spirituality can be found in poems like this:

Wilt thou love God, as he thee! then digest,
My Soule, this wholsome meditation,

How God the Spirit, by Angels waited on

In heaven, doth make his Temple in thy brest.[21]

Recommended Reading

John Donne: Selections from Divine Poems, *Sermons,* Devotions, *and* Prayers, edited by John Booty (New York: Paulist Press, 1990).

John of the Cross (1542–1591)

John of the Cross belongs on everyone's shortlist of must-read mystics. He was a lover of God, a saint, a wisdom keeper, a soul friend, and a non-dualist. Of all the great mystic-poets, he was the greatest. So while I want to acknowledge the breadth of his contribution to Christian mysticism, if there is one quality of his worth celebrating, it is the splendor of his poetry. Indeed, John of the Cross is considered one of the finest poets of the Spanish language.

Juan de Yepes y Álvarez was born into a poor family (his father came from an affluent background but was disowned by his family when he married for love a woman below his social standing). John entered the Carmelite order in 1563, and four years later he met Teresa of Ávila, who inspired him with her plans to establish a Carmelite reform. John was involved in the foundation of the first reformed Carmelite monastery for men and soon became a leader in the reform, which was bitterly opposed by other Carmelites. In 1577, friars hostile to the reform kidnapped John and imprisoned him in a monastery, holding him captive for nearly nine months before he managed to escape. During his imprisonment, in which he spent most of his time in solitude in a small, poorly lit cell, he wrote several of his poems.

After escaping to a friendly convent where he recuperated from the harsh conditions of his incarceration, he resumed leadership in the reform, which became the Order of Discalced Carmelites in 1580. For the rest of his life, John continued to work as a religious reformer, and in addition to his poetry he composed four books of sublime mystical theology: *Ascent of Mount Carmel*, *Spiritual Canticle*, *Living Flame of Love*, and his most renowned work, *Dark Night of the Soul*. Each of these works is structured as a commentary in which he explains the layers of mystical meaning encoded in one of his poems.

The phrase "dark night of the soul" has become almost a cliché in spirituality, describing a period of profound inner purification that "is a privation and purgation of all sensible appetites for the external things of the world, the delights of the flesh, and the gratifications of the will."[22] In other words, the dark night is a period when God strips away from the human soul any appetite, affection, or attachment to worldly or sensual things that could stand in the way of unconditionally loving and serving God. John describes this as an "obscure, dark, and dreadful"[23] process, filled with pain and suffering, as the soul learns to let go of everything that is not God—no matter how much it may love it—in order to be available for nothing but God.

Because of the austerity and uncompromising sternness of John's description of this kind of inner purification, he has developed a reputation as a very difficult and harsh teacher of spiritual wisdom. In fact, though, there is much light and joy in John's writings, which are as lyrical about the love of God as they are harsh in their condemnation of human sin and attachments. Perhaps the best way to enter into the lighter side of John's mystical theology is through his poetry. Here, for example, is his poem "One Dark Night," the poem that forms the basis of the commentary in *Dark Night of the Soul*.

1. On a dark night, Kindled in love with yearnings—oh, happy chance!—
I went forth without being observed, My house being now at rest.

2. In darkness and secure, By the secret ladder, disguised— oh, happy chance!—
In darkness and in concealment, My house being now at rest.

3. In the happy night, In secret, when none saw me, Nor I beheld aught, Without light or guide, save that which burned in my heart.

4. This light guided me More surely than the light of noonday To the place where he (well I knew who!) was awaiting me—A place where none appeared.

5. Oh, night that guided me, Oh, night more lovely than the dawn,
Oh, night that joined Beloved with lover, Lover transformed in the Beloved!

6. Upon my flowery breast, Kept wholly for himself alone, There he stayed sleeping, and I caressed him, And the fanning of the cedars made a breeze.

7. The breeze blew from the turret As I parted his locks;
With his gentle hand he wounded my neck And caused all
my senses to be suspended.

8. I remained, lost in oblivion; My face I reclined on the
Beloved.
All ceased and I abandoned myself, Leaving my cares for-
gotten among the lilies.[24]

Even a casual reading of this poem reveals its mystical secrets. In the poem, the "dark night" implies not only the night of purification, but also the "darkness" of prayer that transcends the "light" of human reason, seeking instead the "darkness" of pure mystical love. "My house being now at rest" implies the silence of contemplative prayer, while going "forth without being observed" suggests the lack of self-consciousness that character- izes true humility. "With his gentle hand he wounded my neck And caused all my senses to be suspended" suggests a kind of mystical ecstasy or rapture that can come in advanced states of contemplative absorption. Finally, "I abandoned myself" points toward the summit of humility, where the love of God enables a mortal soul to engage in such self-abandonment as a response to that love.

Recommended Reading

The Collected Works of Saint John of the Cross, translated by Kieran Kavanaugh and Otilio Rodriguez (Washington, DC: ICS Publications, 1991).

Ramon Llull (ca. 1232–ca. 1315)

Ramon Llull was an intellectual in the Kingdom of Majorca (now part of Spain) who wrote poetry as well as works of fiction, philosophy, and logic. After receiving a mystical vision of Jesus Christ in 1263, he joined the Third Order of Saint Francis. He certainly was no saint: he owned slaves and campaigned actively for the conversion of Jews and Muslims to Christianity. But his masterpiece, *The Book of the Lover and the Beloved*, extols the splendor and beauty of divine love in lyrical, beautiful, and at times soaring language.

Llull had a clear understanding that the heart of the mystical life is love, and he drew comparisons between the beauty of nature and the spiritual life: as the one who fills the sun with light, God can fill our hearts with divine love. Indeed, Llull saw that in our very longing for God, or the tears we cry out of yearning for the Divine, there is evidence for God's infinite love for us.

Recommended Reading

Doctor Illuminatus: A Ramon Llull Reader, translated by Eve Bonner (Princeton, NJ: Princeton University Press, 1985).

Thomas Traherne (ca. 1636–1674)

Thomas Traherne, like John Donne and George Herbert, is considered one of the metaphysical poets of English literature; but by a twist of fate his work is far less known than theirs. A clergyman of the Church of England, with only a few writings published before or shortly after his death from smallpox, during his lifetime he did not have a reputation as either a poet or a mystic. For over two centuries, both Traherne's poetry and a collection of poetic and prose meditations, *Centuries*, remained unpublished. Once the manuscripts were discovered in the late nineteenth century, they were finally published in the early 1900s. Today, Traherne is recognized as a mystic whose writing reflects an ardent and eloquent love of nature, celebrating a simple, almost childlike faith anchored in an intimate relationship with God. At least one literary critic praises Traherne's poetry for its exploration of non-dualism, a key element of mystical wisdom.[25]

> *Divine Impressions when they came*
> *Did quickly enter and my Soul inflame.*
> *Tis not the object, but the Light*
> *That maketh Heaven: 'tis a purer sight.*
> *Felicity*
> *Appears to none but them that purely see.*[26]

Here Traherne describes a child's mystical experience—probably an experience from his own childhood.[27]

In *Centuries*, the poet celebrates the omnipresence of God's love and felicity (happiness): "Our Bridegroom and our King being everywhere, our Lover and Defender watchfully governing all worlds, no danger or enemy can arise to hurt us . . . The essence of God therefore being all light and knowledge, love and goodness, care and providence, felicity and glory, a pure and simple Act, it is present in its operations, and by those Acts which it eternally exerteth is wholly busied in all parts and places of His dominion, perfecting and completing our bliss and happiness."[28]

Recommended Reading

Waking Up in Heaven: A Contemporary Edition of Centuries of Meditation by Thomas Traherne, edited by David Buresh (Spencerville, MD: Hesed Press, 2002).

CHAPTER 5

Saints

Following Christ involves a quest for holiness—for being set apart for God in a special or sacred way. The stereotype of the saint is a "Goody Two-shoes," a holy person with perfect morals and spotless character. Thankfully, such a person doesn't exist— which is a good thing, since we also tend to think of such people as moralistic and judgmental, or at least impossible to emulate.

Even the canonized saints—Christians publicly recognized as embodying heroic virtue—were hardly perfect. Most Christians believe only one person was perfect: Christ himself. (Some also regard Mary his mother as sinless, but even that's not the same thing as perfection.) Even the most pristine saint still had his or her sins and imperfections.

The Catholic and Orthodox Churches will only declare someone a saint after he or she has died and the Church can document the person's exemplary life and even a few miracles attributed to their heavenly intervention. (Part of what makes a heavenly saint so special is that he or she is said to intercede directly with God on our behalf.) Other Christians, like most

Protestants, have a broader understanding of what makes a saint: I once went to a church where the pastor called the congregation "the saints," with the understanding that every believer is a saint of God. It's more democratic, but those churches tend to frown on the idea of praying to the saints to get them to intercede with God on our behalf.

I don't know if anyone has an exact count of how many saints there are in the Catholic/Orthodox sense of the word, but I believe the number is upward of ten thousand. Not every mystic is a canonized saint. (For that matter, not every canonized saint is generally thought of as a mystic, since sainthood is about virtue, not necessarily about mystical union or intimacy with God.) But the saints profiled in this chapter are as famous for their sanctity as for their mystical spirituality.

Learning about the saint-mystics is a reminder that mysticism is about more than just feeling close to God or having an experience of God. At its heart, mysticism is about living in God's presence. To do that naturally implies seeking virtue and holiness as much as it suggests seeking intimacy with God. We who aspire to be mystics need to aspire to be saints, first and foremost. Holiness is a prerequisite for mysticism. The word holiness means "set apart," so if you want to be close to God, start acting like someone who is set aside for God—even if it means some people may think of you as a Goody Two-shoes.

Saint Benedict (480–547)

Saint Benedict is not someone primarily known as a mystic: he barely merits a passing mention in Evelyn Underhill's classic book *Mysticism*. But few figures in the history of Christianity have had more of an impact on the development of mystical spirituality than this important sixth-century monk. Hailing from Nursia, Italy, as a youth Benedict abandoned a promising future in Rome to retreat to a cave in Subiaco, where he lived in solitude for several years, developing a reputation for holiness. He was asked to serve a community of monks as its abbot, but this did not end happily, for it is said that the monks tried to get rid of their unpopular leader by poisoning him. Not surprisingly, Benedict retreated back to his cave, but eventually the monks of Monte Cassino prevailed upon him to be their leader, and it was there where Benedict wrote his rule for monks. More than just a guidebook for running a monastery (although it certainly is also that), *The Rule of Saint Benedict* is an invitation to a committed, conscious spiritual life written for every kind of monk (or nun), from the abbot down to the newest novice. Benedict's rule seems ahead of its time with its emphasis on flexibility, common sense, and recognition that a community is always formed of individuals, so each monk in a monastery has a unique relationship with God.

Benedict encouraged monks to treat their work tools with the same reverence that a priest shows the chalice and paten used to consecrate Holy Communion; he also instructed monks to welcomes guests to the monastery with the same hospitality that they would show if it were Christ himself coming for a visit. These two examples illustrate what is truly beautiful about Benedictine spirituality: it is humble and down to earth but attuned to discerning the presence of God in the most ordinary aspects of life.

Despite the ordinary character of Benedict's teaching, it would be a mistake to dismiss him out of hand for not being a mystic. Even in *The Rule*, there are hints that Benedict had the eyes of a contemplative.

"Let us then at last arise . . . and let us open our eyes to the deifying light,"[1] he instructs his readers in *The Rule*'s prologue. What is he referring to? A conservative interpretation of "the deifying light" is simply a light that comes from God; but the original Latin phrase could also be read as "the light that transfigures us into God." After all, a light that comes from God will do far more than just enable us to see. It will also invite us into union with God, which is the hallmark of the mystical path. Benedict, it seems, recognized that the surest route to such mystical union was a path of humility, community, and ordinary work—but the goal of divine union remains as exalted as anything any mystic could promise.

Recommended Reading

The Rule of St. Benedict: Latin & English, translated by Luke Dysinger (Trabuco Canyon, CA: Source Books, 1997).

Saint Catherine of Genoa (1447–1510)

Saint Catherine of Genoa came from a noble Italian family. At age sixteen, she was married to a man who turned out to be abusive and faithless; she endured the marriage for a decade and then received a dramatic mystical awakening where she felt overwhelmed by God's love while making her sacramental confession. Thus began a life of dedicated prayer and service, particularly to the sick and the poor. Catherine's story includes many "remarkable mental and at times almost pathological experiences,"[2] including extreme fasting, sprinkling bitter herbs on her food, wearing a hair shirt, and other austerities.[3] Her goal was simply to purify herself as a response to the overwhelming love she had encountered. This spirituality of purification would bear fruit in a spiritual treatise on purgatory, probably not written by Catherine herself but based on her mystical spirituality. Unlike the view of purgatory that stresses it as a place of unbearable torment, Catherine sees the pains of purification embedded in joy that emerges from the fact of being one with God. Having encountered "the fiery love of God," she "rejoiced in her union with God in this loving purgatory."[4]

One of the most famous quotes from Saint Catherine of Genoa speaks to the deep sense of unity with God she embodied: "My *me* is God, nor do I know my selfhood except in God."[5]

Recommended Reading

Catherine of Genoa: Purgation and Purgatory: The Spiritual Dialogue, translated by Serge Hughes (New York: Paulist Press, 1979).

Saint Edith Stein (1891–1942)

Saint Edith Stein, also known by her religious name, Teresa Benedicta of the Cross, was a Jewish philosopher who converted to Catholicism, became a Carmelite nun, and was killed at Auschwitz during the Second World War. Regarded as a martyr for her faith (she was one of several hundred Jewish converts to Catholicism that the Nazis imprisoned as retaliation for the

Church in the Netherlands' denunciation of Nazi racism), she was canonized as a saint by Pope John Paul II in 1998.

As a philosopher, Stein was grounded in mystical wisdom; she credited her study of the autobiography of Saint Teresa of Ávila with inspiring her to become a Christian, and one of her most important books is *The Science of the Cross*, a study of the mystical theology of John of the Cross. Her superior had asked her to write this book because 1942 marked the four-hundredth anniversary of John of the Cross's birth; after the Nazis arrested Stein, the other sisters in her community found the manuscript in her room. More than just an academic study, *The Science of the Cross* stands as an overview of mystical spirituality in its own right. Writing about a soul with a mature spiritual life, Stein says, "She no longer needs to meditate in order to love and to come to know God . . . As soon as she sets herself to pray she is with God and, in loving surrender, remains in his presence. Her silence is more precious to him than many words."[6]

Recommended Reading

The Science of the Cross by Edith Stein, translated by Josephine Koeppel (Washington, DC: ICS Publications, 2003).

Saint Francis de Sales (1567–1622)

Saint Francis de Sales is one of the leading spiritual writers of the Catholic world of the seventeenth century. For the last twenty years of his life he was the Bishop of Geneva, Switzerland, although he did not reside there, for at that time Geneva was under Calvinist control. The bishop became renowned as a preacher and teacher dedicated to the spiritual formation not only of priests and nuns but also laypeople. This pastoral concern is revealed in his most renowned book, *Introduction to the Devout Life*, but the saint's mystical side is more readily revealed in his two-volume magnum opus, *On the Love of God*. His friendship with Jane Frances de Chantal resulted in them co-founding a religious order for women, the Order of the Visitation of Holy Mary; the correspondence between de Sales and de Chantal reveals they were both gifted spiritual companions whose relationship reflected their shared love for God and commitment to a life of prayer.

Like many mystics, de Sales draws inspiration from the Song of Songs and reflects on the opening verse in that ancient love poem as symbolizing, with a kiss, the yearning for mystical union. The verse reads, "Let him kiss me with the kisses of his mouth!" (Songs 1:2); to which de Sales comments, "Thus in a kiss one mouth is put to another as testimony to a desire to pour each soul into the other and unite them in a perfect union."[7] "O love eternal, my soul needs and chooses you eternally," prays the saint. "Ah, come Holy Spirit, and inflame our hearts with your love!" His was a mysticism of virtue and duty and sober responsibility, but most of all, it was a mysticism grounded in love.

Recommended Reading

On the Love of God volumes 1 and 2 by St. Francis de Sales, translated by John K. Ryan (Garden City, NY: Image Books, 1963).

Saint Francis of Assisi (ca. 1181–1226)

Saint Francis of Assisi is the Doctor Dolittle of Christian mysticism. For many churches, of various denominations, Saint Francis's feast day (October 4) is a day on which the congregation hosts a "blessing of the animals." Many different kinds of pets, service animals, and even livestock—along with their human companions—gather for the service: dogs, cats, parrots, ferrets, turtles, hamsters, even snakes and skunks. The barking and meowing that join into the prayers of the day make it a worship experience that skids along the thin line between order and chaos. Surely the humble, poor friar from Assisi would approve.

The Patron Saint of Animals and the Environment was born Giovanni Francesco Bernardone in 1181 or 1182—we don't know his exact birthdate. He was the son of an affluent silk merchant, and all indications of Francis's comfortable early life suggested he would follow his father in the family trade. But after spending time as a prisoner of war during a regional conflict in his twentieth year, Francis came home suffering from a serious illness, which fostered in him a commitment to pursue a life of prayer. During a visit to Rome, the wealthy young man was moved by the suffering of poor beggars on the street. Taking seriously Jesus's call to leave all and follow Him, Francis did just that: he abandoned his life of middle-class luxury and adopted voluntary poverty in the name of his faith. Soon others joined him, and the Franciscan Order was born.

Unlike many other mystics, Francis left behind few writings, although a small number of letters, songs, and texts are reliably attributed to saint of Assisi. One of the most loved of Francis's works is the "Canticle of the Sun," perhaps the most succinct statement of how love for God can manifest as a profound sense of delight and kinship with the natural world. This song of praise offers glory and thanksgiving to God by honoring element after element of the natural world. Brother Sun, Sister Moon, Brother Wind, Sister Water, Brother Fire, and Sister Mother Earth are each celebrated in turn.

> *O most high, almighty, good Lord God, to Thee belong praise, glory, honor, and all blessing!*
>
> *Praised be my Lord God with all His creatures, and specially our brother the sun, who brings us the day and who brings us the light; fair is he and shines with a very great splendor: O Lord he signifies to us Thee!*
>
> *Praised be my Lord for our sister the moon, and for the stars, the which He has set clear and lovely in heaven.*
>
> *Praised be my Lord for our brother the wind and for air and cloud, calms and all weather by the which Thou upholdest life in all creatures.*
>
> *Praised be my Lord for our sister water, who is very serviceable unto us and humble and precious and clean.*
>
> *Praised be my Lord for our brother fire, through whom Thou givest us light in the darkness; and he is bright and pleasant and very mighty and strong.*
>
> *Praised be my Lord for our mother the earth, the which doth sustain us and keep us, and bringeth forth divers fruits and flowers of many colors, and grass . . .*[8]

Full of sensuous imagery and poetic descriptions of the beauty of nature, this thoroughly Christian song of praise never fails in declaring that the splendor of creation unites in giving glory to the Maker of All Things. For Francis, love for the poor was equivalent to love for the simplicity of the earth—a mature spiritual understanding that our own age has seen embodied in the first Pope to take the name of Francis.

Few people may feel called to embrace the life of joyful renunciation that marked the lifestyle of Francis and his followers. But while it is not necessary to be poor in order to follow Christ, the Franciscan ideal still has much to say to us. We live in a time when spiraling energy costs and rapidly diminishing resources have forced all of us to rethink what is required in order to protect our natural resources. The spirituality of Saint Francis represents a holistic approach to caring for Mother Earth. Franciscan mysticism recognizes that loving nature is only the first step; equally important is the decision to choose a life of simplicity. Reducing the amount of resources we consume, and reusing and recycling all that we can, are all values consistent with the Franciscan ideal of holy poverty. When we live simply, we love nature. And when we do both, God is glorified.

Recommended Reading

Francis of Assisi in His Own Words: The Essential Writings, translated by Jon Sweeney (Brewster, MA: Paraclete Press, 2013).

Saint Gregory of Narek (951–1003)

Saint Gregory of Narek wrote a lengthy mystical work, *The Book of Lamentations* (translated in English as *Speaking with God from the Depths of the Heart*), consisting of ninety-five luminous and lyrical poem-prayers, filled with mystical longing for union with God. Like so many other mystics, Gregory also wrote a commentary on the Song of Songs, along with various odes and litanies. He has been acclaimed as the first great poet of Armenia. The son of an archbishop, Gregory entered monastic life at an early age and devoted his life to prayer, teaching, and writing. He was something of a Renaissance man, skilled not only in writing but also in music, mathematics, astronomy, and theology.

His prayers express a clear sense that love (compassion) is at the heart of the spiritual life. "When I embark upon the solemn interpretation of the Word, send me first your compassion, and let it speak through me in a manner worthy, useful and pleasing to you, in glory and praise for your Godhead, and in the silence of the universal church."[9] At another point he prays, "By your good will if the light of compassion should shine . . . if the rays of your glory should spread . . . if the drops of your pure love should shower down, . . . if the silenced sound of your beckoning voice, Lord, should again be heard, . . . then with this blessing shall the faith of steady hope be forever mine finding refuge in the Holy Spirit, who with the Father is worshiped with the voice of sweetness and together with you bathed in light too bright for human eyes."[10]

Pope Francis declared Saint Gregory of Narek a Doctor of the Church in 2015.

Recommended Reading

The Festal Works of St. Gregory of Narek, translated by Abraham Terian (Collegeville, MN: Liturgical Press, 2016).

Saint Gregory of Nyssa (ca. 330–ca. 395)

Saint Gregory of Nyssa was both an important early mystic and a significant theologian of his age, one of the fathers of the church. He was one of three important writers known as the Cappadocian Fathers, along with his brother Basil of Caesarea and their colleague Gregory of Nazianzus. The Cappadocian Fathers, named for the region in modern-day Turkey where they lived, were leading Christian thinkers of their day who taught that God is a Trinity. Of the three, Gregory is renowned as having the most mystical voice; his *Life of Moses* is renowned as one of the most important early mystical writings, expressing themes of the hiddenness of God that would later characterize the thought of great mystics like Pseudo-Dionysius and John of the Cross. His other writings include sermons on the Beatitudes and the Song of Songs, treatises on topics like perfection and the resurrection, the life of Saint Macrina the Younger, and, of course, the theology of the Trinity. His mystical writings have been collected in an anthology called *From Glory to Glory*.

"The true vision and the true knowledge of what we seek consists precisely in not seeing, in an awareness that our goal transcends all knowledge and is everywhere cut off from us by the darkness of incomprehensibility."[11] Church historian Martin Laird notes that, for Gregory, themes like darkness or incomprehensibility suggest that the mystical life elevates us beyond the light of human reason into a place where "the contemplation of God is not concerned with the ordinary activities of thought."[12] We encounter the mystical presence of God in a silent place where language and thought fall away.

Recommended Reading

From Glory to Glory: Texts from Gregory of Nyssa's Mystical Writings, edited by Jean Daniélou (Crestwood, NY: St. Vladimir's Seminary Press, 1979).

Saint Isaac the Syrian (ca. 613–ca. 700)

Saint Isaac the Syrian, also known as Isaac of Nineveh, died around the year 700. He had been consecrated the bishop of Nineveh, but apparently administration was not his joy, for he resigned his position after only a few months, retreating to a mountain where he adopted the life of a hermit. Eventually he entered monastic life, where it is said that he studied the Bible so assiduously that it ruined his eyesight and he had to dictate his writings to his students.

More than anything else, Saint Isaac was a mystic of the love of God. Every act of God emerges out of the vast boundlessness of divine love, and our efforts as human beings to respond to that love form the heart of the spiritual life, whether ascetic (the choices we make to let go of everything that stands in the way of divine love) or mystical (the graces showered upon us from

God). Prayer, the heart of the spiritual life, is nothing more than the human response to love.

Isaac taught that turning away from corruption and worldly pleasures was a necessary prerequisite to the joy of contemplating God in stillness, wonder, and light. One distinctive feature of Saint Isaac's teachings involves the "gift of tears"—the tears that flow both when we mortals truly recognize our brokenness because of sin, but also the tears that flow in gratitude and joy as we acknowledge the splendor of God's love. The gift of tears marks the threshold between the old life of worldly desires and carnal appetites and the contemplative life of humility, silence, and deep peace. As a gift, tears are not something we can whip up by our own designs, but rather are a grace bestowed by the same Spirit who sanctifies and deifies us.

Perhaps nowhere is Isaac's mysticism of love more evident than in this fascinating passage from his Ascetical Homily 28, in which he talks about God's love and Gehenna (hell).

> It would be improper for a man to think that sinners in Gehenna are deprived of the love of God. Love is the offspring of knowledge of the truth which, as is commonly confessed, is given to all. The power of love works in two ways: it torments those who have played the fool . . . but it becomes a source of joy for those who have observed its duties. Thus I say that this is the torment of Gehenna: bitter regret. But love inebriates the souls of the sons of Heaven by its delectability.[13]

Hell is one of the thorniest issues in Christian spirituality. Even many children can see the obvious paradox: if God is all-loving and all-forgiving, why would God want to send unrepentant sinners to an eternity of agony in the lake of fire? Isaac's answer is quite simple: we are not punished in eternity like criminals might be sent to prison in their earthly life; but rather, when someone freely chooses to reject God's love, eternity becomes a torment because God keeps on loving us anyway. The torments of hell, in other words, are not external but internal—the "fires" of hell are fueled by our own interior hatred. It's reminiscent of something C. S. Lewis would say over a thousand years later in his darkly brilliant novel about heaven and hell, *The Great Divorce*:

> *Never fear. There are only two kinds of people in the end: those who say to God, "Thy will be done," and those to whom God says, in the end, "Thy will be done." All that are in Hell, choose it. Without that self-choice there could be no Hell. No soul that seriously and constantly desires joy will ever miss it. Those who seek find.*[14]

So hell is not an icon of God's wrath but of human freedom—the freedom to reject even the love of God. Saint Isaac understands that while those who would freely and willingly reject God's love would be tormented by it, everyone who chooses to accept divine love will be forever inebriated by its delectability—as lovely and succinct a statement of mystical ecstasy as one could ever wish for.

Recommended Reading

The Ascetical Homilies of Saint Isaac the Syrian by Isaac of Nineveh (Boston: Holy Transfiguration Monastery, 2011).

Saint John Climacus (ca. 570–ca. 649)

Saint John Climacus was a monk who lived on Mount Sinai. Very little is known about his life; even the dates of his birth and death are subject to much scholarly disagreement. According to one ancient source, John entered what is now called St. Catherine's monastery as a teenager and eventually withdrew into the life of a hermit. In his old age, he was coaxed back into the monastery, where he served as the abbot. John wrote one major work, *The Ladder of Divine Ascent*, which describes how a monk may ascend in the life of holiness (like someone climbing a ladder) by practicing a number of virtues, including detachment, repentance, silence, stillness, and non-possessiveness. The ladder consists of thirty steps, one for each year of Christ's age at the time he was baptized.

Perhaps of particular interest to contemplatives is the eleventh step, "On Talkativeness and Silence." In this, Saint John Climacus speaks of "intelligent silence," which is the inner silence of the mind where thought has been stilled through intentional contemplative awareness. The author says: "Intelligent silence is the mother of prayer, a recall from captivity, preservation of fire, an overseer of thoughts, a watch against enemies, a prison of mourning, a friend of tears . . . a companion of stillness . . . increase of knowledge, a creator of divine vision, unseen progress, secret ascent."[15] He goes on to say, "The friend of silence draws near to God and, by secretly conversing with Him, is enlightened by God."[16] Climacus also understood that deep meditative prayer involves the body as well as the mind: "Let the memory of Jesus be united with your breathing and then you will know the benefit of silence."[17]

The Ladder of Divine Ascent by Saint John Climacus (Boston: The Holy Transfiguration Monastery, 1978).

Saint Nicodemus of the Holy Mountain (ca. 1749–1809)

Saint Nicodemus of the Holy Mountain became a monk on Mount Athos (the Greek "Holy Mountain" for which he is named), making his profession in 1775. The Eastern Orthodox Church recognized him as a saint in 1955. He is probably best known (and most significant for the mystical tradition) for being one of the editors of *The Philokalia*, a multi-volume anthology of Eastern Orthodox mystical and contemplative writings, which was first published in 1782. Its name means "love for what is beautiful." *The Philokalia* gathers together an impressive collection of Orthodox writings on prayer and contemplation, including works by Evagrius Ponticus, John Cassian, Maximus the Confessor, Symeon the New Theologian, Gregory Palamas, and many others. Many of the writings included in it concern praying the Jesus Prayer (the "prayer of the heart") and the quest for *hesychia*, or inner silence.

Nicodemus was not just an editor, however. Among his own writings is a treatise called *A Handbook of Spiritual Counsel* (1801), written for a cousin of his who had been ordained a bishop. But Nicodemus's insight into spiritual psychology can be applied not just to bishops or priests, but to all who seek deeper intimacy with God. It offers "psychological, ethical, and practical"[18] advice to its readers, grounded in the Jesus Prayer tradition, to help them prepare themselves for the gift of union with God. "Everyone finds calm and rest at their center,"[19] notes Nicodemus, but he also acknowledged that spiritual wisdom can be found in nature: "By meditating upon the created beings as mirrors, we contemplate the creator and we praise him and call him by name."[20]

Recommended Reading

Nicodemus of the Holy Mountain: A Handbook of Spiritual Counsel, translated by Peter A. Chamberas (New York: Paulist Press, 1989).

Saint Thomas Aquinas (ca. 1225–1274)

Saint Thomas Aquinas is as much a wisdom keeper as he is a saint—renowned as one of the great medieval philosophers of Western Christianity, his towering unfinished masterpiece *Summa Theologica* gathers in some 3,500 pages the main teachings of the Catholic faith, explained in philosophical terms. Its influence not only on Catholicism but also on Western culture at large cannot be overestimated. He was hardly perfect—his belief that women were naturally inferior to men is particularly odious—but his overall contribution to philosophy remains significant more than seven centuries after his death.

In addition to being a scholar, Aquinas was also a mystic; and on at least one occasion he had a truly extraordinary encounter with the divine mystery. On the feast of Saint Nicholas, several months before Aquinas died—December 6, 1273—he was saying Mass when something extraordinary happened. Afterward, he told his secretary that he was unable to continue his work, for compared to the mystical insight he received that morning, all his writing "seemed like straw" to him.

In other words, a mystical encounter with the splendor of God can make the greatest philosopher of the age see his brilliant writing as virtually worthless.

While the intellectual and philosophical nature of Aquinas's writings may seem overly abstract to the contemplative seeker of the third millennium, his work contains plenty of clues to show that for him spirituality was not just a head trip, but a lived experience. For example,

> It is love of God which fires people to look at his beauty. And because we all enjoy obtaining what we love, the contemplative life culminates in enjoyment, which is a matter of our feelings; and this in turn makes love more intense.[21]

Perhaps it takes a truly brilliant (if flawed) mind to articulate just how deeply the mystical life is really about love.

Recommended Reading

Albert and Thomas: Selected Writings, translated and edited by Simon Tugwell (New York: Paulist Press, 1988).

Saint Teresa of Calcutta (1910–1997)

Saint Teresa of Calcutta is more popularly known around the world as Mother Teresa, the "saint of Calcutta." The winner of the 1979 Nobel Peace Price, the US Presidential Medal of Freedom, and numerous other honors, she is a figure of veneration and devotion among not only Catholics but people of goodwill throughout the world. In addition to her own heroic work among the poor of Calcutta, she founded the Missionaries of Charity, a religious order that now has over 4,500 sisters engaging in works of mercy and contemplative prayer in over 100 countries.

Mother Teresa is not often thought of as a contemplative or a mystic, yet her posthumously published book *Come Be My Light* offers insight into the profound mystery that characterized her faith. The epigraph to this book seems to capture her spirituality well: "If I ever become a Saint—I will surely be one of 'darkness.' I will continually be absent from Heaven—to light the light of those in darkness on earth."[22] While some readers who are not familiar with the mystical tradition of Christianity found the depth of Mother Teresa's darkness and sense of God's absence unsettling, those who know the tradition recognize that her spirituality placed her in the same tradition as *The Cloud of Unknowing, Dark Night of the Soul,* and other great mystical writings that stress God's hiddenness or unknowability. It seems that Mother Teresa's sanctity involves more than her remarkable work on behalf of the poor—she gave herself as generously to the love of God as she did to the love of neighbor.

Recommended Reading

Mother Teresa: Come Be My Light: The Private Writings of the Saint of Calcutta, edited by Brian Kolodiejchuk (New York: Doubleday, 2007).

CHAPTER 6

Heretics

I suspect that readers will have a variety of responses to this chapter. Some will love it, because they see "heretics" as people who think for themselves and who refuse to conform to unrealistic expectations and who refuse to submit to religious bureaucracy. But others might question why heretics are included in this book at all, for they will regard unorthodox mystics as dangerous subversives who destabilized the order of the Christian Church by introducing elements of chaos and discord.

My sense is that many of these heretical mystics fall somewhere between these two extremes. It's important to remember that at least some of the most revered saints of the Christian world were, at one time or another, denounced as heretics—or at least held under a cloud of suspicion (two examples of this would be Thomas Aquinas and Faustina Kowalska). Likewise, some of the more notorious "heretic" mystics worked very hard to defend themselves and their views from what they perceived as unfair attacks. Meister Eckhart claimed that his detractors could accuse him of error, but not of heresy, since an error implies a mistake of the intellect, whereas a heresy implies a defect of the will (a heretic, after all, is someone who chooses to be opposed to accepted Christian teachings; the word *heretic* literally means "chooser"). Eckhart insisted he was a faithful member of the Church and therefore could not be a willful subversive of it; but his critics and enemies disagreed.

This chapter gathers together the troublemakers and rabble-rousers, the loudmouths who were not afraid to question authority or proclaim mystical ideas that came from no source other than their own inner compass. All of them became controversial, although in different ways. Some, like Eckhart or Origen, were formally condemned for their heresy. Other, more recent figures (Thomas Merton and Pierre Teilhard de Chardin) have not been formally labeled heretics but remain controversial among at least some Christians for their outside-the-box views. Then there are the true victims: Madame Guyon, who was imprisoned for her teachings, and Marguerite Porete, who was burned at the stake in 1310 after she refused to recant her beliefs.

What I suppose is remarkable is not that there are many Christian mystics who carry a reputation for heresy, but that there weren't more of them. Whether you are a devout Christian who is suspicious of so-called heretics, or you're the type of person who loves to question authority and therefore are drawn to mystics with a similar personality, hold this notion of "heretic" lightly. After all, today's heretics could be tomorrow's saints (and vice versa).

Clement of Alexandria (ca. 150–215)

Clement of Alexandria is widely considered the first significant Christian mystic after the age of the New Testament. Indeed, when Clement was born (in the middle of the second century), much of the New Testament writings were less than a hundred years old. In the words of Evelyn Underhill, Clement was a seminal figure "who first adapted the language of the pagan Mysteries to the Christian theory of the spiritual life."[1] In writings such as the *Exhortation to the Greeks* and the *Miscellanies*, Clement demonstrated intimate knowledge of Greek religion and philosophy and sought to explain the still-young Christian faith to the larger pagan world.

One of Clement's most profound statements neatly sums up the mystical doctrine of *theosis* (deification): "the Word of God speaks, having become man, in order that such as you may learn from man how it is even possible for man to become a god."[2] This was later succinctly restated by Bishop Athanasius (ca. 296–373), who is credited with saying, "God became human so that humans might become god."[3]

Clement was first accused of heresy by the ninth-century Orthodox patriarch Photios I of Constantinople; in the sixteenth century, the Italian cardinal Cesare Baronius lobbied to have Clement stripped of his status as a Catholic saint. The charges against him include holding unorthodox views about the nature of Christ and about the role of grace in the spiritual life. Because of this, he is not well known outside of academic circles. Ironically, Clement's most famous pupil, Origen of Alexandria, also was a great mystic—and ultimately attacked as an even more notorious heretic.

Recommended Reading

Clement of Alexandria, translated by G. W. Butterworth (Cambridge: Harvard University Press/Loeb Classical Library, 1919).

Evagrius Ponticus (345–399)

Evagrius Ponticus may be the single most important mystical "heretic" in the history of Christian spirituality. Within a generation of his death, prominent church leaders like Saint Jerome were accusing him of heresy, primarily because of his association with the teachings of Origen of Alexandria, the third-century theologian and mystic whose controversial ideas would eventually be formally condemned by church leaders in the sixth century. But it's interesting to trace how Evagrius's writings, in essence, went underground once he was accused of heresy. Generally speaking, once a theologian or mystic was saddled with the accusation of heresy, his or her writings would be destroyed—or at least would no longer be studied by orthodox believers. In Evagrius's case, however, his writings remained in circulation. Jesuit scholar William Harmless notes,

> *Despite persecution, despite posthumous condemnation, that torrent of ideas flowed on. Evagrius's manuscripts were copied and recopied by desert calligraphers. In the Greek-speaking world, calligraphers quietly removed his name from the title page of manuscripts, but they continued both to copy and to imitate his proverblike "chapters."*[4]

Eventually, more orthodox thinkers like Maximus the Confessor in the East, or John Cassian in the West, would incorporate many of Evagrius's ideas and perspectives in their own writings, thus ensuring that this enigmatic desert father's spiritual wisdom would be passed on from generation to generation.

But who exactly was Evagrius? Born into a Christian family in 345 in Pontus, a region on the coast of the Black Sea in what is now Turkey, Evagrius showed promise as a writer and a speaker, working with some of the greatest Christian leaders of the time, including Saint Basil the Great and Saint Gregory of Nazianzus, who ordained him a deacon. But while living in Constantinople, Evagrius fell in love with a married woman and had a dream in which he was imprisoned for the sin of adultery. Horrified, he fled to a monastery near Jerusalem and eventually settled in the desert of Egypt as a monk, where he remained until his death.

This was the golden age of the desert fathers and mothers—hermits, monks, and nuns who lived in the deserts of Egypt, Syria, and Palestine and founded the first Christian monasteries and whose teachings and sayings (gathered in anthologies) remain classics of Christian spirituality. Most of the desert monks and hermits were not writers or theologians—but Evagrius was. So his writings are generally considered to be among the earliest examples of teachings on topics such as contemplative prayer and interior silence, themes that would be central to the wisdom of the Christian mystics.

Many of Evagrius's teachings on prayer, holiness, and interior transformation were committed to writing in the form of brief sentences or short paragraphs, almost like Zen koans. A deep sense of silence, imagelessness, and contemplative calm pervades his teachings. Here is one example:

Stand guard over your spirit, keeping it free of concepts at the time of prayer so that it may remain in its own deep calm. Thus he who has compassion on the ignorant will come to visit even such an insignificant person as yourself. That is when you will receive the most glorious gift of prayer.[5]

But perhaps Evagrius's most lasting and significant contribution to Christian spirituality involved his teaching about the *logismoi*—the eight deadly thoughts of anger, avarice, discouragement, fornication, gluttony, pride, sorrow, and vainglory. Thoughts like these Evagrius considered "deadly" because they could kill the inner calm that a monk sought to cultivate in prayer. These were the thoughts that directly tempted a person to sin. Evagrius understood that sinful behavior began with thoughts that lead a person away from the serenity of prayer. In this sense he was an astute psychologist of the interior life. The list of deadly thoughts was intended to help a person grow spiritually; by identifying which of the afflictive thoughts were assailing a monk, he (or she), along with the guidance of a wise spiritual director, would seek to respond to the thoughts with an appropriate verse from scripture, just as Jesus responded to the temptations of the devil with scripture during his forty-day fast in the desert.

If Evagrius's deadly thoughts seem familiar, that's because this list directly inspired Pope Gregory the Great, who developed the well-known list of "seven deadly sins" (anger, avarice, envy, gluttony, lust, pride and sloth) by adapting Evagrius's list.

Evagrius's reputation within Christianity is slowly being rehabilitated. Over the past centuries, scholars of early church history have begun to recognize just how important Evagrius's ideas were to later figures (like Gregory, Cassian, or Maximus); but this fourth-century contemplative remains relatively unknown outside of academic or monastic circles. This is unfortunate, because Evagrius's insistence on silence, mental clarity, and stability as foundations for contemplative prayer are important principles for the mystical theology that would develop in the following centuries. Evagrius is a fascinating example of how a "heretic" can actually have a profound impact even on "orthodox" spirituality—especially thanks to the many monks who preserved his writings anonymously.

Recommended Reading

Evagrius Ponticus: The Praktikos and Chapters on Prayer, edited by John Eudes Bamberger (Spencer, MA: Cistercian Publications, 1970).

François Fénelon (1651–1715)

François Fénelon enjoyed an illustrious career as a priest, bishop, and courtier in France, but his reputation became suspect because of controversies surrounding some of his writings and his association with Madame Jeanne Guyon, who was condemned as a heretic for allegedly espousing Quietism—a type of spirituality that became popular in southern Europe in the late seventeenth century but was denounced as heresy by the pope in 1687. The term Quietism comes from Teresa of Ávila's concept of the "prayer of quiet"—another name for silent contemplation. But the Quietists were accused of elevating such prayer of quiet to the point that they rejected other legitimate forms of prayer, and of proclaiming that through this kind of passive contemplation one could achieve not only union with God but even a state of sinlessness before death. Fénelon himself signed documents that condemned Quietism, and when in 1699 the pope condemned twenty-three of Fénelon's statements, Fénelon submitted to church authority, recanting his views. He was banished from the royal court and spent the last years of his life living quietly as a provincial archbishop.

Fénelon is remembered as a mystical writer for his letters of spiritual direction and a treatise called *The Maxims of the Saints*. In it he describes contemplation as "the tranquil, uniform exercise of . . . pure love"[6] and proclaims "in the final analysis all interior paths lead to pure love as their destination, and, in life's pilgrimage, the highest of all degrees is the habitual state of this love."[7] Like Bernard of Clairvaux centuries before him, Fénelon saw mysticism first and foremost as growing in ever more refined dimensions of love.

Recommended Reading

Fénelon: Selected Writings, translated by Chad Helms (New York: Paulist Press, 2006).

Jakob Boehme (1575–1624)

Jakob Boehme may be the most renowned and notorious of the Protestant mystics. Since he was never a Catholic, he has never *formally* been denounced as a heretic, but Boehme certainly ran afoul with the local religious authorities during his lifetime—and has remained a controversial figure ever since.

An idiosyncratic visionary who made his living as a cobbler, Boehme's first book of mystical writings was published in 1612, which immediately led to a Lutheran pastor complaining to the municipal authorities, who in turn instructed Boehme to remain silent. In the words of the pastor, "There are as many blasphemies in this shoemaker's book as there are lines; it smells of shoemaker's pitch and filthy blacking. May this insufferable stench be far from us."[8] But by 1618 Boehme was writing again, although many of his works were not published until after his death.

In his book on the history of Christian spirituality, Urban T. Holmes notes that Boehme was "a student of alchemy" who "knew the Jewish Kabbalah, the Neo-Platonism of the Renaissance, and the Hermetic medicine of Paracelsus."[9] He remarks that Boehme's critics have accused the Lutheran visionary of teaching "exotic heresies."[10] He wrote about topics that most orthodox Christian writers avoid, such as magic and astrology. Yet, like so many other "heretical" mystics, Boehme believed his own teachings to be faithful to Christ. "Boehme believed to the last that his explorations of eternity were consistent with the teaching of the Lutheran Church,"[11] notes Evelyn Underhill.

Despite his dubious reputation, Boehme's influence has been remarkable, with admirers as diverse as the English mystic William Law, psychologist Carl Jung, and theologian Paul Tillich. Underhill quotes Boehme approvingly, although she seems to accept that he was not entirely orthodox. Holmes feels that Boehme's unsavory notoriety is unfounded, though he ultimately suggests that this German cobbler's visionary and intuitive writing has little practical advice for spiritual seekers, which may have been the reason why it never found much acceptance in the "action-mode, structured"[12] world of Protestant Christianity.

That may be so, but if nothing else Boehme knew that the doorway into the mystical was contemplative silence. In an imaginary dialogue between a student and a mystical teacher, Boehme declares, "If you could remain silent from all of your willing and sensing for one hour, then you will hear unutterable words of God . . . If you keep silent from sensing and willing of your self, then the eternal hearing, seeing, and speaking will be revealed within you, and God will hear and see through you . . . If you would remain silent, then you are what God was before nature and creatureliness, that from which God created your nature and creatureliness. So hear and see what God saw and heard in you, before your own willing, seeing, and hearing began."[13]

Recommended Reading

Genius of the Transcendent: Mystical Writings of Jakob Boehme, translated and edited by Michael L. Birkel and Jeff Bach (Boston: Shambhala, 2010).

Jeanne Guyon (1648–1717)

Jeanne Guyon, commonly known as Madame Guyon, became infamous in her day as a French heretic, accused of the heresy of Quietism. Like Fénelon, she never explicitly declared herself to be a Quietist, but her writings were accused of espousing the heresy. She spent several years in prison for her views, and to this day she remains ignored by most Catholics. But she had followers even after her release from prison (the most prominent being Fénelon), and the publication of her writings in the

Netherlands after her death led to her work being accepted in at least some Protestant circles.

"Everyone is capable of inward contemplative prayer," she wrote in her most popular text, *A Short and Easy Method of Prayer*, "and it is a terrible shame that almost all people have it in their heads not to do it. We are all called to this prayer as we are all called to eternal life. Contemplative prayer is nothing more than heartfelt affection and love. What is necessary is to love God and to focus on him."[14]

Her writings include her autobiography, poetry, a commentary on the Song of Songs, and a memoir of her stint in prison that has only recently been translated into English.

Recommended Reading

Jeanne Guyon: Selected Writings, translated and edited by Dianne Guenin-Lelle and Ronney Mourad (New York: Paulist Press, 2012).

John Scotus Eriugena (ca. 815–877)

John Scotus Eriugena was a Celtic philosopher (his name means "John of the Gaels, born in Ireland") who spent decades in France in the service of King Charles the Bald, where he led a renowned academy and wrote a number of philosophical, theological, and spiritual treatises. Living in the ninth century, he represents a link between the philosophy of the classical age, particularly that of Plato and his followers, and the coming scholasticism of the high Middle Ages, exemplified by Thomas Aquinas. Eriugena was important, in part, for his work translating and commenting upon the writings of Pseudo-Dionysius.

By making the Greek wisdom of Pseudo-Dionysius available in Latin for the Christians of western Europe, Eriugena influenced the transcendental mysticism that characterized much of Western contemplation for the next seven centuries.

In his book *Listening for the Heartbeat of God*, J. Philip Newell, a Scottish authority on Celtic Christianity, shows how Eriugena stands in a tradition of Celtic wisdom that goes back to the age of saints like Patrick, Columba, and Brigit of Kildare—and extends down to recent times in the work of visionaries like George MacDonald. For Newell, Eriugena represents a flowering of Celtic mysticism.

> *Eriugena tells us that God is in all things, the essence of life; God has not created everything out of nothing, but out of his own essence, out of his very life. This is the light that is in all things . . . The world, therefore, Eriugena regarded as theophany, a visible manifestation of God.*[15]

Eriugena's philosophical writings do not particularly lend themselves to devotional reading, but they offer insight into the wisdom of a mind aflame with the love of God: "raised above all things by the wings of natural contemplation, illuminated and supported by divine grace, you will be able to penetrate by the keenness of your mind the secrets of the Word and, to the extent that it is granted to the human being who seeks signs of God, you will see how all things made by the Word live in the Word and are life."[16]

Eriugena's writings were controversial even during his lifetime for their pantheistic leanings and were formally condemned as heretical in the thirteenth century. But by then his work had already exerted its influence, so that through this Irishman the mysticism of the Orthodox East became known and studied throughout the Catholic West.

Recommended Reading

The Voice of the Eagle: The Heart of Celtic Christianity—John Scotus Eriugena's Homily on the Prologue to the Gospel of St. John, translated by Christopher Bamford (Great Barrington, MA: Lindisfarne Books, 2000).

Marguerite Porete (ca. 1248–1310)

Marguerite Porete died her for mystical beliefs—authorities burned her at the stake for heresy. As a mystic, she authored a book, *The Mirror of Simple Souls*, which was probably composed in the late 1290s in the old French tongue and is considered a literary masterwork filled with beautiful language and striking imagery. But the book ran afoul with the defenders of orthodoxy in Porete's day—it was attacked on multiple occasions, and when its author refused to recant or even cooperate with her trial, she was condemned to die. It is said that Porete faced her cruel execution with such a calm spirit that onlookers were moved to tears.

The Mirror of Simple Souls celebrates the love that flows between God and the soul, often in strikingly beautiful ways. "That which burns has no cold, and the one who swims has no thirst. Thus such a Soul, says Love, is so enflamed in the furnace and fire of Love that she was become properly fire . . . For she is fire in herself through the power of Love who transforms her into the fire of Love."[17]

Why was the book condemned? Apparently because Porete suggested that a soul in union with God, being united to perfection, is itself perfect and therefore not liable to sin. Some observers have suggested that Porete's teachings are actually very similar to those of John of the Cross, who not only became a saint but also a Doctor of the Church.[18] Perhaps her real "crime" was being a few centuries ahead of her time, or of daring to teach in an age when women were expected to be completely submissive to men. Thankfully, scholarly interest in *The Mirror of Simple Souls* ensures that Porete is now seen as an important, if tragic, figure in the annals of medieval Christian mysticism.

Recommended Reading

The Mirror of Simple Souls by Marguerite Porete, edited by Ellen L. Babinsky (New York: Paulist Press, 1993).

Meister Eckhart (ca. 1260–1327)

Meister Eckhart stands alongside Bernard of Clairvaux and John of the Cross as one of the most celebrated Christian mystics; he is also one of the most controversial figures, having a number of his teachings declared as heretical shortly after his death. Today, some scholars believe that the censure of Eckhart's ideas may have been politically motivated and have made efforts to have his name formally cleared by the Vatican.

Eckhart entered the Dominican Order as a youth. After spending some time in Paris, he returned to his native Germany, where he became renowned as a preacher. "Meister" is not his name, but a title, referring to his receiving a master's degree in theology. Eckhart's impressive body of work includes academic treatises in Latin, along with about one hundred sermons in his native German. The German writings generally were his more spiritually daring.

The problem with Eckhart seems to be that his ideas were often expressed using language that could be easily misinterpreted. He has been accused of pantheism (the belief that all things are God) or monism (the idea that there is ultimately no distinction between God and creation). He stressed God as a ground of being present throughout creation—including in the human soul—and that each Christian is invited to give birth to Christ within one's soul. As a preacher, Eckhart saw his sermons as a means of inspiring his listeners to recognize the divine presence within, and in so doing to be "wonderfully united" to God. In his Sermon 5, he offers four goals for his preaching:

> When I preach, I am accustomed to talk about detachment, saying that we should become free of ourselves and of all things. Secondly, I say that we should be in-formed back into the simple goodness, which is God. Thirdly, I say that we should be mindful of the great nobility which God has given the soul in order that we should become wonderfully united with him. Fourthly, I speak of the purity of the divine nature, and of the radiance within it which is ineffable. God is a word: an unspoken word.[19]

Yet to talk about such lofty mystical concerns often meant using language that was paradoxical or playful, which in turn pointed toward an essentially non-dualistic spirituality. In Sermon 83, Eckhart considers the question "How should a person love God?" His answer, while imbued in mystical insight, evokes a spirituality of darkness, unknowing, and profound emptiness. "You should love him as he is a non-God, a nonspirit, a nonperson, a nonimage, but as he is a pure, unmixed, bright 'One,' separated from all duality; and in that One we should eternally sink down, out of 'something' into 'nothing.'"[20]

This non-dualism is expressed even more succinctly in a sentence from Sermon 16, which has become perhaps the most quoted line from his writings: "The eye with which I see God is exactly the same eye with which God sees me. My eye and God's eye are one eye, one seeing, one knowledge and one love."[21]

Eckhart was a philosopher and a man of towering intellect. His body of work includes texts that often seem subtly impenetrable, especially since his writings are not confessional but rather speculative—reflecting on the nature and meaning of mystical union, rather than simply reporting his own experience. But for anyone seeking a stimulating and thought-provoking exploration of Christian mystical theology—who God is, how God acts, and how the human soul can participate in the splendor of the divine nature—Eckhart's writings prove indispensable.

Recommended Reading

Selected Writings of Meister Eckhart (London: Penguin Books, 1994).

Origen (ca. 185–253)

Origen took over Clement of Alexandria's position as the catechist of the Church in that major Egyptian city. Although he was a prolific and influential writer, Origen fell under a cloud of suspicion because some of his teachings were believed to contradict the Bible. He has never been canonized as a saint, and his controversial views are still regarded as heretical in the eyes of orthodox, conservative Christians. Among his controversial views were speculation that the human soul existed prior to birth, and that at the end of time all sentient beings would be reconciled with God, perhaps even including the devil.

Origen's massive body of work includes scripture commentary, sermons, and treatises on a variety of topics, including prayer, martyrdom, and the nature of God. His *Homily XXVII on Numbers* is considered a classic early statement of Christian mystical spirituality, interpreting a verse in the Bible (Numbers 33:1) to suggest that the spiritual life involves an ongoing journey in which a soul ascends, stage by stage, from earth to heaven.

"God is incomprehensible and immeasurable," insisted Origen. "For whatever be the knowledge which we have been able to obtain about God . . . we must of necessity believe that he is far and away better than our thoughts about him."[22] He goes on to insist that it is wrong to interpret the Bible literally, for while all passages in the Bible have a spiritual meaning, some are impossible to believe if understood literally!

On the subject of prayer, Origen was one of the first Christian contemplatives to interpret the Song of Songs—the Hebrew love poem found in the Old Testament—as an allegory of the mystical life, thus launching a tradition in which saints and mystics over succeeding generations (including Gregory of Nyssa, Bernard of Clairvaux, Teresa of Ávila, and Francis de Sales) offered their own commentary on the Song of Songs. He also developed an idea that the soul had "spiritual senses" that correspond to our bodily senses—a spiritual sight, spiritual hearing, spiritual sense of smell, and so forth—which again inspired many mystics of subsequent ages.

Recommended Reading

Origen: Spirit and Fire—A Thematic Anthology of His Writings, translated by Robert J. Daly, edited by Hans Urs von Balthasar (Washington: Catholic University of America Press, 1984).

Pierre Teilhard de Chardin (1881–1955)

Pierre Teilhard de Chardin was not only a Jesuit priest but also a scientist—a paleontologist who participated in the discovery of the Peking Man fossils. The work of this mystic represents a poetic and evocative integration of Christian spirituality and scientific wonder. While regarded in some circles as one of the most important Catholic mystics in the twentieth century, his work has not always been accepted by the Church hierarchy; rather, his writings are considered sufficiently "dangerous" that the Vatican issued a warning about them in 1962, saying that they "abound in such ambiguities and indeed even serious errors, as to offend Catholic doctrine."[23] While this warning has (as of this writing) not been formally rescinded, many prominent Catholic theologians and bishops—including Pope Benedict XVI and Pope

Francis—have quoted Teilhard and even written approvingly of him. Nevertheless, conservative Catholic theologians continue to dismiss the writings of this Jesuit scientist as heretical.

What made Teilhard's writing so controversial? Because he integrated scientific thought into his spiritual vision, Teilhard saw the cosmos in terms of evolution, with the Omega Point, or the final end of the evolutionary arc, being reunion with Christ, who draws all things to himself. Thus, Teilhard regards the material world not as alien to spirituality, but as filled with meaning and purpose and indeed the presence of God. Teilhard was also one of the creators and early advocates of the idea of the noosphere, the sphere of human consciousness, as an evolutionary emergent out of the biosphere (the sphere of life), which in turn emerged from the geosphere (the inert matter of the earth). Because of its evolutionary emphasis, Teilhard's spirituality is optimistic, joyous, and filled with hope.

One of his loveliest pieces is "The Mass on the World" (1923), a fifteen-page prayer written in the Ordos Desert in southern China. Teilhard wrote it for the Feast of the Transfiguration (commemorating the day when Christ took three of his disciples to a mountaintop, where he had a luminous, mystical encounter with Moses and Elijah), on a day when he could not recite the actual Catholic Mass because he was in the field. So he wrote, "I, your priest, will make the whole earth my altar and on it will offer you all the labours and sufferings of the world," going on to pray, "Grant me the remembrance and the mystic presence of all those whom the light is now awakening to the new day."[24]

Teilhard goes on to articulate a rich understanding of God's presence in nature and in fire, finding communion for that day not in the consecrated elements of bread and wine, but throughout the shimmering beauty of the created order.

Teilhard's earth-positive mysticism, despite its lingering controversy, has inspired many later thinkers, both within Christianity and beyond, who have sought to articulate a spirituality friendly to the earth and matter.

Recommended Reading

Hymn of the Universe by Pierre Teilhard de Chardin (New York: Harper & Row, 1965).

Simone Weil (1909–1943)

Simone Weil, born in Paris of a secular Jewish family, grew up in an intellectual environment where she proved to be brilliant, mastering languages like ancient Greek and Sanskrit while still a child. After finishing her education, she became a teacher. Throughout her life, Weil was a political activist. As a youth, she was sympathetic to Marxism, but she later became more of a pacifist and anarchist. Leftist activists in the Europe of her time typically saw Christianity in an unfavorable light (seeing religion as a source of oppression rather than as a means of spiritual liberation), but Weil claimed that even as a child she "always adopted the Christian attitude as the only possible one."[25] In a letter to a priest written in 1942, she talks about visiting a chapel in Assisi where Saint Francis used to pray, at which point "something stronger than I was compelled me for the first time in my life to go down on my knees."[26] Later, after discovering the poem "Love (III)" by the metaphysical poet George Herbert, she found relief in reciting the poem when suffering from a headache. She came to understand that she was not merely reciting the poem, but actually praying it—and "during one of these recitations . . . Christ himself came down and took possession of me."[27]

Despite her own mystical spirituality, Weil maintained at best a troubled relationship with Christianity as an institution. A few months before she died, she spoke with a Catholic priest, but when she insisted that she believed unbaptized infants would go to heaven, the priest refused to baptize her. A friend of hers (who was not a priest or a minister) claimed to have baptized Weil while she was in the hospital suffering from the tuberculosis that would claim her life, but if this happened it was never officially documented.[28] As a woman whose political and philosophical values were grounded in sympathy toward the outsider and the oppressed, it seems fitting that Weil's spirituality would also have an "outsider" characteristic.

Although her writings cover a wide array of topics, several of her books—most notably *Waiting for God* and *Gravity and Grace*—shimmer with spiritual insight. Standing in the tradition of mystics like Pseudo-Dionysius, John of the Cross, and the author of *The Cloud of Unknowing*, Weil's mysticism is shot through with ineffability, darkness, paradox, and a sense of God's mystery. "God can only be present in creation under the form of absence,"[29] she wrote, also saying, "This world, in so far as it is completely empty of God, is God himself . . . This is the mystery of mysteries. When we touch it we are safe."[30] In many ways, Weil's dark mysticism is particularly well suited for the agnostic age in which she lived (and in which we still find ourselves): "To believe in God is not a decision we can make. All we can do is to decide not to give our love to false Gods."[31]

Recommended Reading

Waiting for God by Simone Weil (New York: Perennial, 2000).

Thomas Merton (1915–1968)

Thomas Merton embodied paradox in a most unusual way: thanks to his brilliant writing, he became a famous monk—which makes about as much sense as being an unknown celebrity.

When Merton entered the public eye, World War II had ended only two and a half years earlier, and America was filled with new hope and optimism even as the chill of the Cold War descended around the Northern Hemisphere. For the publication of Merton's memoir, *The Seven Storey Mountain*, in January 1948, expectations were modest; after all, this self-consciously literary autobiography of a young man's search for meaning—that led him from the Communist Party to the Catholic Church, from the glamorous world of Columbia University in New York to the austere silence of a Cistercian monastery in rural Kentucky—simply didn't begin to match the profile of a bestseller.

Several weeks and a hundred thousand copies later, not only had this book become a publishing phenomenon, but its author—a thirty-three-year-old Trappist monk—was launched into his paradoxical role as a cloistered celebrity. For the next twenty years, as his writings chronicled both his spiritual growth within the monastery and his increasingly trenchant criticism of twentieth-century culture and politics, Merton emerged as a powerful and lasting witness to how contemplative spirituality and mystical Christianity remain vitally relevant even in our post-Enlightenment, postmodern world.

Thomas Merton was born in France in 1915 and spent much of his childhood in Europe. Coming to New York in the 1930s, he immersed himself in the worldly pleasures of the day, embracing the naive optimism of the Communist Party and the arty pretensions of the graduate school literary scene. Living a thoroughly secular life, nothing about him suggested that his destiny lay within the cloister; but several influences—the gentle inspiration of a Catholic professor, Merton's own sense of guilt and disgust at his hedonistic life, and the poetic romance of medieval spirituality as described in the writings of philosopher Etienne Gilson—all conspired to nudge this young man toward conversion. When he finally embraced the Catholic Church, the fires of his newfound faith impelled him to seek a vocation, first with the Franciscans (who turned him down after he admitted he had fathered an illegitimate child) and then with the far more austere Trappists, one of the strictest orders of Catholic monks, who accepted him as a novice in December 1941. He arrived at Gethsemani Abbey in Kentucky three days after Pearl Harbor. At that time Merton was not yet twenty-seven years old; he would live another twenty-seven years before dying in a freak accident in 1968, on the anniversary of the date of his arrival at the monastery. So he lived slightly more than half of his short life as a Trappist (Cistercian) monk.

As a graduate student, Merton had shown promise as both a poet and a literary critic; he supposed that he had left that all behind with his entry into the strictly disciplined, tightly controlled, and mostly silent world of the Trappists. His abbot, however, had other ideas; recognizing that this young monk had clear talent, Merton was assigned a variety of writing projects, including translations and essays on various aspects of Cistercian life. Eventually, the abbot encouraged Merton to write his life story, even though he was still a young man. Merton expertly crafted an intelligent if theologically unsophisticated story of modern meaninglessness trumped by the awesome silence of a centuries-old way of life. The memoir covers the young monk's life up until the poignant moment when he learns of his only brother's death in action during World War II. Even though the book is more than four hundred pages, it proved to be a quick read and clearly struck a chord with a public hungry for its own sense of restored meaning after the trauma of the war.

The Seven Storey Mountain launched a boom of vocations among the Trappists[32] and also ignited Merton's literary career. While he would never have another book achieve the kind of success of his autobiography, Merton's prolific output only solidified his position as an important twentieth-century Catholic author. At first, his books were mostly variations on his twin subjects of Catholic devotion and monastic spirituality: he published extracts from his journals, studies of mystics like John of the Cross or Bernard of Clairvaux, and meditative writings designed to support the reader in his or her own spiritual growth.

After about a decade, Merton's work began to take on a more urgent, if not radical, tone. Two issues came to bear on his work: first, his growing concern over some of the critical issues of the day, including civil rights, nuclear proliferation, and the conflict in Vietnam. Just as important, though, was a growing interest in non-Christian forms of mysticism, including Sufism and, in particular, Zen Buddhism. As the excitement of the liberalizing Vatican II council spread through the Catholic Church of the 1960s, Merton evolved from a rather garden-variety Catholic writer to a towering authority whose works were filled with spiritually grounded social and cultural insight.

In many ways, Merton's life came to a stunning climax when all the various threads of his singular intellectual-spiritual journey coalesced when he delivered a paper on Marxism and monasticism at an interfaith conference on the religious life in Bangkok in 1968. Within minutes of delivering the paper, he died in a freak accident, electrocuted when he touched a fan in his room at the conference center. His body was flown back to his monastery in Kentucky on a plane that also carried the remains of soldiers killed in Vietnam.

Like many great contemplatives, Merton rarely wrote about his own encounters with the divine mystery, but at least three times he recounts moments of extraordinary grace and insight. The first happened shortly after he became a Catholic, when he was vacationing in Cuba (this was years before Castro came to power); while attending Mass at a Franciscan parish, as he put it, "It was as if I had been suddenly illuminated by being blinded by the manifestation of God's presence . . . It lasted only a moment, but it left a breathless joy and a clean peace and happiness that stayed for hours and it was something I have never forgotten."[33] But perhaps even more dramatic was an event that has been called Merton's "epiphany," which took place at an ordinary street corner in downtown Louisville. By this time having been a monk for over sixteen years, Merton was on a business errand for the monastery. Yet in a moment of unexpected grace, seeing the ordinary passersby on that ordinary spring day brought Merton to a place of profound wonder and insight.

> *I was suddenly overwhelmed with the realization that I loved all those people, that they were mine and I theirs, that we could not be alien to one another even though we were total strangers. It was like waking from a dream of separateness, of spurious self-isolation in a special world, the world of renunciation and supposed holiness. . . . if only everybody could realize this! But it cannot be explained. There is no way of telling people that they are all walking around shining like the sun. . . . At the center of our being is a point of nothingness which is untouched by sin and by illusion, a point of pure truth, a point or spark which belongs entirely to God . . . It is so to speak his name written in us . . . like a pure diamond, blazing with the invisible light of heaven.*[34]

If the mystical event in Cuba helped inspire Merton to enter the monastery, then the Louisville epiphany metaphorically propelled him into a new chapter of his life as an author, writing about social issues, interfaith dialogue, and criticism of racism and the war in Vietnam. As the 1960s progressed, Merton's interest in interfaith matters became more obvious as he published books clearly indebted to Buddhism, with titles like *Mystics and Zen Masters* and *Zen and the Birds of Appetite*. This interest in Eastern spirituality reached an apex just a few days before Merton died, when he visited the ancient Buddhist sanctuary of Polonnaruwa in Sri Lanka. Once again, Merton entered into a moment of profound mystical insight. As he gazed on the splendid, larger-than-life carved statues of the Buddha, he was "suddenly, almost forcibly, jerked clean out of the habitual, half-tied vision of things, and an inner clearness, clarity, as if exploding from the rocks themselves, became evident and obvious . . . The thing about all this is that there is no puzzle, no problem, and really no 'mystery.' All problems are resolved and everything is clear, simply because what matters is clear . . . everything is emptiness and everything is compassion."[35]

Like so many great writers, Merton's influence and legacy have only grown after his death. Today he is widely regarded as the unofficial founder of the centering-prayer movement as well as of serious interfaith dialogue between contemplatives of different religious traditions. As a keen social critic who spoke prophetically not only against racism and violence but also the consumerism and materialism of Western culture, his words remain as relevant and vital here in the twenty-first century as they were when he wrote them decades ago. Although he was himself cloistered (and in the final years of his life, virtually a hermit), Merton's vision of authentic Christian spirituality proves particularly relevant for those who seek to integrate the splendors of the mystical tradition with the challenges of life immersed in the postmodern world.

Why, then, have I grouped Merton with the heretics? After all, he could fit in almost all of the categories of mystics I've presented here: he was confessional, a poet, and a unitive. But like many heretics, he is the victim of other peoples' attacks. Today, many conservative Catholics view Merton with suspicion, seeing his embrace of Eastern spirituality and his outspoken views on social and political matters as unbefitting a saintly monk. Even worse, Merton wrote candidly in his journals about falling in love with a young nurse after being a monk for nearly twenty-five years. While others might applaud Merton for his honesty and humanity, those who want their spiritual heroes on a pedestal cannot tolerate the idea that the same man who saw God in a Catholic Mass could also find mystical insight in a Buddhist temple. And so, at least in some corners, Merton is dismissed as a heretic rather than honored as the mystic he was.

Recommended Reading

New Seeds of Contemplation by Thomas Merton (New York: New Directions, 1961).

CHAPTER 7

Wisdom Keepers

The Anglican writer Martin Thornton suggested that the most creative expression of Christian spirituality entailed what he called the "affective-speculative synthesis."[1] That's a jargony way of saying that the most expansive and visionary types of contemplatives are ones who integrate head and heart into their spirituality. Certainly, the "head" (our capacity for reason, logic, and intellectual rigor) and the "heart" (our capacity for love, compassion, and meaningful relationship) need each other and thrive best when both are fully alive. But the reality of human nature is that we all have differing gifts, differing strengths, and a variety of personality types. Carl Jung acknowledged in his theory of personality that some people are "feelers" and others are "thinkers." It's not an either-or distinction, of course: thinkers feel and feelers think. But most people tend to favor one or the other, especially in terms of how they discern or make decisions. Thinkers look first to logic, rationality, and consistency, while feelers tend to focus first on relationships, human needs, and ways to alleviate suffering. We need both, but everyone naturally prefers one way over the other.

Among the mystics, too, some tend to be thinkers and others feelers. We've looked at the "lover" mystics, those whose encounters with God tended to be deeply devotional, filled with longing and loving intimacy, and sometimes even embraced the erotic ("Brides of Christ," "the mystical marriage"). Now we're going to look at their brainy counterparts: the wise, sagacious mystics, those whose writings exemplify a deeply philosophical, rational, or intellectual approach to the quest for the presence of God.

This is not to say that the wisdom keepers have no heart: far from it. But they express their love and devotion with erudition and logical precision. These are the mystics who most fully embody Christ's challenge for us to love God with our whole minds. As philosophers, theologians, scientists, and rhetoricians, the wisdom keepers explore both their own minds and the mind of Christ in brilliant, thought-provoking ways. Consequently, their works are among the most challenging of the mystical writings, works that reward the reader who is willing to engage in them slowly and patiently, wrestling with their complex, erudite ideas.

If you love language, logic, and philosophy, you will likely find the writings of the following mystics (along with other learned mystics profiled elsewhere in this book, like Meister Eckhart or Thomas Aquinas) both challenging and rewarding. Otherwise, you might simply find these works daunting. Still, if one or more of these writers intrigues you, give their work a try. Expect a "workout for the mind" when you read them. Like any other workout, it may be difficult, but it is certainly worth the effort.

Albertus Magnus (ca. 1200–1280)

Albertus Magnus, or Albert the Great, taught theology in Paris and Cologne, counting Thomas Aquinas among his students. He was a German Dominican bishop, a scholar, and a prolific writer. Widely considered one of the greatest theologians of his time, he was one of the most important interpreters of Aristotle of his age. His writings covered a breadth of topics, including the sciences (astronomy, geography, zoology), speculative thinking (astrology, alchemy), and philosophy (law, logic, and metaphysics).

His *Commentary on Dionysius's Mystical Theology* reveals the mystical dimension of his thought. As an interpreter of Pseudo-Dionysius, Albertus explores the intimate relationship between the human soul and the Divine: "God is essentially present in the soul, not as any kind of nature of the soul, but as a certain light of the intellect, and this is sufficient for him to be known by the intellect."[2] In other words, God is the light by which all human wisdom is apprehended and understood. And yet, God remains mystically hidden beyond the limits of human understanding: "He who is the pre-eminent cause of all that the senses perceive is not anything perceptible by the senses."[3] Our human wisdom exists only in the light of God's radiance, but when we attempt to perceive God directly, then we are dazzled by his luminous brilliance, just as we would be if we tried to gaze directly at the sun.

Like many teachers, Albertus had the humbling experience of seeing himself surpassed by his greatest pupil; but it is said that he was very fond of Aquinas, and upon learning of his student's death (Aquinas died six years before his master), Albertus remarked that the light of the Church had been extinguished.

In the past it was believed that Albert the Great was the author of the mystical treatise *On Union with God*, but recent scholarship points to a different writer for that particular work.

Recommended Reading:
Albert and Thomas: Selected Writings, translated and edited by Simon Tugwell (New York: Paulist Press, 1988).

Bernard Lonergan (1904–1984)

Bernard Lonergan is not somebody often associated with mysticism; a Jesuit priest from Canada, he was renowned as a philosopher and theologian, a man of ideas rather than devotion. But another Jesuit, Harvey D. Egan, who is an authority on Christian mysticism, argues that Lonergan is essential for understanding how the Christian view of mysticism has evolved over the past century.

> *Under Lonergan's influence, some contemporary scholarship has already shifted the study of mysticism away from the category of "experience" to that of "consciousness," and from the merely "descriptive" to the "explanatory." The term "experience," a highly complex concept, lends itself to a misunderstanding of mysticism as particular feeling or sensible perception that is too easily separated from understanding,*

judging, deciding, and loving . . . The shift toward the cat-
egory of "consciousness" engenders a view of mysticism as
more than unusual sensations. It helps to underscore that
mysticism brings about new ways of knowing and loving that
involve a transformative decision about how one lives. These
new ways of knowing and loving are based on states of aware-
ness in which God is present to our inner acts, not as an
object to be comprehended, but as the direct and transform-
ing center of our lives."[4]

In other words, if we reduce mysticism to merely an *experi-ence* of God, it runs the risk of being lost in a subjective world where every human being has his or her inner spiritual feelings, but without being transformed or transfigured by the encounter with God to become more wise, more loving, more holy, and more truly united with God. This is not to say that experience is bad, or meaningless. But it acknowledges that there is more to mysticism than subjective experience. The "objective" dimension of mystical wisdom resides in love, which we find not in our *experience* but in our *consciousness*—which is to say, our capacity to know and to love—for love is more than just an emotion; it is an act of will.

While many people still equate mysticism with experience, Lonergan's groundbreaking insight is already having an impact. Richard Rohr, Cynthia Bourgeault, Martin Laird, Maggie Ross, and Gerald G. May are just some of the contemplative teachers of the late twentieth and early twenty-first centuries who point out that mystical union with God is more than just an experience: it is a radical deepening of consciousness, grounded in love and service, that emerges from union with God, a union so essential that it occurs at a level both deeper and higher than the mere vicissitudes of human experience.

For Lonergan, religious consciousness can be understood in two ways—as an ordinary way of knowing, but also as a deeper, higher, or "mystical" dimension: "there are two quite different modes of apprehension, of being related, of consciously existing, namely, the commonsense mode operating in the world mediated by meaning and the mystical mode withdrawing from the world mediated by meaning into a silent and all-absorbing self-surrender in response to God's gift of his love."[5] In other words, "ordinary" consciousness (and ways of knowing, including experience) are wrapped up in human constructions of meaning (our language, our philosophy, our ethics, and so forth), while the higher or mystical consciousness emerges only out of deep silence, where human meaning falls away and we are immersed, beyond thought, language, and concept, in the pure love of God.

If you are interested in learning more about Lonergan's philosophy, a good place to start is *Method in Theology*. For understanding the mystical implications of his thought, see Harvey D. Egan's books *Soundings in the Mystical Tradition* and *What Are They Saying about Mysticism?*

Recommended Reading

Method in Theology by Bernard J. F. Lonergan (New York: Herder and Herder, 1972).

Bonaventure (ca. 1217–1274)

Bonaventure was an Italian Franciscan theologian and mystic who studied in Paris, returned to Italy, where he became the head of the Franciscan order, wrote the approved biography of Saint Francis of Assisi, and authored several influential texts, particularly the sublime treatise *The Soul's Journey to God*. Pope Leo XIII declared Bonaventure "the prince of mystics"; he has also been called "the Seraphic Doctor," implying that his teachings are both exalted and angelic.

For Bonaventure, the wisdom of God is difficult for human beings to comprehend, for our finite minds (wounded by sin) are incapable of accessing the full radiance of divine light. "Our mind, accustomed to the darkness of beings and the images of the things of sense, when it glimpses the light of the supreme Being, seems to itself to see nothing. It does not realize that this very darkness is the supreme illumination of our mind, just as when the eye sees pure light, it seems to itself to see nothing."[6] But this should not result in pessimism or cynicism, for divine grace can bestow wisdom upon us that human reason can never achieve.

If you should ask how these things come about, question grace, not instruction; desire, not intellect; the cry of prayer, not pursuit of study; the spouse, not the teacher; God, not man; darkness, not clarity; not light, but the wholly flaming fire which will bear you aloft to God with fullest unction and burning affection.[7]

For Bonaventure, good Franciscan that he was, the created cosmos is a reflection of God, so our "journey to God" begins with a positive appreciation of nature and the world. Through the power of human reason and wisdom, we discern God's glory reflected in creation; but as we climb higher on the ascent into the divine presence, we reach a point where we must lay human reason aside and receive by grace that which can be communicated only through love.

Recommended Reading

Bonaventure: *The Soul's Journey into God, The Tree of Life, The Life of St. Francis*, translated by Ewert Cousins (New York: Paulist Press, 1978).

Francisco de Osuna (ca. 1492–ca. 1542)

Francisco de Osuna, a Franciscan friar, wrote spiritual books that were popular and influential in sixteenth-century Spain. His most significant contribution to Christian mysticism may well be the wisdom he imparted to one of his readers, Teresa of Ávila, the profound visionary, saint, and Doctor of the Church. In her autobiography, Teresa recalls how discovering a book by this writer made an impact in her own spiritual journey:

> *I stopped at the house of this uncle of mine . . . and he gave me a book called Third Alphabet, which treats of the Prayer of Recollection . . . I did not know how to practise prayer, or how to recollect myself, and so I was delighted with this book and determined to follow that way of prayer with all my might.*[8]

Teresa is referring to Francisco's *The Third Spiritual Alphabet*, a widely read spiritual book during her lifetime. And the "prayer of recollection" she mentions is the foundation of contemplative prayer—a prayer in which we "recollect" or recall that God is truly present in our soul, and so when we relax into silence, turning our attention away from the scattered thoughts of our unruly minds and resting in the deep silence within, we are truly resting in the presence of God.

But Francisco's influence did not end with Teresa; indeed, Richard Rohr, who entered the Franciscan order in the early 1960s, has pointed out that Francisco de Osuna's wisdom was still being taught during his novitiate—even though by the mid-twentieth century many Christians had forgotten the mystical wisdom of earlier generations.

> *One friar called it the* no pensar nada *or the* pensar sin pensar *method. We had to kneel in silence for twenty minutes each morning in chapel, but no one was trained to teach us how to "think without thinking." We did not know what to do with our minds during that excruciatingly long time . . . We were victims of our own lost tradition . . .*[9]

The mystical wisdom of *The Third Spiritual Alphabet* is more accessible today than perhaps it has been for centuries, thanks to the renaissance of interest in mysticism and contemplative prayer that began in the twentieth century with writers like Evelyn Underhill, Karl Rahner, and Thomas Merton. Francisco clearly describes the splendor of prayer where love takes precedence over analytical thought: "if [the soul] remains quiet and at rest within itself, it will see the image of God reflected in its own clear waters, more resplendent there than in any other things, provided the disturbing turmoil of thoughts dies down."[10]

Recommended Reading

The Third Spiritual Alphabet by Francisco de Osuna, translated by Mary E. Giles (New York: Paulist Press, 1983).

Gregory Palamas (ca. 1296–1359)

Gregory Palamas, one of the most important mystics of the Eastern Orthodox Church, was a monk of Mount Athos, Greece, before being consecrated as the archbishop of Thessalonica (the home of the Thessalonians, to whom two of the New Testament epistles were addressed). Palamas became renowned as a defender of *hesychasm*, a movement within Eastern Orthodoxy that stressed interior mystical prayer grounded in the continual recitation of the Jesus Prayer. When a philosopher named Barlaam attacked *hesychasm*, denouncing it as a superstitious and presumptuous practice, Palamas responded with his *Triads in Defense of the Holy Hesychasts*, in which he not only defends the practice of the Jesus Prayer, detailing all the ways in which Barlaam misunderstands *hesychasm*, but also spells out key themes of mystical spirituality, including the concept of apophatic spirituality (which stresses God's hiddenness or unknowability), deification in Christ, and God's uncreated glory. In the course of his treatise, Palamas offers sublime language about the nature of contemplation and the light contemplatives receive directly from God:

Those who possess not only the faculties of sensation and intellection, but have also obtained spiritual and supernatural grace, do not gain knowledge only through created beings, but also know spiritually, in a manner beyond sense and intelligence, that God is spirit, for they have become entirely God, and know God in God. It is therefore by this mystical knowledge that divine things must be conceived . . . We must transcend ourselves altogether, and give ourselves entirely to God, for it is better to belong to God, and not to ourselves.[11]

Recommended Reading

The Triads by Gregory Palamas, edited by John Meyendorff (New York: Paulist Press, 1983).

Johannes Tauler (ca. 1300–1361)

Johannes Tauler is, along with Henry Suso, one of the greatest disciples of Meister Eckhart, the German Dominican mystic whose brilliant, philosophically nuanced insight into the divine nature unfortunately left him at the end of his life accused of heresy. A friar like Eckhart, Tauler entered the Dominicans as a young man and may have known the great mystic, since he studied in Strasbourg when Eckhart was teaching there (though we do not know for sure what relationship the two men may have had).

The Dominicans are an order dedicated to preaching, and true to form, Tauler's literary work consists entirely of sermons—more than seventy-five of which have survived. His sermons reveal not only his own keen knowledge of mystical theology, but also his zeal for instructing his listeners in the contemplative life. Like his mentor, Tauler counseled his listeners to a spirituality grounded in detachment, the virtues, and seeking rest in God—and the "birth" of God in the soul. Like many great mystics, he recognized and proclaimed the importance of contemplative silence. "There is no better way of serving the Word than by silence and by listening,"[12] he proclaims in Sermon 1, exhorting his audience to "Cherish this deep silence within, nourish it frequently, so that it may become a habit, and by becoming a habit, a mighty possession."[13] Then, in Sermon 76, when describing the characteristics of a soul that has advanced far into the love of God, "It enters upon another path, way above itself, where the spirit rests in God's Spirit, in the secret silence of the divine Essence."[14]

Recommended Reading

Sermons by Johannes Tauler, translated by Maria Shrady (New York: Paulist Press, 1985).

Karl Rahner (1904–1984)

Karl Rahner, a German Jesuit priest, is now considered one of the great theologians of the twentieth century and a towering intellect of his time. He authored numerous works of theology and philosophy, along with several works of a more explicitly spiritual or mystical nature. He is famous for saying "the Christian of the future will be a mystic or will not exist at all."[15] Like other twentieth-century mystics such as Evelyn Underhill or Thomas Merton, he saw mysticism not as some sort of elite spirituality, but rather accessible to anyone who truly seeks the presence of God in their lives. Indeed, an anthology of his spiritual writings published after his death is called *The Mystical Way in Everyday Life*.

Ironically, Rahner was an exact contemporary of Bernard Lonergan, another Christian thinker known more as a philosopher and a theologian than a mystic but whose wisdom helped to shape ways of thinking about spirituality for the twentieth and twenty-first centuries.

Despite (or perhaps because of) the brilliance of his mind, Rahner understood that the heart of spirituality is love. In his devotional masterpiece *Encounters with Silence*, he expresses the centrality of such love:

> *Only in love can I find you, my God. In love the gates of my soul spring open, allowing me to breathe a new air of freedom and forget my own petty self. In love my whole being streams forth out of the rigid confines of narrowness and anxious self-assertion, which make me a prisoner of my own poverty and emptiness. In love all the powers of my soul flow out toward you, wanting never more to return, but to lose themselves completely in you, since by your love you are the inmost center of my heart, closer to me than I am to myself.*[16]

Recommended Reading

The Mystical Way in Everyday Life by Karl Rahner (Maryknoll, NY: Orbis Books, 2010).

Nicholas of Cusa (1401–1464)

Nicholas of Cusa enjoyed great success in his earthly career, a philosopher and theologian involved in the political controversies of his time and being appointed not only a bishop but also a cardinal by Pope Nicholas V in recognition for his service to the Church. Living as he did at the height of the European Renaissance (and just one generation before the Protestant Reformation), Nicholas of Cusa represents the end of the line of mystical theology as a topic endorsed by the Christian establishment. Contemplative writer Maggie Ross flatly says, "The last great exponent of silence within the hierarchy of the institution was Nicholas of Cusa."[17] He was an "exponent of silence" precisely because of the depth and wisdom of his vocation as a mystical theologian, whose great masterpiece, *On the Vision of God*, encompassed both the theological foundation and practical meditations on the great contemplative act of beholding the mystery of God, in silence and unknowing.

Coming from a prosperous merchant family of the German city of Kues, Nicholas was trained as a canon lawyer and entered into an academic career as a young priest, teaching at the University of Cologne before embarking on a successful career in the church, serving bishops and popes in a variety of positions, while continuing his academic work and publishing his theological and philosophical treatises. In 1437, Nicholas was part of a papal delegation sent to Constantinople to seek reconciliation and reunion between the Catholic and Orthodox Churches. The trip from Rome to Constantinople was arduous and lasted over two months; his encounter with Orthodox spirituality helped to shape his own formation as a mystic. When Nicholas returned from the east, he underwent a mystical encounter with God: "by what I believe was a celestial gift from the Father of Lights, from whom comes every perfect gift, I was led to embrace incomprehensibles incomprehensibly in learned ignorance, by transcending those incorruptible truths that can be humanly known."[18] In other words, in a moment of profound insight, Nicholas was given the gift of "incomprehensible" divine knowledge that cannot be attained by human reason or logic. Following this mystical awakening, and influenced by the writings of great mystics like Pseudo-Dionysius and Meister Eckhart, Nicholas wrote *On Learned Ignorance* (1440), arguing that human knowledge and reason are ultimately incapable of apprehending the inscrutable mysteries of God, which can be accessed only through the knowledge attained by faith through grace. Nicholas did not repudiate human reason and argued that such reason remained necessary for all earthly modes of knowledge—but to fully approach truth, particularly mystical truth, human knowledge had to be supplanted by divine wisdom, accessed only through silence and contemplation.

Various other writings followed, but more than a dozen years would pass before Nicholas penned his most lasting contribution to mystical wisdom, *On the Vision of God* (1453), written for the monks of the Benedictine Abbey of Tegernsee, where Nicholas had made retreat and inspired the brothers with his contemplative wisdom. When Nicholas sent the book to the monks, he included an icon—an image he describes as "an all-seeing figure . . . an icon of God."[19] He encouraged the brothers to display the icon on a wall and to gaze upon it so that they could see for themselves that, by looking at the icon, they would realize they were being looked at by the iconic figure of God. Apparently this figure was "omnivoyant," meaning that its eyes appeared to be looking at a person no matter where he or she stood in relation to it. This uncanny sense of always being seen (by Christ, or by God) underlines the heart of Nicholas's mystical teaching: that the vision of God is possible only because we human beings are in fact gazed upon by God; on an even deeper level, even our human seeing is anchored in the presence of God: we are gazed upon by God even in our own seeing.

As Maggie Ross notes, silence was an essential component of Nicholas's understanding of contemplation. "When I rest in the silence of contemplation," he writes, "you, Lord, answer me within my heart."[20] But *On the Vision of God* also relies on paradox, particularly in terms of darkness and light, to convey its mystical teachings using imagery that echoes the work of other great mystics such as John of the Cross or the author of *The Cloud of Unknowing*.

> *This cloud, mist, darkness or ignorance into which whoever seeks your face enters when one leaps beyond every knowledge and concept is such that below it your face cannot be found except veiled. But this very cloud reveals your face to be there beyond all veils, just as when our eye seeks to view the light of the sun ... since the eye seeks to see the light which it cannot see, it knows that so long as it sees anything, what it sees is not what it is seeing.*[21]

Because God cannot be captured by the human mind or human language, we are left with metaphor, symbolism, paradox, and analogy to attempt to encounter God, as best we can, in human understanding grounded in contemplation, wonder, and unknowing. But the vision of God, like Nicholas's moment of mystical insight on the boat from Constantinople, takes us beyond all these earthly categories of knowledge into the deep silence where the eye of God meets the eye of the human in a limitless encounter of love.

Recommended Reading

Nicholas of Cusa: Selected Spiritual Writings, translated by H. Lawrence Bond (New York: Paulist Press, 2005).

Pseudo-Dionysius (Fifth to Sixth Century)

Pseudo-Dionysius, perhaps the most important Christian mystic of the first millennium, wrote several treatises, including a short but influential work called *Mystical Theology*. Active around the year 500, this writer is so shrouded in mystery that we have no idea what his name was—his works historically have been attributed to a minor figure in the New Testament.

Dionysius the Areopagite appears in only one verse in the entire Bible: Acts 17:33 mentions that when the Apostle Paul preached in Athens, among those who followed him was a man named Dionysius, "a member of the Areopagus"—in other words, a political leader in Athens. That's all we know about Dionysius—but an obscure mystic, writing around the turn of the fifth and sixth centuries (in other words, some 450 years after the life of Paul) called himself Dionysius in his small collection of deeply mystical writings.

Why would he do such a thing? Perhaps this was a kind of literary self-effacement: the author (who was probably a Syrian monk) didn't want to take credit in his own name for his writings—that would be a sign of pride. So he attributed them to a figure in the Bible, perhaps the single most obscure character in the entire New Testament. But what this author did as a way of humbly disguising his identity had an electrifying effect on Christian philosophers in the Middle Ages. Accepting at face value that these writings were by Dionysius the Areopagite, who was a direct disciple of Saint Paul, Christians in the Middle Ages (like Thomas Aquinas, the great philosopher) assumed that Dionysius's writings were almost as authoritative as the Bible itself (after all, Dionysius was mentioned in the Bible, even if only briefly). So for centuries, the philosophy of the author we now call Pseudo-Dionysius remained profoundly influential among Christian philosophers and theologians, helping to foster the medieval worldview where mysticism flourished.

But during the Renaissance, scholars finally began to question whether Pseudo-Dionysius really could have been the man who knew Saint Paul. In all of the writings of the early Church fathers, no one ever quoted from (or even mentioned) the writings of "Dionysius the Areopagite" until the year 533. Meanwhile, the philosophy of pagan Greeks like Plotinus (who lived in the third century) and Proclus (who died in 485) clearly influenced the writings of Pseudo-Dionysius. In other words, it was obvious that these writings must have been composed between 485 and 533, which is why scholars now place the author at approximately the year 500.

Clearly, he was not who he said he was.

Once this was figured out, the backlash was enormous. Scholars went from admiring Pseudo-Dionysius as an important teacher to dismissing him as a fraud. Some attacked his ideas for being too Greek, too pagan, too philosophical. His writings were consigned to the footnotes of scholarship.

Fortunately, though, because Pseudo-Dionysius did have such an impact on Christian thought for almost a thousand years, it's impossible to simply write him off as a fake. Maybe he didn't deserve to be considered a major voice in the world of philosophy or theology, but there's no denying that his writings, especially *Mystical Theology*, were profoundly influential for centuries—and remain crucial for anyone wanting to understand the philosophy of mysticism.

In his writings, Pseudo-Dionysius stressed order and hierarchy (he may have coined that term). For him, God was the apex of the cosmos, and all created things—angels, humanity, other sentient beings—had a natural place in the order of things. Pseudo-Dionysius depicted the angels as hierarchically organized in a series of nine "choirs," each one higher than the next (and, therefore, closer to God). Likewise, humanity had a hierarchy of its own, found in the church, where bishops, priests, deacons, monks, laypeople, and penitents also fit into a neat social structure. It's tempting to dismiss this idea as too, well, hierarchical—the word itself has fallen out of favor in modern thinking, where we tend to dismiss these kinds of social structures as dominating and limiting. But Pseudo-Dionysius was not trying to legitimize domination; rather, he felt that all of creation had a natural order so that the glory and light of God could be transmitted by means of the hierarchy. In other words, the higher choirs of angels may have been closer to God, but their job was to receive glory from God and pass it on to the lower choirs. The same dynamic was at play with the earthly hierarchy of the church: the job of the bishops was to transmit the glory of God to the priests, who passed it on to the deacons, and so forth. So while on one hand Pseudo-Dionysius's ideas about hierarchy might seem oppressive, seen from another perspective his vision of the cosmos was like an ever-blossoming flower, where all beings are connected in a vast network and pass on divine light and glory throughout that network.

But even more important than his ideas about hierarchy is Pseudo-Dionysius's recognition of the hidden (mystical) nature of God. *Mystical Theology* is not a discussion of visions, or exalted states of consciousness, or experiences of union with God—none of the topics that someone in our day might associate with mysticism. Rather, it is a powerful and poetic meditation on the fact that God is so far beyond the limits of human language, human thought, even human imagination, that God must necessarily always remain shrouded in mystery to us. Even the greatest of philosophers (Augustine, Aquinas), when faced with the inscrutable mystery of God, ultimately recognize that all their profound ideas and intricate logic about God is ultimately just straw.

Consider the powerful opening lines of *Mystical Theology*:

O Trinity beyond being, beyond divinity, beyond goodness, and guide of Christians in divine wisdom, direct us to the mystical summits more than unknown and beyond light, there the simple, absolved, and unchanged mysteries of

theology lie hidden in the darkness beyond light of the hidden
mystical silence, there, in the greatest darkness, that beyond
all that is most evident exceedingly illuminates the sightless
intellects.[22]

Here is a vision of God that is luminously dark. Dark not in the sense of evil or dangerous, but in the sense of so utterly beyond anything the human mind can fathom or comprehend that even the very light and glory of God appear to us as darkness and mystery.

Pseudo-Dionysius was a mystical wisdom keeper who understood the importance of humility in the quest to understand or comprehend God. Because of God's limitlessness, and because of the relative smallness of the human heart and mind, we can only approach God with humility, acknowledging that anything we may think, or feel, or experience in terms of God is ultimately only a tiny approximation of what the divine majesty truly is. As such, *Mystical Theology* and the other writings of Pseudo-Dionysius have inspired mystics and contemplatives through the centuries, reassuring them that their profound sense of God's unfathomable mystery is, in fact, the way things are. God is a mystery, and to say otherwise is to run the risk of turning our human ideas about God into an idol. Worshipping an idol (even if the "idol" is our cherished ideas about God) is always a dead end; the only road to life is the road that takes us deep into the unknowing mystery of divine love.

Recommended Reading

The Divine Names and The Mystical Theology by Pseudo-Dionysius, translated by John D. Jones (Milwaukee, WI: Marquette University Press, 2011).

Raimon Panikkar (1918–2010)

Raimon Panikkar has been called one of the most original scholars of world religions; even in his family life, he embodied inter-spirituality: he was the son of a Spanish Catholic mother and a Hindu Indian father. Panikkar became a Catholic priest after a life-changing trip to India in 1954. Of that trip, he later said, "I left Europe as a Christian, I discovered I was a Hindu and returned as a Buddhist without ever having ceased to be Christian."[23] He devoted the rest of his life not only to Christian spirituality but to deep engagement with the wisdom of other traditions. Panikkar wrote over forty books, many of which dealt with contemplative spirituality, inter-religious dialogue, and spiritual practice.

One of the richest statements of his spiritual vision is *Christophany*, published six years before he died. Panikkar's concept of Christophany provides a spiritual alternative to Christology. The academic/theological field of Christology entails the study of Christ (a left-brain, cognitive, dogmatic approach), trapped in the limitations of human language, logic, and rational thought; by contrast, Christophany invites a person into direct, existential encounter with Christ as a living presence. In forming his understanding of Christophany, Panikkar drew not only from Christian spirituality but also from science and Eastern mysticism. The result is a richly woven and deeply textured Christian wisdom for our time.

"What we seek cannot be elsewhere than in ourselves,"[24] proclaimed Panikkar, who also notes that "The Beginning is Silence."[25] Just as God's Word emerges out of the silence of eternity, so also all human thought, language, and reason emerge out of the eternal silence found within us. "Let us not forget that the Word is the ecstasy of Silence,"[26] he goes on to say. But like nearly all mystics, Panikkar's wisdom ultimately points to love, which is the fountain of the unitive life. "Love is a nondualistic experience . . . Love is neither equality nor otherness, neither one nor two."[27]

Recommended Reading

Christophany: The Fullness of Man by Raimon Panikkar (Maryknoll, NY: Orbis Books 2004).

Richard of St. Victor (ca. 1110–1173)

Richard of St. Victor hailed from Scotland, but he lived and wrote in the Monastery of St. Victor near Paris, one of several important medieval theologians associated with that particular abbey. His writings cover a variety of topics; his most important contemplative or mystical writings include *The Twelve Patriarchs, The Mystical Ark,* and *Book Three of the Trinity*. Richard is considered to be one of the first theologians to attempt to explain contemplation in a systematic fashion, drawing on the story of the Hebrew patriarch Jacob, his wives, concubines, and children to explain various aspects of the spiritual life. This intricate allegory sees Joseph's children as representing various virtues that govern human will, thoughts, and deeds, preparing for the two youngest children, the sons of Rachel (who symbolizes reason): Joseph, who represents self-knowledge, and Benjamin, who represents ecstatic contemplation. Rachel dies giving birth to Benjamin, symbolizing that we must surrender reason in order to enter into the grace of heavenly contemplation.

Richard describes the transfiguring splendor of contemplation as an "alienation of mind," suggesting that in mystical ecstasy the human mind becomes alienated from all earthly cares or distractions. "Certainly by meditation it [the human soul] is raised to contemplation; by contemplation, to wonder; by wonder, to alienation of mind."[28] He also notes the mystical life consists in "understanding," then "contemplation," which finally leads to "astonishment," where the mystic silences the mind in order to receive ecstasy.[29]

Richard's medieval way of thinking and categorizing can seem needlessly intricate to us in the third millennium, yet his psychological approach to understanding the inner dynamics of meditation and contemplation provides rich food for thought and insight into the terrain that mystical spirituality covers.

Recommended Reading

Richard of St. Victor: The Twelve Patriarchs, The Mystical Ark, Book Three of the Trinity, translated by Grover A. Zinn (New York: Paulist Press, 1979).

William Law (1686–1761)

William Law's *A Serious Call to a Devout and Holy Life* (1728) is considered a masterpiece of eighteenth-century evangelical piety. But it was also steeped in Christian mysticism, for Law found inspiration from the writings of mystics like Johannes Tauler and John Ruusbroec. With its emphasis on everyday spirituality, virtuous living, and a balance between vocal prayer and "mystic intercourses with God in silence,"[30] it became an instant classic, counting among its readers John Wesley, the founder of Methodism.

Later in life, Law became a student of the German esoteric mystic Jakob Boehme. This influence is evident in Law's mature work, including his books *The Spirit of Prayer* and *The Spirit of Love*. Indeed, the latter work clearly spells out the heart of Law's mystical wisdom:

> *For the spirit of love, wherever it is, is its own blessing and happiness because it is the truth and reality of God in the soul, and therefore is in the same joy of life and is the same good to itself, everywhere and on every occasion . . . For love is the one only blessing and goodness and God of nature; and you have no true religion, are no worshipper of the one true God but in and by that spirit of love which is God Himself living and working in you.*[31]

Recommended Reading

A Serious Call to a Devout and Holy Life: The Spirit of Love by William Law, edited by P. G. Stanwood (New York: Paulist Press, 1978).

CHAPTER 8

Soul Friends

"Go forth and eat nothing until you get a soul friend, for any-one without a soul friend is like a body without a head."[1] Thus spoke Brigit of Kildare, one of the great saints of the Irish Celtic tradition and, if the stories about her are even somewhat true, certainly a mystic in her own right. Here she is giving advice to a young person who asked her for a word of wisdom; and her reply applies to everyone, not just the youth to whom she spoke. We all need companions who share our commitment to grow in grace and response to the love of God. But a soul friend is more than just a regular friend. He or she is someone with whom we pray, and with whom we listen together for the silent whispers of the prompting of the Holy Spirit, seeking guidance and direction for our ongoing journey to wholeness and union with, and in, God.

A soul friend can go by many names, including spiritual director, spiritual companion, mentor, or guide. Such a person is not really a guru, as that Eastern word is commonly understood in the West. A guru carries the connotation of a spiritual master who leads the disciple toward enlightenment, a transformation of the student from darkness into light. In the Christian tradition, no human being has that kind of power; only God—the Holy Spirit—can enlighten us or dispel our darkness. So in a Christian sense, a spiritual director is a fellow traveler, a friend who might be a bit older and wiser (and in that sense is a guide) but who shares in the common character of humanity—since all of us, no matter how "advanced" we are spiritually, need the healing mercy of the Spirit.

In a way, every mystic is a type of soul friend, for they all seek to share with others, through their writings, insight into the adventure of receiving grace and transfiguration in the Spirit.

But the ones whom I profile in this chapter seem to embody in a singular or remarkable way this down-to-earth quality of friendliness and willingness to help others along the way. Some of the writers included here are known specifically for their mentoring or guidance: *The Cloud of Unknowing* and Walter Hilton's *The Scale of Perfection* are renowned texts written specifically to provide guidance to a particular reader. When we read these books, we become "fellow directees," able to receive the benefits of the author's wisdom, even if we might have to translate some of their directives into the circumstances of twenty-first century life.

The soul-friend mystics are some of the most approachable and accessible spiritual writers. Their books are warm, inviting, and encouraging. They remind us that anyone who truly hungers for the love of God can embark with hope and confidence on the mystical path.

Aelred of Rievaulx (1110–1167)

Aelred of Rievaulx has long been overshadowed by his Cistercian contemporaries, Saint Bernard of Clairvaux and William of St.-Thierry. But this twelfth-century monk made his own contribution to contemplative spirituality with an impressive collection of writings. A courtier to King David of Scotland, Aelred entered monastic life as a young man, eventually becoming abbot of the monastery in Rievaulx, in the north of England. Bernard of Clairvaux asked Aelred to write a manual for novice monks, *The Mirror of Charity*; other writings include saints' lives, treatises on a variety of topics, and the work generally considered to be his masterpiece, *Spiritual Friendship*. Based on Cicero's classical treatise *On Friendship*, Aelred's work presents a dialogue between the author and two other monks, discussing the nature and beauty of friendship in Christ. For Aelred, a friendship between monks is meant to be a way of deepening both of the friends' relationships with Christ.

"A friend is the partner of your soul," wrote Aelred, "to whose spirit you join and link your own and so unite yourself as to wish to become one from two, to whom you commit yourself as to another self, from whom you conceal nothing, from whom you fear nothing."[2]

Although his influence on later writers and mystics has been limited, Aelred deserves recognition as an important voice on the spirituality of friendship, which has found fruition in our time with the ministries of spiritual direction and spiritual accompaniment.

Recommended Reading

Aelred of Rievaulx: Spiritual Friendship, translated by Lawrence C. Braceland, edited by Marsha L. Dutton (Trappist, KY: Cistercian Publications, 2010).

Brother Lawrence of the Resurrection (ca. 1610–1691)

Brother Lawrence of the Resurrection died without knowing that he was the author of a mystical classic. Originally named Nicholas Herman, this simple French Carmelite entered religious life in Paris after a career as a soldier, fighting in the Thirty Years' War. As a lay brother, he performed menial labor in the Carmelite priory, working in the kitchen for many years and then in the priory shoe shop after his health declined. But the humility of his station did not prevent others from discerning his holiness, and soon he became known as a wise spiritual guide. Brother Lawrence wrote letters to his spiritual friends and also kept a notebook of maxims; these were collected by the friar's superior, Fr. Joseph de Beaufort, who published two small volumes in the years following Brother Lawrence's death; those two books were combined to form *The Practice of the Presence of God*, itself a slender book (a recent paperback edition is only 112 pages).

The title of the book alone has become a classic description of intentional spirituality, as recognizable to Christian contemplatives as "the cloud of unknowing" or "the dark night of the soul." The idea of "practicing the presence of God" in a general way refers to any effort to cultivate an awareness of God's ever-presence, through prayer, meditation, contemplation, *lectio divina*, or works of mercy.

Brother Lawrence counsels simplicity, peace, and tranquility, and a willingness to return one's thoughts to God whenever distractions arise. Some of his language is surprisingly maternal:

My most usual method is this simple attentiveness and this loving gaze upon God to whom I often feel myself united with greater happiness and satisfaction than that of an infant nursing at his mother's breast; also for the inexpressible sweetness which I taste and experience there, if I dared use this term, I would willingly call this state "the breasts of God." If sometimes by necessity or weakness I am distracted from this thought, I am soon recalled to it by interior emotions so delightful and so entrancing that I am ashamed to speak of them.[3]

Such humility interlaced with such clear love for and joy in God makes Brother Lawrence's simple book for soul friends still relevant and meaningful more than three centuries after his death.

Recommended Reading

The Practice of the Presence of God by Brother Lawrence of the Resurrection, translated by John J. Delaney (Garden City, NY: Image Books, 1977).

Friedrich von Hügel (1852–1925)

Friedrich von Hügel is known for writing an influential book on the study of mysticism, *The Mystical Element of Religion*. But he was also a noted spiritual director, with his most renowned directee being Evelyn Underhill. In von Hügel's letters we find a fascinating correspondence with Underhill where he challenges her to accept Christianity not merely as a religion of mystical ideas, but to see in it the work of God in, and through, human history. With correspondents ranging from well-known priests to schoolgirls on the eve of their confirmation, von Hügel demonstrates both a keen mind and a warm heart for assisting those who came to him with their unique spiritual journeys. "You are a mystic," he bluntly tells one directee. "You have never found, you will never find, either Church, or Christ, or just simply God, or even the vaguest spiritual presence and conviction, except in deep recollection, purification, quietness, intuition, love."[4]

Recommended Reading

Spiritual Counsel and Letters by Baron Friedrich von Hügel, edited by Douglas V. Steere (New York: Harper & Row, 1964).

Howard Thurman (1899–1981)

Howard Thurman may be remembered first and foremost as a mentor to Martin Luther King Jr., but he is also widely regarded as one of the greatest African American spiritual leaders of the twentieth century. Over a long ministry, which included serving as dean of the chapel at Howard University and Boston University, he became renowned not only as a gifted preacher but also a prolific author of more than twenty-eight books. His writing and his sermons reveal a deep contemplative sensibility, grounded in the encounter with the God who is Love that informed his commitment to social justice and nonviolence.

Thurman was born in Daytona Beach, Florida, and graduated from Morehouse College in Atlanta. Ordained a Baptist minister, he befriended the Quaker mystic Rufus Jones; in 1935, he traveled to India and met Mahatma Gandhi, who told Thurman that he wished he had done more to promote nonviolence—and thought that the African American community could be the champions for nonviolence in America. These prophetic words bore fruit in the spiritual friendship that blossomed between Thurman and King at Boston University in the early 1950s—shortly before King would change history when he led the Montgomery Bus Boycott in Alabama in 1955–6. Throughout Dr. King's leadership of the civil rights movement, he continued to correspond with Thurman, who counseled him to remain grounded in nonviolence, which was the way not only of Gandhi but also of Jesus. It is said that Martin Luther King Jr. carried Howard Thurman's book *Jesus and the Disinherited* with him at all times.

These facts alone mark Thurman as a true, if underappreciated, hero; but when we consider also the rich mystical sensibility that characterizes Thurman's sermons and writings, he emerges as one of the great twentieth-century Christian contemplatives. Even the titles of his books display his mystical heart: *Deep Is the Hunger, Meditations of the Heart, Mysticism and the Experience of Love, The Inward Journey, The Luminous Darkness*, and *The Centering Moment* all speak to Thurman's rich recognition that the heart of Christian spirituality concerns how inner transformation shapes outer behavior.

Thurman brought a keen intellect to his study of spirituality, but he always recognized that Christian mysticism is grounded in love. He defined mysticism as "the response of the individual to a personal encounter with God within his own spirit."[5] Recognizing that God is love, Thurman understood that love is something other than our human tendency to judge, and that authentic love is related to vulnerability, to freedom, and to the willingness to suffer with and on behalf of the beloved. Thus, "God is Love" means something far more than mere sentimentality: it is an invitation into an awe-inspiring power that can literally change the world.

"The mystic experiences unity, not identity, but it is a unity that penetrates through all the levels of consciousness and fills him with a sense of the Other," wrote Thurman. "He discovers, however, that it is not possible to keep the consciousness of the presence of God alive at a high point in his experience over long time intervals ... He comes upon the fact that deep within the structure of his own personality and life are the things which obscure and blot out his vision."[6] For Thurman, the key to retaining the consciousness of such divine unity was found in what he termed "disciplines of the spirit," including growing in wisdom, suffering, prayer, and reconciliation—all key elements not only in inner, spiritual growth, but also in the challenging but necessary work of struggling for social justice.

Perhaps Thurman's best-known quote is this: "Don't ask what the world needs. Ask what makes you come alive, and go do it. Because what the world needs is people who have come alive."[7] This conveys a profound mystical truth: that the heart of union with God (union with Love) consists precisely in awakening to who we truly are, and in such coming alive, we give ourselves joyously to God and to others.

Recommended Reading

A Strange Freedom: The Best of Howard Thurman on Religious Experience and Public Life, edited by W. E. Fluker and Catherine Tumber (Boston: Beacon Press, 1998).

Recommended Listening

The Living Wisdom of Howard Thurman: A Visionary for Our Time. 6-CD set (Boulder, CO: Sounds True, 2010).
Many of Dr. Thurman's audio recordings are available online at http://hgar-srv3.bu.edu/web/howard-thurman/virtual-listening-room.

Jean-Pierre de Caussade (1675–1751)

Jean-Pierre de Caussade, like Brother Lawrence before him (and Thomas R. Kelly after him), is a great spiritual writer whose masterpiece was published after he died. A French Jesuit priest, for seven years he served as a spiritual director for a convent of Visitation Sisters (the order founded by Saint Francis de Sales and Saint Jane de Chantal). After leaving that position, he continued to correspond with the nuns, and his letters of spiritual direction were collected and edited by another Jesuit over a century after his death, when they were published as *Abandonment to Divine Providence.* Filled with gentle common sense and a fervent devotion to God, the author presents the path to holiness as consisting of complete, trusting surrender to divine will.

He also emphasizes the importance of living in the present moment (at least one translation of this book has been titled *Sacrament of the Present Moment*). "The whole essence of the spiritual life consists in recognizing the designs of God for us in the present moment,"[8] writes de Caussade. By recognizing God's action and abandoning ourselves to his presence, we consent to divine union. "The presence of God which sanctifies us is the indwelling of the Blessed Trinity, who take up their abode in the depths of our hearts when we submit to the divine will. The presence of God that results from contemplation effects this intimate union in us only in the same way as other things that are part of God's design. Contemplation, however, ranks first among these things because it is the greatest means of uniting ourselves to God when the divine will bids us make use of it."[9]

Recommended Reading

Abandonment to Divine Providence by Jean-Pierre de Caussade, edited by Dennis Billy (Notre Dame, IN: Ave Maria Press, 2010).

John Cassian (ca. 360–435)

John Cassian is widely regarded as the person who brought monasticism (and, therefore, contemplative spirituality) from the deserts of the Middle East to western Europe. His birthplace is uncertain, but by the 380s he was living in a monastery in Bethlehem; subsequently he left to travel the deserts of Egypt, where he and his spiritual friend Germanus received spiritual direction from the desert fathers. The story of this journey, along with the wisdom the two young monks gleaned, is recorded in Cassian's *The Conferences*, one of two important books he wrote toward the end of his life, after he settled in Europe (near Marseille, France), where he established what is generally regarded as the first European monastery. His other book, *The Institutes*, largely concerns the administration of a monastery, whereas

The Conferences is a more explicitly spiritual book. As a record of instruction from several of the desert dwellers of the fourth century, Cassian's writing is priceless; two of the conferences specifically deal with instructions on prayer, providing one of the earliest written records of contemplative teaching in the Christian faith.

Cassian reports that Abba Isaac taught him and Germanus both the importance and the manner of contemplative prayer. "The end of every monk and the perfection of his heart direct him to constant and uninterrupted perseverance in prayer,"[10] declared the old man. Abba Isaac saw perpetual prayer as the result of a tranquil mind that has been liberated from earthly passions. He discusses different forms of prayer, including supplication, vows, intercession, and thanksgiving. But beyond these forms of vocal prayer, "a still more sublime and exalted condition follows . . . fashioned by the contemplation of God alone and by fervent charity, by which the mind, having been dissolved and flung into love of him, speaks most familiarly and with particular devotion to God."[11] Abba Isaac goes on to point out that true prayer arises from the love of God (who first loved us) and leads to union—not only with God, but also with all others who share our devotion to Christ. Everyone "who longs for the continual awareness of God should be in the habit of meditating on it ceaselessly in his heart, after having driven out every kind of thought"[12]—a sentence which reveals how the ancients saw thought as emanating not from the brain, but from the heart.

But how does one "drive out every kind of thought" in order to meditate and cultivate an ongoing awareness of the presence of God? Cassian reports that Abba Isaac recommends using a verse from scripture as a continual prayer word, to be repeated continually: "O God, come to my assistance; O Lord, make haste to help me." (Psalm 69:2, Douay-Rheims version).[13]

This simple meditation practice—of reciting a Bible verse repeatedly as a way to train one's attention on God rather than on extraneous distractions—became the foundation of the Orthodox Jesus Prayer discipline (as celebrated in *The Way of a Pilgrim* and *The Philokalia*) and also can be seen as the earliest form of contemplative practices such as promoted by *The Cloud of Unknowing* or the modern-day centering-prayer movement.

Prayer was not the only topic that Cassian wrote about. *The Conferences* includes discussions of vice and virtue, spiritual knowledge, and friendship. In the conference on friendship, Cassian (quoting the desert father Abba Joseph) offers practical advice on the psychology and ethics of friendship, recognizing that true spiritual friendship must be grounded in the love of God, for God is love.

Recommended Reading

The Conferences by John Cassian, translated by Boniface Ramsey (New York: Paulist Press, 1997).

Kenneth Leech (1939–2015)

Kenneth Leech, an Anglican priest, political activist, prolific writer, and humble contemplative, is the author of *Soul Friend*, one of the most influential books in the twentieth-century revival of popular Christian spirituality, and a major factor in the explosion of spiritual companionship as a contemplative Christian ministry. Leech (whom I met on several occasions) was a deeply humble man. To the best of my knowledge, he never talked or wrote about having any supernatural visions, extraordinary experiences, or moments of profound non-dual consciousness. If anything, he tended to be suspicious of a spirituality that was rooted in "inner experience" as a kind of psychological diversion that religious people with economic or social privilege would use to distract themselves from the real-world issues of poverty, racism, sexism, and other forms of injustice. But he was a sterling example of how "still waters run deep," for beneath his unassuming demeanor was a man passionately in love with God, and who understood that to be in love with God meant to be lovingly engaged with the messiness and brokenness of our world, racked as it is by addiction, abuse, despair, and inequality. Leech knew that it was possible to see God face to face—as long as you were willing to look for God in the slums, the ghettoes, the homeless shelters, or the safe houses.

Born on the eve of World War II, Leech grew up in a secular home in the north of England. As a youth, he met Alasdair MacIntyre (who later became famous for his renowned study of postmodern moral theory, *After Virtue*) and realized that it is possible to have a critical, inquiring mind while also being a person of faith. He embraced the Anglo-Catholic tradition of the Church of England and was ordained a priest. Leech served most of his ministry in the same neighborhood of the east end of London, where for more than four decades he engaged with a variety of social and economic challenges, including homelessness, drug abuse, racism, and religious prejudice. (His neighborhood became a home for immigrants, particularly from the Muslim world.)

Leech was a prolific writer. His first books dealt with topical issues such as the drug problem, but early on he recognized that the youth culture of the 1960s and 1970s had a strong interest in spirituality, which led him to begin writing about the treasures of the Christian tradition. It was his work with people suffering on the margins of society that made him realize the need for literature on spiritual companionship; when *Soul Friend* was published in 1977, it became a minor modern spiritual classic. Subsequent titles explored topics such as God, prayer, the crucifixion, and theology; but issues of social and economic justice were never far from Leech's mind. Toward the end of his life, a comprehensive anthology of his best writing was published with the title *Prayer and Prophecy*.

Those two words really sum up Leech's spirituality and ministry. As a prophet of our times, he spoke out on behalf of those whom society (and, all too often, the Church) tended to ignore. But his political activism was always grounded in a down-to-earth understanding of relationship as the heart of spirituality. Leech's tireless work on behalf of the poor, the homeless, the addicted, the victims of racism or religious prejudice, was always anchored in his faith in Jesus Christ and his unwavering belief that the Church, the community of faith, is called to be a countersign to the "principalities and powers" of our world (which includes oppressive economic and political systems that keep some people marginalized even as they benefit those with privilege).

Leech called himself a "community theologian," recognizing that the best theology comes not from the ivory tower, but from the gritty realities of life on the street. Yet he always understood that prayer came first. When I read *Prayer and Prophecy* the first time, I was profoundly moved by the following quotation—an eloquent and insightful commentary on how contemplative spirituality (which is to say, mystical spirituality) links the depths of our inner selves (our souls) with the realities of the world in which we live.

> *Contemplation has a context: it does not occur in a vacuum. Today's context is that of the multinational corporations, the arms race, the strong state, the economic crisis, urban decay, the growing racism, and human loneliness. It is within this highly deranged culture that contemplatives explore the waste of their own being. It is in the midst of chaos and crisis that they pursue the vision of God and experience the conflict which is at the core of the contemplative search. They become part of that conflict and begin to see into the heart of things. The contemplative shares in the passion of Christ which is both an identification with the pain of the world and also the despoiling of the principalities and powers of the fallen world-order.*[14]

Anyone who struggles with what Buddhists call "the monkey mind" might take comfort in Leech's wisdom here. Traditionally, Christian mystics insisted that the mind was noisy and distracted as a result of original sin. Leech's perspective, while not repudiating that traditional view, offers a more down-to-earth yet no less compelling analysis: we have noisy (chaotic) minds because we live in a noisy, chaotic culture, a culture wounded by alienation and the hoarding of resources by the wealthy to the detriment of the poor. To be a contemplative means facing down our inner chaos, but that only makes sense if we simultaneously work to alleviate the suffering in the world in which we live.

Like all mystics, Leech understood that to "explore the waste of our own being" we needed not only prayer, but silence.

> *The practice of silence is, of course, inseparable from the discovery of one's own inner depths. For when one descends into the depths of one's spirit, there is a realisation of the closeness of God, the ground of one's being, the depth in which our own soul stands.*[15]

I know of no other writer, from our time or of any age, who so eloquently made the case for the integral unity between Christian spirituality and social action. Leech's powerful proclamation—that the breathing in of contemplation is essentially linked to the breathing out of working for justice and mercy—shines boldly and powerfully in his writings and calls us to embody in our own lives that mystical place where prayer and prophecy unite in an integral act of love.

Recommended Reading

Prayer and Prophecy: The Essential Kenneth Leech, edited by David Bunch and Angus Ritchie (New York: Seabury Books, 2009).

Rufus Jones (1863–1948)

Rufus Jones taught Quaker history and philosophy and became renowned as one of the most important American religious thinkers of the early twentieth century. As a Quaker, Jones developed a keen interest in mysticism, and he can be seen as the American counterpart to Evelyn Underhill, the British writer who lived and wrote at the same time, who also devoted her life to making mysticism accessible for the twentieth-century seeker.

Jones helped to promote the idea of the "inner light" as a core Quaker principle—the spiritual insight that acknowledges "that which is of God" in every human soul.

But perhaps Jones's most significant achievement was his role as a mentor and spiritual friend to Howard Thurman, a mystic in his own right, who in turn mentored Martin Luther King Jr. In this sense, Jones could be seen as an honorary "godfather" of the American Civil Rights movement, particularly in terms of its commitment to peace and nonviolence.

Like Evelyn Underhill, Karl Rahner, and Thomas Merton, Rufus Jones championed the idea that mysticism is not an "elite" form of spirituality but rather belongs to humanity at large. "I am convinced by my own life and by wide observation of children that mystical experience is much more common than is usually supposed . . . They have more room for surprise and wonder. They are more sensitive to intimations, flashes, openings. The invisible impinges on their souls and they feel its reality as something quite natural."[16] He goes on to say, "The world within is just as real as the world without until events force us to become mainly occupied with the outside one."[17]

Recommended Reading

Rufus Jones: Essential Writings by Rufus Jones, edited by Kerry S. Walters (Maryknoll, NY: Orbis Books, 2001).

Thomas R. Kelly (1893–1941)

Thomas R. Kelly, a Quaker philosopher and educator, discovered Christian mysticism while under the tutelage of Rufus Jones, one of his professors in graduate school. Kelly died young, of a heart attack, which ironically occurred the same day he received word from Harper & Brothers, who wanted to publish a collection of his essays. That book, *A Testament of Devotion*, has become a minor classic of twentieth-century spirituality.

In her book *The Mystic Way of Evangelism*, Elaine A. Heath profiles Kelly as a mystic whose identity was forged by his struggle against the evangelical piety that had shaped his childhood and young adult years. With Jones as his spiritual guide, he studied both Western and Eastern philosophy but suffered a deep disappointment when he failed an oral exam at Harvard University, where he was pursuing a PhD. Although initially depressed, he found in his academic failure the freedom to find himself not in external achievements but solely in the love of God. After a mission trip to Germany on the eve of World War II, Kelly became the leader of a small spiritual formation community at the school where he taught, thereby passing on the spiritual nurture he had received from Jones to the next generation.[18]

"When we are drowned in the overwhelming seas of the love of God," wrote Kelly, "we find ourselves in a new and particular relation to a few of our fellows. The relation is so surprising and so rich that we despair of finding a word glorious enough and weighty enough to name it . . . For a new kind of life-sharing and of love has arisen of which we had had only dim hints before."[19]

For Kelly, the mysticism of loving God naturally overflowed into the love for other human beings.

Recommended Reading

A Testament of Devotion by Thomas R. Kelly (New York: Harper & Row, 1988).

Walter Hilton (ca. 1340–1396)

Walter Hilton is to Julian of Norwich and the author of *The Cloud of Unknowing* what George Harrison of the Beatles was to John Lennon and Paul McCartney. In other words, Harrison was an excellent songwriter in his own right who was almost totally overshadowed by the two geniuses in his band; so, too, Walter Hilton sadly gets overlooked because of the two mystical legends who were his contemporaries in late fourteenth-century England. That's unfortunate, because in some ways Hilton's writings, especially his masterpiece *The Scale of Perfection*, are more accessible and user-friendly than the visionary poetry of Julian or the apophatic austerity of *The Cloud*.

Hilton was born probably in the 1340s and died in 1396; little is known about his life, although he likely studied law at Cambridge before becoming an Augustinian priest. His writings, mostly in Middle English, were popular during his lifetime

and in the following century. In his work, Hilton demonstrates
a keen understanding of the psychology of contemplative life
and (like *The Cloud*) reveals considerable talent as a soul friend.
The Scale of Perfection, written specifically to provide spiritual
direction to a nun, concerns the ongoing process of inner transfiguration that marks perseverance in contemplation. Hilton
follows the longstanding mystical tradition that understands
the human soul as created in the image and likeness of God,
and presents the contemplative life as a gradual reformation of
the soul in order to restore the Divine's image that has been
defaced by sin.

Hilton equates humility with truth,[20] so his emphasis as a
spiritual director is on authenticity—understanding the limitations of human nature, set against the splendor of divine grace.
But humility is also equated with love: anyone who "truly has
the gift of perfect humility . . . has the gift of perfect love."[21]
Furthermore, true spiritual humility, grounded in a sustaining
love for God in Christ, is not a cause for sorrow or great effort
(in Hilton's words, "sullenness or striving"), but is grounded in
"pleasure and gladness" that come from beholding the truth of
God's goodness and beauty, in Christ, through the Holy Spirit.
"For the heart of a true lover of Jesus is made so great and so
large through a little sight of him and a little feeling of his spiritual love, that all the pleasure and all the joy of the whole world
cannot suffice to fill a corner of it."[22]

Early in *The Scale*, Hilton provides insightful instruction
in *lectio divina*, one of the most time-honored spiritual practices of the Christian mystical tradition. Describing it as "the
means that bring a person to contemplation,"[23] Hilton details

the three preliminary steps of this practice as "the reading of holy scripture and of holy teaching, spiritual meditation, and diligent prayer with devotion."[24] These three steps—reading the Bible or other sources of spiritual wisdom, reflecting on such wisdom and how it applies to one's own life, and responding to this insight to God with words of prayer—all prepare one for the grace of contemplation, which is found not through striving or effort, but simply by resting in the mystical presence of God, cultivating interior silence as a way to be obediently present to the divine mystery.

Some readers might be put off by Hilton's insistence that spirituality includes seeing the human self, and all our good works, as "nothing"—because, to Hilton, God is "everything." A superficial reading of Hilton's language might lead to the erroneous conclusion that he is advocating a kind of self-hating or masochistic spirituality. But that is not the case. For Hilton, like many mystics in the Christian tradition, viewing oneself as "nothing" is not grounded in hatred of the self, but rather liberation from narcissism and egocentrism. Spiritual maturity comes not from self-contempt, but self-forgetfulness. And the object of forgetting one's self is always to seek to be found in the heart of divine love. Indeed, Hilton delineates between two kinds of humility: the lesser kind focuses on the nothingness of the self, but the greater, more perfect humility is anchored in, and focused on, the beauty and splendor of God, who is Love.

Recommended Reading

Walter Hilton: The Scale of Perfection, translated by John P. H. Clark and Rosemary Dorward (New York: Paulist Press, 1991).

The Cloud of Unknowing (ca. 1375)

The Cloud of Unknowing, a great classic of Christian mystical literature composed in Middle English, dates from around the same time Julian of Norwich and Walter Hilton were living and writing. We know almost nothing about the author, aside from a few speculations that scholars have put together based on *The Cloud* and several shorter works written by the same person. He was likely a monk, probably of the Carthusian Order—a rigorous order that stresses deep silence and solitude as essential foundations to the contemplative life. *The Cloud*'s author translated several mystical classics into Middle English, including writings by Pseudo-Dionysius and Richard of St. Victor. Clearly, he was educated in the contemplative tradition, and he devoted his writings to passing this wisdom on to the next generation. Indeed, *The Cloud of Unknowing* appears to be written with a specific, younger monk in mind—perhaps a novice to whom this author provided spiritual direction. It is a practical, down-to-earth manual of instruction in contemplative prayer. As such, it is a priceless text and one of the towering classics of Christian mysticism.

Some Christians, who unfortunately are uncomfortable with mystical or contemplative spirituality, argue that followers of Jesus should not engage in silent prayer or meditation—that such practices are foreign intrusions, imported from Vedanta or Zen, and are therefore not authentically Christian. Yet *The Cloud of Unknowing*, along with other key texts such as the works of Evagrius Ponticus or the Eastern Orthodox writings anthologized in *The Philokalia*, proves that Christianity actually has a long heritage of meditation and intentional silence as key forms of prayer.

> *Lift up your heart towards God with a humble stirring of love; and think of himself, not of any good to be gained from him. See, too, that you refuse to think of anything but him, so that nothing acts in your intellect or will but God himself. And do what you can to forget all of God's creations and all their actions, so that your thoughts and desires are not directed and do not reach out towards any of them, in general or in particular. But leave them alone, and pay no heed to them.*[25]

Here, in a nutshell, is *The Cloud* author's teaching: pray with your heart lifted to God, surrendering the activity of your mind or will so that your attention rests on God alone, with all thoughts, imagination, and other mental activity suspended beneath what the author calls "the cloud of forgetting," a mental veil drawn between the present moment and all distracting thoughts or feelings. However, the author acknowledges that "thinking of God" is itself problematic, for a similar metaphorical "cloud" separates human knowing from God—this being the titular cloud of unknowing.

The purest type of contemplative prayer, the author says, consists not of many words (like most "normal" prayers in Christian devotion or worship), but rather a single word that can be used to focus the attention so that it is not continually distracted by various (even pious or holy) thoughts. For contemplative prayer is not meant to be directed by our cognitive minds, but rather by our loving hearts:

a naked intention directed to God is fully sufficient, without any other goal than himself. If you want to have this intention wrapped and enfolded in one word, so that you can hold on to it better, take only a short word of one syllable; that is better than one of two syllables, for the shorter it is, the better it agrees with the work of the spirit. A word of this kind is the word GOD or the word LOVE.[26]

This one-word prayer became the foundation of the centering-prayer movement in the twentieth century, which advocates a profoundly silent and still form of prayer, centered on a single prayer word that you can repeat in the rhythm of your breath, allowing your awareness to be focused on this single word so that you may more fully rest in the vast, open silence of God.

There is much more to *The Cloud of Unknowing* than this simple instruction in contemplative prayer, although that may be its greatest contribution to Western mysticism. The text also explores the relationship between contemplative prayer and social action, considers the importance of virtues such as humility to the spiritual life, and offers trenchant criticism of what it calls "false contemplatives"—people who lust after spiritual experiences rather than surrendering themselves to the uncontrollable mystery of God. Of the author's minor works, perhaps the most important is *The Book of Privy Counseling*, a shorter book of spiritual direction that offers profound theological insight into the mystery of God and the function of prayer as the giving of oneself to that divine mystery.

Recommended Reading

The Cloud of Unknowing and Other Works, translated by A. C. Spearing (London: Penguin, 2001).

Theologia Germanica (ca. 1350)

Theologia Germanica, like *The Cloud of Unknowing*, is the work of an unknown author. Its title means "the German theology." Probably written in the fourteenth century by a priest from Frankfurt, it was not widely circulated until the early sixteenth century, when Martin Luther discovered it and published it, saying "Next to the Bible and Saint Augustine no other book has come to my attention from which I have learned—and desired to learn—more concerning God, Christ, man, and what all things are."[27]

The Way of a Pilgrim includes an interesting section where its anonymous author offers advice to those who cannot find a spiritual director.[28] While continuing to seek such a guide, along with praying and practicing mindfulness, the seeker may turn to spiritually nurturing books as a type of vicarious spiritual guidance. It seems that, for Luther, *Theologia Germanica* functioned like this—as a kind of spiritual director in written form.

Theologia Germanica offers insight into what it means to have a relationship with Christ, the importance of surrendering the human will to Christ's will, and the primacy of love. While it lacks the daring speculation of other northern European mystics like Meister Eckhart or John Ruusbroec, *Theologia Germanica* still conveys a rich sense of contemplative wisdom: for example, "all things dwell as beings in God's being; their being is more truly in God than in themselves."[29]

Recommended Reading

The Theologia Germanica of Martin Luther, translated by Bengt Hoffman (New York: Paulist Press, 1980).

CHAPTER 9

Unitives

The Christian mystical life has been described as consisting of three stages: purification, illumination, and union. In other words, the quest for divine union begins with self-knowledge and humility, as we begin to notice all the ways that we fail to embody the heavenly love that we seek. To use traditional language, we are sinners, "mistake-makers" who hunger for God's love to be poured into and through us, and yet our choices and inclinations often prevent us from letting that love in. So the purification stage is a period of radical letting-go: letting go of all that is not-love to create space in our lives for that which is truly Love.

The humility of purification leads to the compassion of illumination: for as we persevere on the path to God, we begin to discover that by grace (not our own efforts) God's love really does flow through us, and it reveals its presence by our capacity to truly love our neighbors, our family and friends, and even our enemies. We are illuminated by love, and knowing that love is available to us only heightens our effort to let go of everything that is not love.

Finally comes union: the insight that God is not elsewhere, that we are not separate from God, that we are "partakers of the Divine Nature" (II Peter 1:4), that we are one with Christ, who in turn is one with God (John 10:30). The Greeks call this *theosis*, translated into English as "deification" or "divinization," words that point to union with God, like a drop of water united with the ocean. The drop is one with the ocean, yet it does not become the entire ocean. Some Christians, nervous that this could be misinterpreted as pantheism, may prefer to say *communion* with God, rather than union with God, but mystically speaking communion and union are the same.

The following mystics, each in their own way, testify that this non-dual unitive life can be at least tasted here on earth, even if it finds its fullest expression only in heaven. With their witness to the beauty and splendor of divine union, they are representing the flowering of Christian mysticism—its fullest expression and most refulgent hope.

Many unitive mystics drink deeply from the well of interreligious dialogue and interspirituality. I think this is because unitive consciousness can be found in all mystical traditions, and those who realize union with God are often inspired by encountering similar depth in the teachings and adherents of other contemplative paths.

What can we learn from the unitive mystics? Their message is both hopeful and humbling: union with God is not something we *achieve*, but rather something that by grace we *receive*. It's not what we do; it's who we are (in God). We read the words of the unitive mystics to be inspired and encouraged, even if we recognize that we may still have a lot of purifying and illuminating to do in our own lives. For the paradox is this: no one on this side of death ever becomes sinless or mistake-less; purification and illumination are not stages to pass through, but lifelong commitments as we strive to make ourselves worthy of God's call.

Unitive consciousness is a gift; it's not something within human control. We can make ourselves ready for it by doing the slow and steady work of knowing ourselves better, accepting our imperfections, striving to let go of anything that impedes the flow of love in our lives, and then actively giving that love away to our friends, family, neighbors, and enemies. If we keep doing those down-to-earth things, then the heavenly joy of divine union will overtake us when we least expect it.

Abhishiktananda (1910–1973)

Abhishiktananda is one of numerous Christians from the West who traveled to the East to discover wisdom by engaging in the practice of a mystical tradition other than that into which he was born. Hailing from western France, he was baptized with the name Henri Le Saux. At the age of nineteen he entered a Benedictine monastery and spent almost two decades in the cloister, except for a short stint as a sergeant during World War II. In 1948 he departed for India, where he lived for the rest of his life. He was motivated to leave Europe because of his desire for a deeper, more authentic contemplative life than he felt the Catholic monasteries of the mid-twentieth century could support. Once in India, he turned to Hindu sages like Sri Ramana Maharshi and Sri Gnanananda Giri for guidance and training in the practice of meditation.

Along with another French priest, Le Saux founded the Saccidananda Ashram, also called Shantivanam, in 1950, intending it to be a place of interspiritual practice, where Christians and Hindus could come together for meditation, contemplation, and silent communion. It was at this time that Le Saux took his Sanskrit name, Abhishiktananda, which means "Bliss of the Anointed Lord." He remained at Shantivanam until 1968, at which time he embraced a life of solitude and teaching of his own disciple until his death by a heart attack at the age of sixty-three.

Among his many writings, Abhishiktananda's *Prayer* is an excellent introduction to his thought. He could just as easily have called the book *Contemplation*, for in discussing the shape and climate of Christian prayer, the author invites the reader into a place of deep silence and rest. Like his own life journey, the spirituality in *Prayer* is shaped by interfaith dialogue: one chapter explores the relationship between yoga and silence, while quotations from Hindu sacred texts such as the Rig Veda or the Upanishads appear almost as often as citations from the Bible. But Abhishiktananda is not trying to create some sort of blended spirituality; rather, he draws on Eastern wisdom to unpack the mysteries of Christian spirituality more deeply.

For Abhishiktananda, non-duality means simply that God is present, always present, whether we feel this presence or not. Likewise, prayer and contemplation are simply means "to realize God's presence in the depth of our being, in the depth of every being, and at the same time beyond all beings, beyond all that is within and all that is without."[1]

And while the author acknowledges that "God is hidden in his own mystery,"[2] he also declares, "Truly there is nothing in the created universe, in all time and all space, which does not manifest God and reveal his glory."[3] In other words, prayer, contemplation, spirituality, and mysticism are not means to attain non-dual union with God. Rather, they are simply doorways through which we might see that such union already exists.

Recommended Reading

Prayer by Abhishiktananda (Norwich, England: Canterbury Press, 2006).

Anthony de Mello (1931–1987)

Anthony de Mello, one of the most accessible of recent Christian contemplative writers, uses parables, stories, and exercises to invite his readers to explore the heart of all mystical spirituality, bridging the divide between East and West. An Indian Jesuit priest and psychotherapist, de Mello became a popular author after the publication of his first book, *Sadhana: A Way to God*. By encouraging readers to attend to silence, attentiveness, posture, and the breath, de Mello offered an embodied approach to spiritual growth. Drawing not only on his own Catholic identity but also on wisdom of other traditions such as Buddhism, Taoism, and Hinduism, he offered an approach to mysticism that is truly interspiritual in nature.

Here's an example of his teaching method, in this instance on the topic of emptiness:

Sometimes there would be a rush of noisy visitors and the Silence of the monastery would be shattered. This would upset the disciples; not the Master, who seemed just as content with the noise as with the Silence. To his protesting disciples he said one day, "Silence is not the absence of sound, but the absence of self."[4]

Themes of non-duality or the unitive life showed up in his writing in subtle ways. De Mello was not interested in expounding theory, but rather inviting his readers to see spiritual truth for themselves. Thus, for example, he comments on the difference between dualistic knowledge and unitive enlightenment: "When you have knowledge, you use a torch to show the way. When you are enlightened, you become a torch."[5]

De Mello died suddenly of a heart attack at age fifty-five. Sadly, after his death his writings were criticized by the Vatican for their mystical and interspiritual content.[6]

Recommended Reading

Anthony de Mello: Writings, edited by William V. Dych, (Maryknoll, NY: Orbis Books, 1999).

Bede Griffiths (1906–1993)

Bede Griffiths was an English Benedictine monk who studied at Oxford University under C. S. Lewis, eventually discerning a vocation to monastic life, which he pursued after becoming a

Roman Catholic in 1931. He was ordained a priest a few years later and lived in several different monasteries throughout Great Britain before receiving permission to go to India in 1955, where he spent the rest of his life. In India, he worked with several other figures prominent in East-West dialogue, like Abhishiktananda and the Cistercian monk Francis Acharya, establishing or supporting several "Christian ashrams," which consisted of Christian communities modeled after Hindu ashrams, where teachings of the East are explored in dialogue with Christian wisdom. Eventually, Griffiths settled at Saccidananda Ashram, which was founded by Abhishiktananda in 1950. Griffiths became the leader of that community until his death following a series of strokes in 1993.

Even before he traveled to India, Griffiths exhibited a propensity for mystical consciousness; he writes beautifully of an ecstatic experience in nature as a youth:

One day during my last term at school I walked out alone in the evening and heard the birds singing in that full chorus of song, which can only be heard at that time of the year at dawn or at sunset. I remember now the shock of surprise with which the sound broke on my ears. It seemed to me that I had never heard the birds singing before ... Everything then grew still as the sunset faded and the veil of dusk began to cover the earth. I felt inclined to kneel on the ground, as though I had been standing in the presence of an angel; and I hardly dared to look on the face of the sky, because it seemed as though it was but a veil before the face of God.[7]

Yet it was in India that Griffiths truly discovered the heart of the mystery. As he wrote in *Return to the Center*, "There is a window in my consciousness where I can look out on eternity, or rather where this eternal Reality looks out on the world of space and time through me."[8] In an interview conducted just a few months before his death, he said,

> When we go to a deeper level of consciousness, we should not lose the diversity of things and their individuality. On the contrary, the diversity, the multiplicity, is taken up into the unity. It cannot be put into words properly, and it cannot be explained rationally. It is simply an experience of advaita. The more one reads from the Hindu or the Buddhist or the Taoist or the Christian mystics, the more one realizes that this non duality has been the great discovery beyond the rational mind with all its dualities of good and evil, light and darkness, black and white, conscious and unconscious, male and female. All these divisions are there, but they are contained in a unity. That is the important thing.[9]

Griffith's apprehension of *advaita* (Sanskrit for "non-duality") was reflected not only in his interior unitive consciousness but also in his life work of fostering dialogue between Christianity and Eastern spirituality, particularly Vedanta. Griffiths inspired many others to carry on in this work, including Bruno Barnhart, Sara Grant, and Wayne Teasdale.

Recommended Reading

The One Light: Bede Griffiths' Principal Writings, edited by Bruno Barnhart (Springfield, IL: Templegate Publishers, 2001).

Bruno Barnhart (1931–2015)

Bruno Barnhart was a monk of the New Camaldoli Hermitage in Big Sur, California. Camaldolese monks follow the rule of Saint Benedict, only with a greater emphasis on solitude than is typically found among other Benedictines. Fr. Bruno authored several books, all dedicated to the reclamation of "Sapiential Christianity," or Christianity as a wisdom tradition (which, in essence, is mysticism by another name). His books include *The Good Wine* (a commentary on the Gospel of John), *Second Simplicity*, and *The Future of Wisdom*.

Non-duality, or unitive reality, is a theme at the heart of the Sapiential tradition, so not surprisingly it is prominent in Fr. Bruno's writings. "Unitive reality lives at the heart of the Western spiritual traditions, but it has rarely been expressed there with the directness and purity with which we find it in the Hindu and Buddhist literature,"[10] he admits. Still, the heart of Christian contemplation is "an awakening of pure consciousness, an unconditioned illumination and realization of the core of the Person, the point of a primordial oneness with God."[11] Barnhart also acknowledges that the heart of mystical Christianity is divinization, or deification: "the union of God with the human person that brings about a divine humanity."[12]

How is such wisdom realized? "Silent meditation is one of the most direct ways . . . downward into the ground and inward to the center. Still we are in the realm of metaphor; we cannot speak directly of this reality of the Source."[13] Silence, the heart of contemplation, is our portal into wisdom, but even deeper than that, it is the means by which we encounter the God who is not "other" than us. Barnhart points out that this mystical wisdom is not some novel notion imported into Christianity from the East, but is grounded in the Bible itself. "The New Testament is anything but an abstract textbook treatise on unitive reality or knowledge; it is an initiation into unitive experience, into contemplation."[14]

Recommended Reading

Second Simplicity: The Inner Shape of Christianity by Bruno Barnhart (New York: Paulist Press, 1999).

Gerald G. May (1940–2005)

Gerald G. May was a psychiatrist, spiritual director, and contemplative writer. After practicing psychiatry for many years, May joined the Shalem Institute for Spiritual Formation in 1973, eventually becoming a senior fellow for that ecumenical Christian organization, training spiritual directors and supporting clergy and laypersons in fostering contemplative spirituality. May's work helped deepen the understanding of the distinct benefits of psychology and spirituality. He felt that healing was measured by how loving one might become, not how adjusted.

"It seems quite certain, in fact, that rather than saying, 'I have consciousness,' it would be far more accurate to say, 'consciousness has me.'"[15] This koan-like statement offers insight into May's non-dual spirituality.

A prolific author, May is perhaps best known for *Addiction and Grace*, a consideration of the spiritual nature of addiction and recovery. Other works include *Simply Sane, The Awakened*

Heart, and *The Wisdom of Wilderness.* May is also one of the contributing authors in the Fetzer Institute's project *Deepening the American Dream.* Yet his most significant contribution to contemplative spirituality is probably *Will and Spirit,* which is the most eloquent statement of his integral understanding of spirituality and mental wellness.

Will and Spirit offers a comprehensive introduction to the psychology of contemplation. It covers categories such as good and evil, love and fear, and unity and duality. May begins his exploration by reflecting on the distinction between willfulness, the tendency for a human being to assert his or her will to seek power and control in any life circumstance, and willingness, the impulse or possibility of self-surrender, which May sees as the appropriate response to the mystery of God—and the threshold to the contemplative path. It is a natural characteristic of the human will that we seek autonomy, freedom, and the ability to control or define our self and our choices in life; by contrast, the spirit is by nature that dimension within us that seeks connection and even union with others, with the universe, and with "the mysterious Source of all."[16] The contemplative life, therefore, is a gradual process of surrendering the autonomy of the will into the unitive encounter with the Divine, where God and the self are "not two," and in the vast openness of this nondual place, growth in humility, compassion, and love naturally ensues.

May goes on to point out that this kind of unitive, self-forgetful spaciousness is not something we can manufacture on demand—that would just be our willfulness reasserting itself. It's always a gift, always grace. Thankfully, though, God is always willing to give this mystical gift to those who gently, humbly, and silently seek it.

Recommended Reading

Will and Spirit: A Contemplative Psychology by Gerald G. May (San Francisco: Harper & Row, 1982).

John O'Donohue (1956–2008)

John O'Donohue hailed from the west of Ireland, where he spoke Gaelic and intuitively learned the mystical wisdom of his Celtic ancestors, which he integrated with his vocation as a Catholic priest. He became internationally renowned with the publication of his luminous book *Anam Ċara*. Deeply meditative and shimmering with wonder, his book appealed to readers from all walks of life; he followed it up with several other books of meditative prose, as well as a few volumes of poetry and a book of blessings.

For O'Donohue, the unitive life begins and ends in love, which he expresses in a humbly domestic way. "Love is absolutely vital for a human life," he writes, "for love alone can awaken what is divine within you. In love, you grow and come home to your self. When you learn to love and to let your self be loved, you come home to the hearth of your own spirit. You are warm and sheltered. You are completely at one in the house of your own longing and belonging."[17]

His Celtic sensibility allowed O'Donohue to see the limitations in ordinary western European/American modes of thought. "When time is reduced to linear progress, it is emptied of presence,"[18] he wryly remarked. Along these lines, he even invoked Meister Eckhart to challenge the very idea that the mystical life involves a journey or process. "If there were a spiritual journey, it would be only a quarter inch long, though many miles deep. It would be a swerve into rhythm with your deeper nature and presence. The wisdom here is so consoling. You do not have to go away outside yourself to come into real conversation with your soul and with the mysteries of the spiritual world. The eternal is at home—within you."[19] The takeaway is that unitive mysticism is not something we achieve, but rather something we receive through grace—merely by being alive. Mystical spirituality means simply remembering who we truly are.

Recommended Reading

Anam Ċara: A Book of Celtic Wisdom by John O'Donohue (New York: Cliff Street Books, 1997).

Recommended Listening

Anam Ċara: Wisdom from the Celtic World by John O'Donohue (Boulder, CO: Sounds True, 1996).

John Ruusbroec (1293–1381)

John Ruusbroec had a fan in Evelyn Underhill. She referred to him as "great," "mighty," "supreme," and "the most transcendental of all mystics." She notes that Ruusbroec "seems often to use [Meister] Eckhart's ideas as a means of expressing his own experiences, but the ardour and realism with which he invests them are his own."[20] Who was this relatively obscure figure Underhill so admired?

Unlike Meister Eckhart, Ruusbroec was never formally charged with heresy. In fact, Ruusbroec has been beatified by the Catholic Church—one step short of being declared a saint. So while institutional Christianity accepts him as orthodox, his work is arguably every bit as radical as that of the more notorious Eckhart.

Born in the Flemish village of Ruisbroek (in modern day Belgium) in the late thirteenth century, young John began studying for the priesthood with his uncle when he was only eleven years old. After his ordination in 1318, he served as a parish priest until 1343, when he and two other priests retired to the forest of Groenendal, near Brussels, to become hermit contemplatives. Eventually, though, their small community became an Augustinian friary, with Ruusbroec serving as the community leader until his death in December 1381.

Ruusbroec was a prolific writer, usually composing his works in Flemish rather than Latin in order to reach a wider audience. His most important work is *The Spiritual Espousals*, a luminous meditation on how Christ, the bridegroom, unites human nature with his own in a sacred marriage officiated by the Holy Spirit.

Structured as an extended commentary on Matthew 25:6 ("See, the bridegroom is coming. Go out to meet him"), *The Spiritual Espousals* considers the life of faith in three forms: the active live, the interior life, and the contemplative life. According to Ruusbroec, Jesus (the bridegroom) "comes" in three ways: in his earthly life in the past as Jesus of Nazareth, in the present day as mystically united with those who love him, and at the end of time he will return to judge the living and the dead. Like many mystics, Ruusbroec insists that the cultivation of virtues like humility, patience, kindness, and compassion is an essential preliminary to the exaltation of the mystical life. Moving into his discussion of the interior life, Ruusbroec begins to reveal his exalted teachings. In the words of Ruusbroec scholar James A. Wiseman, OSB, "there is the movement inward toward 'the dark silence' and toward rest in the 'superessential Unity,' while . . . simultaneously, a movement outward in the generation of the Son and the breathing forth of the Holy Spirit."[21] For Ruusbroec, God is paradoxically present in both activity (doing good works) and repose (contemplative rest). Therefore, the highest expression of mystical spirituality is a life in which action and rest, meditation and good work, are equally immersed in the presence of God.

At its summit, the mystical life equals complete union with God: "To comprehend and understand God as he is in himself, above and beyond all likenesses, is to be God with God, without intermediary or any element of otherness which could constitute an obstacle or impediment."[22] Nevertheless, Ruusbroec warns that this mystery requires that a mystic have fully died to his narcissistic or egocentric self: "Whoever, then, wishes to understand it must have died to himself and be living in God and must turn his gaze to that eternal light which is shining in the ground of his spirit, where the hidden truth is revealing itself without intermediary."[23]

The contemplative life requires a willingness to let go of all thoughts, feelings, affections, and distractions and rest "in a state devoid of particular form or measure, a state of darkness in which all contemplatives blissfully lose their way . . . In the abyss of this darkness in which the loving spirit has died to itself

. . . an incomprehensible light is born and shines forth; this is the Son of God, in whom a person becomes able to see and to contemplate eternal life . . . The spirit ceaselessly becomes the very resplendence which it receives."[24]

Once a person who has cultivated a life grounded in virtue "dies to the self" by surrendering all claims for self-identity into the silent abyss of interior darkness, he or she consents to the radiant birth of Christ within his or her own soul, a birth that brings forth unity in Christ—for in receiving the splendor of Christ's light, our spirit becomes one with that very splendor. Masterful words from a remarkable mystic, whose command of language created a lovely and lyrical description of the supreme destiny available to anyone who, with a pure heart and total self-donation, surrenders everything to God's call to be One with Him.

Recommended Reading

John Ruusbroec: The Spiritual Espousals and Other Works, translated by James A. Wiseman (New York: Paulist Press, 1986).

Richard Rohr (1943–)

Richard Rohr is a Franciscan friar and the author of several books, including *Everything Belongs* and *The Naked Now*. He is one of the leading proponents of contemplative and mystical spirituality in the early twenty-first century, proclaiming a positive message that appeals both to Christians and to the larger community of spiritual seekers. Non-dual, or unitive, consciousness is a major theme in his writing. "Jesus was the first nondual religious teacher of the West," wrote Rohr, "and one reason we have failed to understand so much of his teaching, much less follow it, is because we tried to understand it with a dualistic mind."[25] In other words, Jesus himself embodies mystical consciousness, and to truly understand the power and wisdom of his teachings, we must approach his words with the eyes of unitive love, cultivated through silence, compassion, and contemplative prayer.

Recommended Reading

The Naked Now: Learning to See As the Mystics See by Richard Rohr (New York: Crossroad, 2009).

Sara Grant (1922–2002)

Sara Grant, born in England of Scottish parents, described herself as "haunted from childhood by the obsessive need to discover the secret bond of union drawing all things into one."[26] She entered religious life during World War II, joining the Society of the Sacred Heart. Grant moved to India in 1956 as a Catholic missionary, where she immersed herself in interreligious dialogue and the exploration of the deep resonance between Hindu spirituality (specifically Advaita Vedanta) and Christian mysticism. She became a close friend and an associate of Abhishiktananda and wrote a biography of him that was published toward the end of her life. She also wrote an autobiography, based on lectures delivered at Cambridge University and Bristol University, in which she labeled herself as a "nondualist Christian." A collection of her essays on contemplation,

Catholicism, and interreligious dialogue, *Lord of the Dance*, was published in 1987.

Sara Grant says, quoting one of the Upanishads to illustrate her point, "It is in a very real sense impossible to get out of God's presence—there is 'neither without nor within,' since every creature is simply a manifestation of him."[27] After a distinguished career as a philosopher at Sophia College in Bombay, in 1972 she joined the Christa Prema Seva Ashram in Pune, India, an ecumenical/interfaith center where Anglican and Catholic Christians worked together to integrate the wisdom of Hindu spirituality and practice with their devotion to Christ. She devoted most of the rest of her life to the ashram and the larger goal of fostering a spirituality grounded in "contact with other movements in an atmosphere of encounter and reconciliation."[28]

Recommended Reading

Toward an Alternative Theology: Confessions of a Non-Dualist Christian by Sara Grant (Notre Dame, IN: University of Notre Dame Press, 2002).

Thomas Keating (1923–)

Thomas Keating, a Trappist monk and popular spiritual writer, says, "The Christian religion is primarily about a transformation of consciousness. This takes spiritual practice and the cultivation of wisdom . . . the main thing is to be transformed into God, what the early church called deification, *theosis*, divinization."[29] Although not as widely known as his slightly older contemporary Thomas Merton, Keating—who has authored numerous books and been featured in many audio and video recordings—may be just as influential. As one of several monks who developed the centering-prayer method of attending to the presence of God in silence, Keating has been at the forefront of the efforts in the late twentieth and early twenty-first centuries to make contemplative forms of prayer part of mainstream Christianity.

Thomas Keating was born in the spring of 1923 and just twenty-one years later entered the Cistercian order at St. Joseph's Abbey, located at the time in Rhode Island. In 1958 he became the superior of a fledgling monastery in Colorado, but he returned to the East Coast in 1961 when he was elected the abbot of St. Joseph's, a position he held for twenty years. It was during this time that he, along with fellow monks M. Basil Pennington and William Meninger, developed the centering-prayer method of spiritual practice. Drawing on Christian sources like the writings of the desert fathers and *The Cloud of Unknowing*, but also influenced by Eastern practices like zazen and transcendental meditation, centering prayer involves using a repetitive prayer word to allow the mind and heart to rest in the openness of silence, without being lost in the distracting zone of endless mental activity. Practitioners are taught to silently repeat the prayer word, returning to it whenever the mind wanders. But if one's attention simply rests in boundless silence, it is okay for the prayer word to cease, allowing oneself simply to be present in the vast, limitless openness of this sacred moment. Of course, the mind inevitably generates more distracting thoughts, so the prayer word remains important as a way to center back in the present.

After resigning as abbot, Keating returned to Colorado and devoted his energy to leading Contemplative Outreach, a ministry for promoting the practice of centering prayer. Through his many books and recordings, Keating has become a leader among intentional Christian seekers. His work symbolizes the great transition of our time, as Christian mystical spirituality becomes less centered in monasteries and more available to "ordinary" Christians.

As a unitive, Keating insists that the key to spirituality is "dismantling the monumental illusion that God is absent or even distant."[30] In other words, mystical practices (like centering prayer) do not *achieve* union with God; such union is already given to us! The purpose behind all mystical disciplines is simply to remember who we already are—and the union we have already been given.

Recommended Reading

Invitation to Love: The Way of Christian Contemplation by Thomas Keating (New York: Continuum, 1999).

Wayne Teasdale (1945–2004)

Wayne Teasdale embraced the wisdom of the world's religious traditions and became a leading advocate for what he termed *interspirituality*—the weaving together of spiritual wisdom and insight in a way that integrates the teachings and practices of two or more religious traditions. Interspirituality can take many forms, but it always entails engaging with multiple spiritual paths from a place of respect, appreciation, and desire for illumination and insight. After writing a dissertation on Bede Griffiths, Teasdale taught theology at several different colleges, spent time in India, and eventually made a profession as a "monk in the world" before the archbishop of Chicago. He participated in a number of interfaith organizations, such as the North American Board for East-West Dialog, which later became Monastic Interreligious Dialogue. He helped to revive the Parliament of the World's Religions and founded the Community of The Mystic Heart (originally The Universal Order of Sannyasa) as a dispersed order of interspiritual mystics and contemplatives.

"Every one of us is a mystic," notes Teasdale. "We may or may not realize it; we may not even like it. But whether we know it or not, whether we accept it or not, mystical experience is always there, inviting us on a journey of ultimate discovery."[31] Drawing from both Christian and Eastern sources, he affirmed the nondual nature of union with the Divine as the end point of all mystical seeking: "Mystical spirituality is also *unitive*; it seeks integration with the infinite. All theistic types of mysticism are interested in this integration, for the goal is to be invited into a permanent, divine union with God. This unity is the heart of all mysticisms. It is awareness of nonduality and non-separation, of no distance between ourselves, the ultimate mystery, and all other beings. The unitive level of consciousness is both integration with the divine and nondual awareness or perception."[32]

Recommended Reading

The Mystic Heart: Discovering a Universal Spirituality in the World's Religions by Wayne Teasdale (Novato, CA: New World Library, 1999).

Willigis Jäger (1925–)

Willigis Jäger is a Benedictine monk and also a Zen master. Born in Hösbach, Germany, Jäger spent several years in Japan, where he received authorization to teach Zen in 1981. He returned to Germany and became a popular teacher of both zazen and Christian contemplation, culminating in the Church hierarchy censuring him in 2002. While the Vatican criticized Jäger specifically for his interspiritual activities, his books reveal a rich spirituality grounded in interreligious dialogue and especially in the wisdom of the Christian mystics. His works include *The Way to Contemplation* (1986), *Contemplation* (1994), *Search for the Meaning of Life* (1995), and *Mysticism for Modern Times* (2006).

Jäger's writings are filled with insight into communion and union with God, which he equates with "enlightenment, liberation, satori, samadhi, and so on, in various religions."[33] Inspired by the mystical wisdom of figures like John of the Cross, Meister Eckhart, and the author of *The Cloud of Unknowing*, Jäger writes,

> *In every case, the experience at the end of the journey is of oneness and emptiness. But oneness and emptiness, or nothingness, are not to be understood negatively. The words point to the ultimate reality that cannot be named. Even words such as "God," "Jesus" or "Christ," and the experience of one's own being must be transcended. In the end, there is not even a person. There is only being itself in which everything has its continued existence.*[34]

Recommended Reading

The Way to Contemplation: Encountering God Today by Willigis Jäger, translated by Matthew J. O'Connell (New York: Paulist Press, 1986).

Conclusion

This book features 108 Christian mystics (twelve in each of nine categories), representing nearly every century of church history, homelands as far flung as Egypt, Syria, Germany, and America, who originally wrote in languages from Latin to Greek, from Syriac to Flemish, from English to Spanish. Space prohibited me from giving you more than just a brief introduction to each figure. Think of this book as a kind of spiritual "speed dating"— you meet a lot of people in a hurry, gather plenty of information for further contact, but at the end of the night there are really only one or two individuals you're interested in seeing again. You reach out to the ones who appeal to you, and you hardly give anyone else a second thought. And so it is with the Christian mystics. If you try to dutifully read a book or two by every one of the 108 figures profiled in this survey, you will in all probability quickly get bogged down.

It's not you; it's them.

Remember the quotation from Richard Rohr in my Introduction, where he admitted that reading the desert mystics from the third and fourth centuries can sometimes be an exercise in frustration. Even the mystics you naturally feel connected to might be challenging in some ways. For example, Julian of Norwich is one of my favorite mystics, and her poetic recounting of a night of visions still moves me even thirty years after first discovering her writing. But one of her favorite themes is talking about the crucifixion of Jesus—in bloody, gory detail. As someone who was repulsed by the gratuitous violence of Mel Gibson's *The Passion of the Christ*, I have to keep reminding myself that Julian wrote in an era when devotion to the horrors of the cross was a way to make sense of the terrors of her own day, like the bubonic plague. My point is this: if I had given up on reading Julian because I found her devotion to the crucifixion unappealing, I would have missed the splendor of her lyrical celebration of divine love. And that would have been a significant loss.

Still, it's only natural that some mystics will appeal to you more than others, so I encourage you, especially if you are new to the topic of the Christian mystics, to select just one or two of the figures profiled here, and try to learn a bit more about them. At the end of each profile, I've recommended a book for further exploration; if you'd like a handy online reference to all of the recommended titles in this book, visit *www.carlmccolman.net/christian-mystics*. I encourage you to visit your library or local bookstore to pick up one or two of the writings of the great mystics and begin to taste their wisdom for yourself.

Another approach might be to pick up an anthology of mystical writings. This gives you a chance to sample the words of many of the mystics at once, which can provide much insight into the direction in which you might wish to take your further study. My favorite anthology of the mystics, by far, is Bernard

McGinn's *The Essential Writings of Christian Mysticism*. This book provides not only a generous sampling of the mystics in their own words but also helpful introductions and commentary from McGinn, a leading scholar of the mystics who is adept at making their sometimes inscrutable language accessible to the average reader. McGinn avoids a chronological approach, arranging the writings in a thematic way. So reading the entire book gives you a wonderful overview of the sweep and grandeur of Christian mystical thought in its entirety.

Two other anthologies worth exploring are Harvey D. Egan's *An Anthology of Christian Mysticism* and Louis Dupré and James Wiseman's *Light from Light*. These books arrange the writings of the mystics chronologically rather than topically, which is less helpful for those who wish to read the mystics devotionally; but they are nevertheless excellent overviews of mystical writings and fine places to start on your journey into contemplative wisdom.

One of the challenges we face in reading the mystics is the temptation to read them in an academic or scholarly way, as opposed to a devotional way. There's nothing wrong with reading the mystics like a student reads a textbook—and if your interest in the mystics is mostly a matter of historical or literary curiosity, that may be perfectly satisfying for you. But I wrote this book specifically for people who want to encounter the mystics not for the purpose of learning a few interesting bits of trivia, but for the far nobler purpose of allowing the wisdom and vision of the mystics to directly and profoundly impact your own spiritual journey. Put another way, we are reading the mystics not to gather *information*, but to receive *formation*—to allow the Holy Spirit to directly and lovingly impact our own lives, transfiguring us on the journey to restoring the likeness of God in our own hearts and minds. We read the mystics not to become smarter (worthy a goal though that may be), but rather to become, by God's grace, holy.

With this in mind, I strongly encourage you to read the mystics using the ancient monastic exercise known as *lectio divina*. *Lectio divina* means "sacred reading" and refers to a prayerful, meditative approach to reading sacred scripture that was first mentioned by Saint Benedict in his rule for monasteries and then more fully explained by a medieval monk, Guigo II, in his twelfth-century treatise *The Ladder of Monks*. Walter Hilton also mentions it in *The Scale of Perfection*. *Lectio* was originally intended specifically as a discipline for reading the Bible, and some purists still maintain that the Bible is the only appropriate book for *lectio*; but I believe the method of sacred reading can be used just as profitably with other spiritual writings, including the writings of the mystics. The purpose behind *lectio* is to allow the words we read to become part of us by weaving them into a larger practice that includes prayer, meditation, and contemplation. In this way, the reading becomes not just an exercise in gathering facts (information) but rather a tool for asking the Holy Spirit to enter into our lives and shape us into the person God calls us to be (formation). My wife has as the signature line in her emails, "Be the love you were created to be!" This is the goal of all creative spirituality, and of positive spiritual exercises like *lectio divina*.

The practice of *lectio* is really very simple. Whether you are reading the Bible, the writings of a great mystic, or some other spiritually nourishing text, begin with the intention that you are setting aside this time to grow closer to God. *The purpose of lectio is to grow closer to God, not to finish a reading assignment.* If you are a speed-reader or otherwise in the habit of plowing through books quickly, set aside your normal style of reading. This is not a race. It's a time to savor your desire for God (and God's yearning for you).

When practicing *lectio*, read only until a word or phrase seems to "jump out" and speak to you directly. At that point, stop reading. You might find that you get only a paragraph or even just a few sentences read before moving on to the next stages of the *lectio* process. That's fine! In fact, it's more than fine—it's good. *Lectio* works better when the reading is done slowly, deliberately, in a relaxed and unhurried way. It's a time to savor those words that invite you closer to God. It's a time to let God speak to you through those words.

Maybe you've only read a sentence or two; maybe you've read a page or two. If by then nothing has particularly jumped out at you, I'd recommend moving on anyway to the second stage, which is *meditatio* (meditation). This is not meditation in the sense of focusing your mind silently on a prayer word or your breath, but rather in the sense of pondering, or reflecting on, the words you have just read. Take some time to gently, thoughtfully review the reading you've just done, especially the words/phrases that seem to directly speak to you. Notice your feelings: did these words fill you with joy, or insight, or wonder, or did they leave you confused, angry, and filled with resistance? Any response is okay; it's your response. The purpose behind this meditation is to become more fully aware of, and present to, the way that these words you've just read seem to be speaking to you, directly, here and now.

Meditation leads to the third phase of *lectio*, which is *oratio* (praying). In a way, the entire process of *lectio divina* is a type of prayer, but the *oratio* stage is where we most directly respond to the words we've read, offering our own thoughts and words to God. Some people like to use this part of *lectio* to write in their journals; others prefer nonverbal activities such as dancing or drawing a picture. You can be creative or simply say your prayers; the point is to offer yourself to God—your thoughts, your feelings, your response to what you've just read. It's a way of opening yourself to the source of all life and love.

Another way of entering into *oratio* is by using our imagination. Ignatius of Loyola, the founder of the Jesuits, particularly recommended the imagination as a tool for encountering Jesus by visualizing ourselves entering into a scene from the Gospels. That can be especially useful as part of *lectio divina*, although the imagination can seek to communicate with God in an almost infinite variety of ways. Whether you feel most connected to God through language, through visualization, or through some other creative means, open your heart and mind to God in the way that's right for you.

Of course, God already knows everything that is taking place deep in our hearts and minds. But the act of praying is something we give not only to God but also to ourselves. It makes us more receptive, more open to the love and creative process that the Holy Spirit eagerly longs to give to us.

Whether your prayer lasts for five seconds or fifteen minutes, eventually you'll reach a point where you feel like you've shared all you have to say to God. This leads to the final (and to my mind, the most important) stage of *lectio*: *contemplatio* (contemplation), or resting in the deep silence of God. Think of it this way: *lectio* is reading about God, meditation is thinking about God, prayer is talking to God, and now comes contemplation, or listening to God, in silence. For most people, when we listen to God we encounter deep and restful silence. This is not a bad thing. God gives us silence so that He may speak to us at a level deeper than our conscious awareness. Resting in silence is a way to allow the Holy Spirit to touch our lives without us trying to control or manage the interaction. It's very humbling, but also deeply nourishing.

I could say much more about the *lectio divina* process, but this is enough to get you started. Here's the most important point: when we read the mystics, we are reading the wisdom of men and women who have encountered the splendor, the joy, the shimmering radiance, and the profound awe of the presence of God. By embracing this wisdom, we are invited by God to make ourselves available for a similar encounter in our own lives. We may not be a visionary like Julian of Norwich, a philosopher like Meister Eckhart, or a saint like Mother Teresa. Our relationship with God may be very simple and humble and down to earth. But it's still a real relationship, and if we let it, it can transfigure our lives, igniting in our hearts a living flame of love that both responds to, and is nourished by, the divine love that moves the sun and other stars. That's the adventure that the mystics call us to. So when we read their words, let's keep that promise in mind. The rest will be up to God.

Acknowledgments

This book is a companion volume to *The Big Book of Christian Mysticism*. I originally envisioned including a section in that book that would serve as a sort of who's who of mysticism, with entries for all the major figures, that gave biographical information, key teachings or ideas, and a representative quote or two. For a variety of reasons, that never came to pass, and so *The Big Book of Christian Mysticism* included only a list of significant mystics and contemplatives of the Christian tradition.

Here at last is my who's who. I've written this not as a scholar or an academic, but as a spiritual practitioner—which means this is not meant to be an encyclopedia of facts and figures, but really an invitation for you to discover the riches of mystical wisdom in order to cultivate your own marvelous and wonderful relationship with God.

In writing this book, I relied on the following resources; I list them here to encourage you to explore further if you so desire.

Over the years, a number of wonderful books have been published that offer historical overviews of the mystical tradition with insights into the most remarkable or significant wisdom keepers and teachers. Some of the books that have helped me to appreciate this tradition include *Mysticism* and *The Mystics of the Church* by Evelyn Underhill, *The Story of Mysticism* by Hilda Graef, *A History of Christian Spirituality* by Urban T. Holmes, *Christian Mystics* by Ursula King, *Two Worlds Are Ours* by John MacQuarrie, *Soundings in the Christian Mystical Tradition* by Harvey D. Egan, *The Oxford Dictionary of the Christian Church* edited by F. L. Cross, *The Study of Spirituality* edited by Cheslyn Jones, Geoffrey Wainwright, and Edward Yarnold, and two wonderful series: *The Presence of God* by Bernard McGinn, and *A History of Christian Spirituality* by Louis Bouyer, Jean Leclercq, and François Vandenbroucke.

I also must acknowledge the incredible Classics of Western Spirituality series of mystical writings published by Paulist Press. This collection of scholarly editions of mystical writings, translated into contemporary English, is absolutely essential for anyone wishing to explore the wisdom of the mystics. (In addition to Christian mystical texts, this series also includes Jewish, Sufi, and Native American writings.)

Online resources I've consulted include Christian Classics Ethereal Library, New Advent, Wikipedia, and Wikiquote, along with other websites that are documented in the notes.

Finally, there's no way that a project of this magnitude could have been completed without the benefit of an amazing library, with a wonderful and helpful staff: the John Bulow Campbell Library of the Columbia Theological Seminary in Decatur, Georgia.

Naturally, I have made every effort to be precise and careful in my description of the mystics, their lives, their significance, and their key ideas or teachings. But I'm only human, so I imagine that discerning and informed readers may spot a blunder here or there. I leave it to such eagle eyes to ferret out my errors. Write to me if you find any. And as one of my favorite musicians, Kate Bush, says, please "be kind to my mistakes."

Now I'd like to offer a few special words of thanks to those who, in big or small ways, have supported the creation of this book.

First, to my best friend, life partner, and beloved, Fran McColman—thank you for being there. Every day with you is a joyful day. I am honored to be your husband.

I appreciate Greg Brandenburgh, who planted the seed for this book, and Linda Roghaar, who watered it (and helped me stay on task). CeCe Balboni, Lerita Coleman Brown, Fr. Mark Horak, SJ, Kevin Johnson, Kurt Johnson, and especially Br. Elias Marechal, OCSO, all offered helpful insights and suggestions on various mystics included herein. Of course, any blemishes or errors in this book remain entirely my responsibility.

Many years ago (right after I graduated from high school), David Hamilton gave me a copy of Evelyn Underhill's *Mysticism*. That book changed my life. David, thank you for helping me to discern one of my great, abiding passions. Likewise, my gratitude goes out to Linda Smith, my eighth grade English teacher, whose encouragement helped a shy youth to embrace a lifelong love of language and writing.

Special props go to Fr. Thomas Francis, OCSO, Br. Cassian Russell, OCSO, Fr. Steve Yander, Malika and Paco Ambrosetti, Julie Hliboki, Georges Hoffmann, Rosary Mangano, Linda Mitchell, Jack Moran, Mike Morrell, Nancy and Dan O'Neill,

Kate Sheehan Roach, and Wendy Smith, for their friendship, advice, support, and spiritual encouragement.

Finally, many thanks to the numerous people who visit my blog, read my books, or attend retreats or classes with me. Your engagement with my work, your comments and questions, and your love for the Christian mystics makes this all worthwhile, and truly you are all my best and most faithful teachers. A deep bow of gratitude.

Carl McColman
Feast of the Visitation 2016
Clarkston, Georgia

Notes

Introduction

1. Evelyn Underhill, *Practical Mysticism* (New York: E. P. Dutton, 1960), 1–2.

2. See Thomas Dubay, *Fire Within: St. Teresa of Avila, St. John of the Cross, and the Gospel, on Prayer* (San Francisco: Ignatius Press, 1989), 3.

3. Karl Rahner, *Theological Investigations*, (Baltimore: Helicon Press, 1961), 149.

4. William McNamara, *Earthy Mysticism: Contemplation and the Life of Passionate Presence* (New York: Crossroad, 1983), ix.

5. The Cistercian monks are an order of monks founded in France in 1098. Several mystics, notably Bernard of Clairvaux and Thomas Merton, are Cistercians.

6. "Richard Rohr's Daily Meditation," email from the Center for Action and Contemplation, May 3, 2015.

7. See Evelyn Underhill, *The Mystics of the Church* (Cambridge, England: James Clarke, 1975); Hilda C. Graef, *The Story of Mysticism* (Garden City, NY: Doubleday, 1965); and Ursula King, *Christian Mystics: Their Lives and Legacies throughout the Ages* (Mahwah, NJ: Hidden Spring, 2001).

Chapter 1: Visionaries

1. Evelyn Underhill, *Mysticism: The Nature and Development of Spiritual Consciousness* (Oxford, NY: Oneworld Publishing, 1993), 268.

2. "Doctor, Convert, and Mystic: The Life and Work of Adrienne von Speyr," Ignatius Press, accessed October 21, 2015, *http://www.ignatiusinsight.com/authors/adrienne_von_speyr.asp*.

3. Adrienne von Speyr, *The Boundless God* (San Francisco: Ignatius Press, 2004), chapter 8.

4. *Birgitta of Sweden: Life and Selected Revelations* (New York, Paulist Press, 1990), 146.

5. *Elisabeth of Schönau: The Complete Works*, trans. Anne L. Clark (New York: Paulist Press, 2000), 46–47.

6. George MacDonald, *Unspoken Sermons*, Series One, "The New Name," accessed May 28, 2016, *http://www.online-literature.com/george-macdonald/unspoken-sermons/5/*.

7. J. Philip Newell, *Listening for the Heartbeat of God: A Celtic Spirituality* (New York: Paulist Press, 1997), 61.

8. *Hildegard of Bingen: Scivias*, trans. Mother Columba Hart and Jane Bishop (New York: Paulist Press, 1990), 161.

9. *Hildegard of Bingen*, trans. Hart and Bishop, 164.

10. *Maria Maddalena de' Pazzi: Selected Revelations*, trans. Armando Maggi (New York: Paulist Press, 2000), 59.

11. *Marie of the Incarnation: Selected Writings*, ed. Irene Mahoney (New York: Paulist Press, 1989), 202.

12. "The Assumption of Our Lady," Belgravia Catholic Church of St. Anne, Archdiocese of Johannesburg, last modified August 14, 2015, accessed October 8, 2015, *http://www.saintannes.co.za/Sts%20Mechtildis%20%26%20Gertrude.htm*.

13. Acts 22:6–11.

14. II Corinthians 12:3.

Chapter 2: Confessors

1. *Angela of Foligno: Complete Works*, trans. Paul Lachance (New York: Paulist Press, 1993), 234.

2. *Saint Augustine: Confessions*, trans. Henry Chadwick (Oxford: Oxford University Press, 2008), 3.

3. Dag Hammarskjöld, *Markings* (New York: Knopf, 1964), 91.

4. Hammarskjöld, *Markings*, 122.

5. Hammarskjöld, *Markings*, 174.

6. Hammarskjöld, *Markings*, 59.

7. *The Journal of George Fox*, ed. Rufus Matthew Jones (Richmond, IN: Friends United Press, 1983), 76.

8. *The Journal of George Fox*, 212.

9. *Henry Suso: The Exemplar, with Two German Sermons*, trans. and ed. Frank Tobin (New York: Paulist Press, 1989), 5.

10. *Henry Suso*, 86.

11. *Ignatius of Loyola: Spiritual Exercises and Selected Works*, ed. George E. Ganss (New York: Paulist Press, 1991), 109.

12. *John and Charles Wesley: Selected Prayers, Hymns, Journal Notes, Sermons, Letters and Treatises*, ed. Frank Whaling (New York: Paulist Press, 1981), 107.

13. *John and Charles Wesley*, 315.

14. *John and Charles Wesley*, 316.

15. Martin Thornton, *English Spirituality: An Outline of Ascetical Theology According to the English Pastoral Tradition* (Cambridge, MA: Cowley, 1986), 222.

16. *The Book of Margery Kempe: A New Translation*, trans. John Skinner (New York: Image Books/Doubleday, 1998), 74.

17. *On the Cosmic Mystery of Jesus Christ: Selected Writings from St. Maximus the Confessor*, trans. Paul M. Blowers and Robert Louis Wilken (Crestwood, NY: St. Vladimir's Seminary Press, 2003), 16.

18. *On the Cosmic Mystery of Jesus Christ*, 126.

19. *On the Cosmic Mystery of Jesus Christ*, 125–6.

20. Richard Wheatley, *The Life and Letters of Mrs. Phoebe Palmer* (New York: Garland Publishing, 1984), 39.

21. *Story of a Soul: The Autobiography of Saint Thérèse of Lisieux*, trans. John Clarke (Washington, DC: ICS Publications, 1996), xi.

22. *Story of a Soul*, 15.

23. Urban T. Holmes, *A History of Christian Spirituality: An Analytical Introduction* (New York: Seabury Press, 1980), 145.

24. *The Way of a Pilgrim and The Pilgrim Continues His Way*, trans. Helen Bacovcin (New York: Image Books, 2003), 10.

25. *The Way of a Pilgrim and The Pilgrim Continues His Way*, 75–6.

Chapter 3: Lovers

1. My source for this entry is Jerome Kroll and Roger de Ganck's "Beatrice of Nazareth: Psychiatric Perspectives on a Medieval Mystic," *Cistercian Studies Quarterly* XXIV, no. 4 (1989): 301–23.

2. *Bernard of Clairvaux: Selected Works* (New York: Paulist Press, 1987), 255.

3. *Bernard of Clairvaux*, 255.

4. *John and Charles Wesley*, 107.

5. Blaise Pascal and Honor Levi, *Pensées and Other Writings* (New York: Oxford University Press, 2008), 178.

6. Catherine of Siena, *The Dialogue*, trans. Suzanne Noffke (New York: Paulist Press, 1980), 65.

7. Harvey D. Egan, *An Anthology of Christian Mysticism* (Collegeville, MN: Liturgical Press, 1991), 556.

8. Gertrude of Helfta, *The Herald of Divine Love*, trans. and ed. Margaret Winkworth (New York: Paulist Press, 1993), 190.

9. Gertrude of Helfta, *The Herald of Divine Love*, 96–97.

10. *Gertrude the Great of Helfta: Spiritual Exercises*, trans. Gertrud Jaron Lewis and Jack Lewis (Kalamazoo, MI: Cistercian Publications, 1989), back cover.

11. *Gertrude the Great of Helfta*, 82–83.

12. Harvey D. Egan, *Soundings in the Christian Mystical Tradition* (Collegeville, MN: Liturgical Press, 2010), 113.

13. Hadewijch, *The Complete Works*, ed. Columba Hart (New York: Paulist Press, 1980), 272.

14. Hadewijch, *The Complete Works*, 84.

15. *Diary of Saint Maria Faustina Kowalska: Divine Mercy in My Soul* (Stockbridge, MA: Marian Press, 2005), paragraph 181.

16. Mechthild, *The Flowing Light of the Godhead*, ed. Frank J. Tobin (New York: Paulist Press, 1998), 52.

17. Mechthild, *The Flowing Light of the Godhead*, 102.

18. *The Oxford Dictionary of the Christian Church*, ed. F. L. Cross and Elizabeth A. Livingstone (New York: Oxford University Press, 1974), 1275.

19. George A. Maloney, *The Mystic of Fire and Light: St. Symeon the New Theologian* (Denville, NJ: Dimension Books, 1975).

20. *Divine Eros: Hymns of St. Symeon the New Theologian*, trans. Daniel K. Griggs (Crestwood, NY: St. Vladimir's Seminary Press, 2010).

21. Symeon the New Theologian, *The Discourses* (New York: Paulist Press, 1980), 205–6.

22. Symeon the New Theologian, *The Discourses*, 143.

23. Symeon the New Theologian, *The Discourses*, 148.

24. Symeon the New Theologian, *The Discourses*, 10.

25. Pauline Maud Matarasso, *The Cistercian World: Monastic Writings of the Twelfth Century* (London: Penguin, 1993), 115.

26. *The Works of William of St Thierry: Vol. 1: On Contemplating God, Prayer, Meditations* (Kalamazoo, MI: Cistercian Publications, 1977), 60–61.

Chapter 4: Poets

1. Johann Scheffler (Angelus Silesius), "Morgenstern in finst'rer Nacht," trans. Catherine Winkworth, from *Christian Singers of Germany* (1869). Public domain text accessed online March 9, 2016, *www.ccel.org/ccel/winkworth/singers.h44.html*.

2. C. S. Lewis, *Letters to Malcolm: Chiefly on Prayer: Reflections on the Intimate Dialogue between Man and God* (San Diego, Harcourt, 1992), 61.

3. Lewis, *Letters to Malcolm*, 62.

4. C. S. Lewis, *Till We Have Faces: A Myth Retold* (New York: Harcourt, Brace, 1957), 306–7.

5. C. S. Lewis and Pauline Baynes, *The Chronicles of Narnia* (New York: Harper Trophy, 2000), 243–4.

6. William McNamara, *Earthy Mysticism*, ix.

7. Caryll Houselander, *The Reed of God* (Allen, TX: Christian Classics, 1995), 116.

8. Houselander, *The Reed of God*, 28.

9. Houselander, *The Reed of God*, 119.

10. Underhill, *Mysticism*, 2.

11. Coventry Patmore, *The Rod, the Root, and the Flower* (Freeport, NY: Books for Libraries Press, 1968), 27 (Aurea Dicta XIII).

12. *The Poems of Coventry Patmore*, ed. Frederick Page (London: Oxford Editions of Standard Authors, 1949), 457.

13. Ephrem Syrus, *Hymns Against Heresies 22*, trans. Adam McCollum, accessed March 11, 2016, *www.archive.org/details /EphremSyrusHymnsAgainstHeresies22*.

14. *Ephrem the Syrian*, trans. Kathleen E. McVey (New York: Paulist Press, 1989) 371.

15. Evelyn Underhill, *Immanence: A Book of Verses* (London: J. M. Dent & Sons Ltd., 1912), 1.

16. "From *The Temple (1633)*, by George Herbert: Love (III)," Christian Classics Ethereal Library, accessed October 21, 2015, *www.ccel.org/h/herbert/temple/Love3.html*.

17. Simone Weil, *Waiting for God* (New York: Perennial, 2000), 27.

18. Jacopone da Todi, *Laud 90*, trans. Mrs. Theodore Beck, in *Jacopone da Todi* by Evelyn Underhill (London: J. M. Dent & Sons Ltd., 1919), 369.

19. *The Oxford Dictionary of the Christian Church*, 420.

20. *John Donne: Selections from* Divine Poems, *Sermons*, Devotions, *and Prayers*, ed. John E. Booty (New York: Paulist Press, 1990), 189.

21. John Donne, *Holy Sonnets*, last accessed March 11, 2016, *en.wikisource.org/wiki/Holy_Sonnets/Holy_Sonnet_15*.

22. *The Collected Works of Saint John of the Cross*, trans. Kieran Kavanaugh and Otilio Rodriguez (Washington, DC: ICS Publications, 1991), 78.

23. *The Collected Works of Saint John of the Cross*, 78.

24. John of the Cross, *Dark Night of the Soul*, trans. and ed. E. Allison Peers. Christian Classics Ethereal Library, last accessed March 11, 2016, *www.ccel.org/ccel/john_cross/dark_night.vi.html.*

25. James Charlton, *Non-dualism in Eckhart, Julian of Norwich and Traherne: A Theopoetic Reflection* (New York: Bloomsbury, 2013).

26. Thomas Traherne, "The Preparative," in *The Book of Restoration Verse,* ed. William Stanley Braithwaite (London: Duckworth and Company, 1909), 587.

27. Charlton, *Non-dualism in Eckhart*, 21.

28. Thomas Traherne, *Centuries* (Wilton, CT: Morehouse-Barlow, 1986), 228.

Chapter 5: Saints

1. *The Rule of St. Benedict: Latin & English*, trans. Luke Dysinger (Trabuco Canyon, CA: Source Books, 1997), 3.

2. *The Oxford Dictionary of the Christian Church*, 253.

3. Carol Flinders, *Enduring Grace: Living Portraits of Seven Women Mystics* (San Francisco, CA: HarperSanFrancisco, 1993), 142.

4. Catherine of Genoa, *Purgation and Purgatory: The Spiritual Dialogue* (New York: Paulist Press, 1980), 71.

5. Underhill, *Mysticism*, 396.

6. Edith Stein, *The Science of the Cross*, trans. Josephine Koeppel (Washington, DC: ICS Publications, 2002), 116–17.

7. St. Francis de Sales, *On the Love of God*, trans. John K. Ryan (Garden City, NY: Image Books, 1963), vol. 1, 74.

8. "Canticle of the Sun," translated by Matthew Arnold. Christian Classics Ethereal Library, last accessed March 14, 2016, *www.ccel.org /ccel/schaff/hcc5.ii.x.x.html?highlight=canticle,of,brother,sun#highli ght.*

9. Gregory of Narek, *Speaking with God from the Depths of the Heart: The Armenian Prayer Book of St. Gregory of Narek*, 3rd edition (Yerevan, Armenia: Vem Press, 2005), Prayer 34.

10. Gregory of Narek, *Speaking with God from the Depths of the Heart*, Prayer 25.

11. Gregory of Nyssa, *From Glory to Glory: Texts from Gregory of Nyssa's Mystical Writings*, ed. Jean Daniélou and Herbert Musurillo (Crestwood, NY: St. Vladimir's Seminary Press, 1979), 118.

12. Martin Laird, *Gregory of Nyssa and the Grasp of Faith: Union, Knowledge, and Divine Presence* (New York: Oxford University Press, 2004), 50.

13. Isaac of Nineveh, *The Ascetical Homilies of Saint Isaac the Syrian* (Boston: The Holy Transfiguration Monastery, 2011), 266.

14. C. S. Lewis, *The Great Divorce: A Dream* (San Francisco: HarperSanFrancisco, 2001), 72.

15. John Climacus, *The Ladder of Divine Ascent*, ed. and trans. Archimandrite Lazarus (Boston: The Holy Transfiguration Monastery, 1978), 92.

16. Climacus, *The Ladder of Divine Ascent*.

17. Quoted in Nicodemus, *A Handbook of Spiritual Counsel*, ed. Peter A. Chamberas (New York: Paulist Press, 1989), 168.

18. Nicodemus, *A Handbook of Spiritual Counsel*, 4.

19. Nicodemus, *A Handbook of Spiritual Counsel*, 167.

20. Nicodemus, *A Handbook of Spiritual Counsel*, 197.

21. *Albert and Thomas: Selected Writings*, trans. and ed. Simon Tugwell (New York: Paulist Press, 1988), 541.

22. *Mother Teresa: Come Be My Light: The Private Writings of the Saint of Calcutta*, ed. Brian Kolodiejchuk (New York: Doubleday, 2007), ix.

Chapter 6: Heretics

1. Underhill, *Mysticism*, 455.

2. *Clement of Alexandria*, trans. G. W. Butterworth (Cambridge, MA: Harvard University Press, 1919), 23.

3. Athanasius, *De Incarnatione*, 54. My translation.

4. William Harmless, *Mystics* (New York: Oxford University Press, 2008), 155.

5. *Evagrius Ponticus: The Praktikos and Chapters on Prayer*, ed. John Eudes Bamberger (Spencer, MA: Cistercian Publications, 1970), 66.

6. *Fénelon: Selected Writings*, ed. Chad Helms (New York: Paulist Press), 212–3.

7. *Fénelon*, 213.

8. Dr. Hans Lassen Martensen, *Jacob Boehme: His Life and Teaching or Studies in Theosophy*, trans. T. Rhys Evans (London: Hodder and Stoughton, 1885), 13.

9. Holmes, *A History of Christian Spirituality*, 128–29.

10. Holmes, *A History of Christian Spirituality*, 128–29.

11. Underhill, *Mysticism*, 96.

12. Holmes, *A History of Christian Spirituality*, 130.

13. *Genius of the Transcendent: Mystical Writings of Jakob Boehme*, trans. and ed. Michael L. Birkel and Jeff Bach (Boston: Shambhala, 2010), 33.

14. *Jeanne Guyon: Selected Writings*, trans. and ed. Dianne Guenin-Lelle and Ronney Mourad (New York: Paulist Press, 2012), 57.

15. J. Philip Newell, *Listening for the Heartbeat of God: A Celtic Spirituality* (New York: Paulist Press, 1997), 35.

16. *The Voice of the Eagle: The Heart of Celtic Christianity—John Scotus Eriugena's Homily on the Prologue to the Gospel of St. John*, trans. Christopher Bamford (Great Barrington, MA: Lindisfarne Books, 2000), 87.

17. Marguerite Porete, *The Mirror of Simple Souls*, ed. Ellen L. Babinsky (New York: Paulist Press, 1993), 107.

18. "Marguerite Porete," Wikipedia, last accessed October 22, 2015, *https://en.wikipedia.org/wiki/Marguerite_Porete*.

19. Meister Eckhart, *Selected Writings* (London: Penguin UK, 1994), 127–28.

20. *Meister Eckhart, the Essential Sermons, Commentaries, Treatises, and Defense*, trans. Edmund Colledge and Bernard McGinn (New York: Paulist Press, 1981), 208.

21. Eckhart, *Selected Writings*, 179.

22. Origen, *On First Principles*, trans. G. W. Butterworth, ed. John C. Cavadini (Notre Dame, IN: Ave Maria Press, 2013), 12–13.

23. "Warning Regarding the Writings of Father Teilhard de Chardin," Eternal World Television Network, last accessed October 6, 2015, *https://www.ewtn.com/library/CURIA/CDFTEILH.HTM*.

24. Pierre Teilhard de Chardin, *Hymn of the Universe* (New York: Harper & Row, 1965), 19.

25. Weil, *Waiting for God*, 22.

26. Weil, *Waiting for God*, 26.

27. Weil, *Waiting for God*, 27.

28. Diogenes Allen and Eric O. Springsted, *Spirit, Nature, and Community: Issues in the Thought of Simone Weil* (Albany, NY: State University of New York Press, 1994), 5.

29. Simone Weil, *Gravity and Grace* (New York: Routledge, 2002), 109.

30. Weil, *Gravity and Grace*, 109.

31. *Simone Weil*, ed. Eric O. Springsted (Maryknoll, NY: Orbis Books, 1998), 74.

32. A Trappist monk read an early draft of this manuscript to offer me feedback and suggestions; when he came to this sentence, he wrote in the margin of the manuscript, "Mine too."

33. *A Thomas Merton Reader*, ed. Thomas P. McDonnell (Garden City, NY: Image Books, 1974), 83.

34. *A Thomas Merton Reader*, 345–7.

35. Thomas Merton, *The Asian Journal of Thomas Merton*, ed. Naomi Burton, Brother Patrick Hart, and James Laughlin (New York: New Directions, 1975), 233–5.

Chapter 7: Wisdom Keepers

1. Thornton, *English Spirituality*, 156.

2. *Albert and Thomas*, 61.

3. *Albert and Thomas*, 186.

4. Egan, *Soundings in the Christian Mystical Tradition*, 345–46.

5. Bernard J. F. Lonergan, *Method in Theology* (New York: Herder and Herder, 1972), 273.

6. *Bonaventure*, ed. Ewert H. Cousins (New York: Paulist Press, 1978), 96–97.

7. Bonaventure, *The Mind's Road to God*, trans. George Boas, Christian Classics Ethereal Library, chapter 7, paragraph 6, last accessed March 15, 2016, *www.ccel.org/ccel/bonaventure/mindsroad.xii.html*.

8. *The Life of Teresa of Jesus: The Autobiography of Teresa of Ávila*, trans. and ed. E. Allison Peers (New York: Image Books, 2004), 80.

9. Richard Rohr, *The Naked Now: Learning to See As the Mystics See* (New York: Crossroad Publishing, 2009), 113.

10. Francisco de Osuna, *The Third Spiritual Alphabet*, trans. Mary E. Giles (New York: Paulist Press, 1983), 566.

11. Gregory Palamas, *The Triads*, ed. John Meyendorff (New York: Paulist Press, 1983), 69.

12. *Johannes Tauler: Sermons*, trans. Maria Shrady (New York, Paulist Press, 1985), 38.

13. *Johannes Tauler: Sermons*, 40.

14. *Johannes Tauler: Sermons*, 172.

15. Karl Rahner, *Concern for the Church* (New York: Crossroad, 1981), 149.

16. Egan, *An Anthology of Christian Mysticism*, 626.

17. Maggie Ross, *Silence: A User's Guide* (Eugene, OR: Cascade Books, 2014), 218.

18. *Nicholas of Cusa: Selected Spiritual Writings*, trans. H. Lawrence Bond (New York: Paulist Press, 2005), 206.

19. *Nicholas of Cusa*, 235.

20. *Nicholas of Cusa*, 247.

21. *Nicholas of Cusa*, 244.

22. Pseudo-Dionysius, *The Divine Names and The Mystical Theology*, trans. John D. Jones (Milwaukee, WI: Marquette University Press, 1980), 211.

23. William Grimes, "Raimon Panikkar, Catholic Theologian, Is Dead at 91," *New York Times*, September 4, 2010. Last accessed October 8, 2015, *http://www.nytimes.com/2010/09/05/us/05panikkar.html?_r=3&hpw*.

24. Raimon Panikkar, *Christophany: The Fullness of Man* (Maryknoll, NY: Orbis Books, 2004), 31.

25. Panikkar, *Christophany*, 41.

26. Panikkar, *Christophany*, 54.

27. Panikkar, *Christophany*, 57.

28. *Richard of St. Victor: The Twelve Patriarchs, The Mystical Ark, Book Three of the Trinity*, trans. Grover A. Zinn (New York: Paulist Press, 1979), 327.

29. *Richard of St. Victor*, 327.

30. William Law, *A Serious Call to a Devout and Holy Life: The Spirit of Love*, ed. P. G. Stanwood (New York: Paulist Press, 1978), 216.

31. Law, *A Serious Call to a Devout and Holy Life*, 358, 389.

Chapter 8: Soul Friends

1. *The Martyrology of Oengus the Culdee*, ed. and trans. Whitley Stokes (London: Henry Bradshaw Society, 1905), 65.

2. *Aelred of Rievaulx: Spiritual Friendship*, trans. Lawrence C. Braceland, ed. Marsha L. Dutton (Trappist, KY: Cistercian Publications, 2010), 89.

3. Brother Lawrence of the Resurrection, *The Practice of the Presence of God*, trans. John J. Delaney (Garden City, NY: Image Books, 1977), 69–70.

4. Friedrich von Hugel, *Spiritual Counsel and Letters*, ed. Douglas V. Steere (New York: Harper & Row, 1964), 56.

5. Howard Thurman, *Mysticism and the Experience of Love* (Wallingford, PA: Pendle Hill, 1961), 6.

6. Howard Thurman, *A Strange Freedom: The Best of Howard Thurman on Religious Experience and Public Life*, ed. Walter Earl Fluker and Catherine Tumber (Boston: Beacon Press, 1998), 110.

7. Gil Bailie, *Violence Unveiled: Humanity at the Crossroads* (New York: Crossroad, 1995), xv.

8. Jean-Pierre de Caussade, *Abandonment to Divine Providence*, ed. Dennis Billy (Notre Dame, IN: Ave Maria Press, 2010), 36.

9. de Caussade, *Abandonment to Divine Providence*, 40.

10. John Cassian, *The Conferences*, trans. Boniface Ramsey (New York: Paulist Press, 1997), 329.

11. John Cassian, *The Conferences*, 340.

12. John Cassian, *The Conferences*, 379.

13. Most Protestant and newer Catholic Bibles number the Psalms differently from the Douay-Rheims version. In such versions, this verse is Psalm 70:1.

14. *Prayer and Prophecy: The Essential Kenneth Leech*, ed. David Bunch and Angus Ritchie (New York: Seabury Books, 2009), 230.

15. Kenneth Leech, *Soul Friend: Spiritual Direction in the Modern World* (London: Darton, Longman and Todd, 1994), 174.

16. *Rufus Jones: Essential Writings*, ed. Kerry S. Walters (Maryknoll, NY: Orbis Books, 2001), 80.

17. *Rufus Jones*, 80.

18. Elaine A. Heath, *The Mystic Way of Evangelism: A Contemplative Vision for Christian Outreach* (Grand Rapids, MI: Baker Academic, 2008), 72–77.

19. Thomas R. Kelly, *A Testament of Devotion* (New York: Harper & Row, 1988), 77.

20. *Walter Hilton: The Scale of Perfection*, trans. John P. H. Clark and Rosemary Dorward (New York: Paulist Press, 1991), 225.

21. *Walter Hilton*, 274–5.

22. *Walter Hilton*, 273.

23. *Walter Hilton*, 87.

24. *Walter Hilton*, 87–88.

25. *The Cloud of Unknowing and Other Works*, trans. A. C. Spearing (London: Penguin, 2001), 21–22.

26. *The Cloud of Unknowing and Other Works*, 29.

27. *The Theologia Germanica of Martin Luther*, trans. Bengt Hoffman (New York: Paulist Press, 1980), 54.

28. *The Pilgrim's Tale*, trans. T. Allan Smith (New York: Paulist Press, 1999), 208–9.

29. *The Theologia Germanica of Martin Luther*, 134.

Chapter 9: Unitives

1. Abhishiktananda, *Prayer* (Norwich, England: Canterbury Press, 2006), 5.

2. Abhishiktananda, *Prayer*, 19.

3. Abhishiktananda, *Prayer*, 21.

4. Anthony de Mello, *One Minute Wisdom* (New York: Doubleday, 1988), 126.

5. *Anthony de Mello: Writings*, ed. William V. Dych (Maryknoll, NY: Orbis Books, 1999), 88.

6. Joseph Card. Ratzinger and Tarcisio Bertone, "Notification Concerning the Writings of Father Anthony de Mello, CJ," The Vatican, last accessed October 27, 2015, *http://www .vatican.va/roman_curia/congregations/cfaith/documents/ rc_con_cfaith_doc_19980624_demello_en.html*.

7. *Bede Griffiths: Essential Writings*, ed. Thomas Matus (Maryknoll, NY: Orbis Books, 2004), 27–28.

8. Quoted in Andrew Harvey, *The Essential Mystics: The Soul's Journey into Truth* (Edison, NJ: Castle Books, 1998), 215.

9. *The One Light: Bede Griffiths' Principal Writings*, ed. Bruno Barnhart (Springfield, IL: Templegate Publishers, 2001), 217.

10. Bruno Barnhart, *Second Simplicity: The Inner Shape of Christianity* (New York: Paulist Press, 1999), 17.

11. Barnhart, *Second Simplicity*, 18.

12. Barnhart, *Second Simplicity*, 237.

13. Barnhart, *Second Simplicity*, 16.

14. Barnhart, *Second Simplicity*, 36.

15. Gerald G. May, *Will and Spirit: A Contemplative Psychology* (San Francisco: Harper & Row, 1983), 46.

16. May, *Will and Spirit*, 3.

17. John O'Donohue, *Anam Ċara: A Book of Celtic Wisdom* (New York: Cliff Street Books, 1997), 7.

18. O'Donohue, *Anam Ċara*, 89.

19. O'Donohue, *Anam Ċara*, 89–90.

20. Underhill, *The Mystics of the Church*, 136–7.

21. *John Ruusbroec: The Spiritual Espousals and Other Works*, trans. James A. Wiseman (New York: Paulist Press, 1986), 11.

22. *John Ruusbroec*, 146.

23. *John Ruusbroec*, 146.

24. *John Ruusbroec*, 147.

25. Rohr, *The Naked Now*, 34.

26. Bertha Wilcox and Josef Neuner, "In Memoriam: Sara Grant, RSCJ," *The Bede Griffiths Sangha Newsletter* 12, no. 1 (2011): 4.

27. Sarah Grant, *Lord of the Dance* (Bangalore, India: Asian Trading Corporation, 1987), 32.

28. Wilcox and Neuner, "In Memoriam: Sara Grant, RSCJ," 5.

29. Thomas Keating, *Spirituality, Contemplation, and Transformation: Writings on Centering Prayer* (New York: Lantern Books, 2008), 12.

30. *The Thomas Keating Reader: Selected Writings on Centering Prayer from the Contemplative Outreach Newsletter* (New York: Lantern Books, 2012), 122.

31. Wayne Teasdale, *The Mystic Heart: Discovering a Universal Spirituality in the World's Religions* (Novato, CA: New World Library, 1999), 3.

32. Teasdale, *The Mystic Heart*, 23.

33. Willigis Jäger, S*earch for the Meaning of Life: Essays and Reflections on the Mystical Experience* (Liguori, MO: Liguori/Triumph, 2003), Kindle locations 789–790.

34. Willigis Jäger, *The Way to Contemplation: Encountering God Today* (New York: Paulist Press, 1986), 25.

Bibliography

Abhishiktananda. *Prayer.* Norwich, England: Canterbury Press, 2006.

Aelred of Rievaulx. *Aelred of Rievaulx: Spiritual Friendship.* Translated by Lawrence C. Braceland. Edited by Marsha L. Dutton. Trappist, KY: Cistercian Publications, 2010.

Allen, Diogenes, and Eric O. Springsted. *Spirit, Nature, and Community: Issues in the Thought of Simone Weil.* Albany, NY: State University of New York Press, 1994.

Angela of Foligno. *Angela of Foligno: Complete Works.* Translated by Paul Lachance. New York: Paulist Press, 1993.

Augustine of Hippo. *Saint Augustine: Confessions.* Translated by Henry Chadwick. Oxford: Oxford University Press, 2008.

Bailie, Gil. *Violence Unveiled: Humanity at the Crossroads.* New York: Crossroad, 1995.

Barnhart, Bruno. *Second Simplicity: The Inner Shape of Christianity.* New York: Paulist Press, 1999.

Benedict of Nursia. *The Rule of St. Benedict: Latin & English.* Translated by Luke Dysinger. Trabuco Canyon, CA: Source Books, 1997.

Bernard of Clairvaux. *Bernard of Clairvaux: Selected Works.* Translated by G. R. Evans. New York: Paulist Press, 1987.

Birgitta of Sweden. *Birgitta of Sweden: Life and Selected Revelations.* Edited by Marguerite Tjader Harris. Translated by Albert Ryle

Kezel. New York: Paulist Press, 1990.

Boehme, Jakob. *Genius of the Transcendent: Mystical Writings of Jakob Boehme.* Translated and edited by Michael L. Birkel and Jeff Bach. Boston: Shambhala, 2010.

Bonaventure. *Bonaventure.* Edited by Ewert H. Cousins. New York: Paulist Press, 1978.

Braithwaite, William Stanley. *The Book of Restoration Verse.* London: Duckworth and Company, 1909.

Brother Lawrence of the Resurrection. *The Practice of the Presence of God.* Translated by John J. Delaney. Garden City, NY: Image Books, 1977.

Cassian, John. *The Conferences.* Translated by Boniface Ramsey. New York: Paulist Press, 1997.

Catherine of Genoa. *Purgation and Purgatory: The Spiritual Dialogue.* New York: Paulist Press, 1979.

Catherine of Siena. *The Dialogue.* Translated by Suzanne Noffke. New York: Paulist Press, 1980.

Charlton, James. *Non-dualism in Eckhart, Julian of Norwich and Traherne: A Theopoetic Reflection.* New York: Bloomsbury, 2013.

Climacus, John. *The Ladder of Divine Ascent.* Boston: The Holy Transfiguration Monastery, 1978.

Clement of Alexandria. *Clement of Alexandria.* Translated by G. W. Butterworth. Cambridge, MA: Harvard University Press, 1919.

da Todi, Jacopone. *The Lauds.* Translated by Serge Hughes and Elizabeth Hughes. New York: Paulist Press, 1982.

de Caussade, Jean-Pierre. *Abandonment to Divine Providence.* Edited by Dennis Billy. Notre Dame, IN: Ave Maria Press, 2010.

de l'Incarnation, Marie. *Marie of the Incarnation: Selected Writings.* Edited by Irene Mahoney. New York: Paulist Press, 1989.

de Mello, Anthony. *Anthony de Mello: Writings.* Edited by William V. Dych. Maryknoll, NY: Orbis Books, 1999.

———. *One Minute Wisdom.* New York: Doubleday, 1988.

de Osuna, Francisco. *The Third Spiritual Alphabet.* Translated by

Mary E. Giles. New York: Paulist Press, 1983.

de'Pazzi, Maria Maddalena. *Maria Maddalena de' Pazzi: Selected Revelations*. Translated by Armando Maggi. New York: Paulist Press, 2000.

Donne, John. *John Donne: Selections from Divine Poems, Sermons, Devotions, and Prayers*. Edited by John E. Booty. New York: Paulist Press, 1990.

Dubay, Thomas. *Fire Within: St. Teresa of Avila, St. John of the Cross, and the Gospel, on Prayer*. San Francisco: Ignatius Press, 1989.

Eckhart, Meister. *Meister Eckhart: the Essential Sermons, Commentaries, Treatises, and Defense*. Translated by Edmund Colledge and Bernard McGinn. New York: Paulist Press, 1981.

———. *Selected Writings*. London, UK: Penguin, 1994.

Egan, Harvey D. *An Anthology of Christian Mysticism*. Collegeville, MN: Liturgical Press, 1991.

———. *Soundings in the Christian Mystical Tradition*. Collegeville, MN: Liturgical Press, 2010.

Elisabeth of Schönau. *Elisabeth of Schönau: The Complete Works*. Translated by Anne L. Clark. New York: Paulist Press, 2000.

Ephrem the Syrian. *Ephrem the Syrian: Hymns*. Translated by Kathleen E. McVey. New York: Paulist Press, 1989.

Eriugena, John Scotus. *The Voice of the Eagle: The Heart of Celtic Christianity—John Scotus Eriugena's Homily on the Prologue to the Gospel of St. John*. Translated by Christopher Bamford. Great Barrington, MA: Lindisfarne Books, 2000.

Evagrius Ponticus. *Evagrius Ponticus: The Praktikos and Chapters on Prayer*. Edited by John Eudes Bamberger. Spencer, MA: Cistercian Publications, 1970.

Fénelon, François. *Fénelon: Selected Writings*. Edited by Chad Helms. New York: Paulist Press, 2006.

Flinders, Carol. *Enduring Grace: Living Portraits of Seven Women Mystics*. San Francisco, CA: HarperSanFrancisco, 1993.

Fox, George. *The Journal of George Fox*. Edited by Rufus M. Jones.

Richmond, IN: Friends United Press, 1983.

Francis of Assisi. *Francis and Clare: The Complete Works.*
Translated by Regis J. Armstrong and Ignatius C. Brady. New York:
Paulist Press, 1982.

Gertrude of Helfta. *Gertrude the Great of Helfta: Spiritual Exercises.*
Translated by Gertrud Jaron Lewis and Jack Lewis. Kalamazoo, MI:
Cistercian Publications, 1989.

———. *The Herald of Divine Love.* Translated and edited by Margaret
Winkworth. New York: Paulist Press, 1993.

Graef, Hilda C. *The Story of Mysticism.* Garden City, NY: Doubleday,
1965.

Grant, Sarah. *Lord of the Dance.* Bangalore, India: Asian Trading
Corporation, 1987.

Gregory of Narek. *Speaking with God from the Depths of the Heart:
The Armenian Prayer Book of St. Gregory of Narek.* Third edition.
Yerevan, Armenia: Vem Press, 2005.

Gregory of Nyssa. *From Glory to Glory: Texts from Gregory of Nyssa's
Mystical Writings.* Edited by Jean Daniélou and Herbert Musurillo.
Crestwood, NY: St. Vladimir's Seminary Press, 1979.

Griffiths, Bede. *The One Light: Bede Griffiths' Principal Writings.*
Edited by Bruno Barnhart. Springfield, IL: Templegate Publishers,
2001.

Griffiths, Bede, and Thomas Matus. *Bede Griffiths: Essential
Writings.* Maryknoll, NY: Orbis Books, 2004.

Guigo II. *The Ladder of Monks: A Letter on the Contemplative Life
and Twelve Meditations.* Edited by Edmund Colledge. Kalamazoo,
MI: Cistercian Publications, 1981.

Guyon, Jeanne. *Jeanne Guyon: Selected Writings.* Translated and
edited by Dianne Guenin-Lelle and Ronney Mourad. New York:
Paulist Press, 2012.

Hadewijch. *The Complete Works.* Edited by Columba Hart. New
York: Paulist Press, 1980.

Hammarskjöld, Dag. *Markings.* New York: Knopf, 1964.

Harmless, William. *Mystics.* New York: Oxford University Press,
2008.

Harvey, Andrew. *The Essential Mystics: The Soul's Journey into Truth.* Edison, NJ: Castle Books, 1998.

Heath, Elaine A. *The Mystic Way of Evangelism: A Contemplative Vision for Christian Outreach.* Grand Rapids, MI: Baker Academic, 2008.

Hildegard of Bingen. *Hildegard of Bingen: Scivias.* Translated by Mother Columba Hart and Jane Bishop. New York: Paulist Press, 1990.

Hilton, Walter. *Walter Hilton: The Scale of Perfection.* Translated by John P. H. Clark and Rosemary Dorward. New York: Paulist Press, 1991.

Holmes, Urban T. *A History of Christian Spirituality: An Analytical Introduction.* New York: Seabury Press, 1980.

Houselander, Caryll. *The Reed of God.* Allen, TX: Christian Classics, 1995.

Ignatius. *Ignatius of Loyola: Spiritual Exercises and Selected Works.* Edited by George E. Ganss. New York: Paulist Press, 1991.

Isaac the Syrian. *The Ascetical Homilies of Saint Isaac the Syrian.* Boston, MA: The Holy Transfiguration Monastery, 2011.

Jäger, Willigis. *Search for the Meaning of Life: Essays and Reflections on the Mystical Experience.* Liguori, MO: Liguori/Triumph, 2003.

———. *The Way to Contemplation: Encountering God Today.* New York: Paulist Press, 1986.

John of the Cross. *The Collected Works of Saint John of the Cross.* Washington, DC: ICS Publications, 1991.

———. *Dark Night of the Soul.* Translated by E. Allison Peers. New York: Image Books, 1959.

Jones, Rufus Matthew. *Rufus Jones: Essential Writings.* Edited by Kerry S. Walters. Maryknoll, NY: Orbis Books, 2001.

Keating, Thomas. *Spirituality, Contemplation and Transformation: Writings on Centering Prayer.* New York: Lantern Books, 2008.

———. *The Thomas Keating Reader: Selected Writings on Centering Prayer from the Contemplative Outreach Newsletter.* New York: Lantern Books, 2012.

Kelly, Thomas R. *A Testament of Devotion.* New York: Harper & Row, 1988.

Kempe, Margery. *The Book of Margery Kempe: A New Translation.* Translated by John Skinner. New York: Image Books, 1998.

Kowalska, Maria Faustina. *Diary of Saint Maria Faustina Kowalska: Divine Mercy in My Soul.* Stockbridge, MA: Marian Press, 2005.

King, Ursula. *Christian Mystics: Their Lives and Legacies throughout the Ages.* Mahwah, NJ: Hidden Spring, 2001.

Laird, Martin. *Gregory of Nyssa and the Grasp of Faith: Union, Knowledge, and Divine Presence.* New York: Oxford University Press, 2004.

Law, William. *A Serious Call to a Devout and Holy Life: The Spirit of Love.* Edited by P. G. Stanwood. New York: Paulist Press, 1978.

Leech, Kenneth. *Prayer and Prophecy: The Essential Kenneth Leech.* Edited by David Bunch and Angus Ritchie. New York: Seabury Books, 2009.

———. *Soul Friend: Spiritual Direction in the Modern World.* London: Darton, Longman and Todd, 1994.

Lewis, C. S. *The Great Divorce: A Dream.* San Francisco: HarperSanFrancisco, 2001.

———. *Letters to Malcolm: Chiefly on Prayer: Reflections on the Intimate Dialogue between Man and God.* San Diego: Harcourt, 1992.

———. *Till We Have Faces: A Myth Retold.* New York: Harcourt, Brace, 1957.

Lewis, C. S., and Pauline Baynes. *The Chronicles of Narnia.* New York: Harper Trophy, 2000.

Light from Light: An Anthology of Christian Mysticism. Edited by Louis Dupré and James A. Wiseman. New York: Paulist Press, 2001.

Llull, Ramon. *Doctor Illuminatus: A Ramon Llull Reader.* Edited by Anthony Bonner. Princeton, NJ: Princeton University Press, 1993.

Lonergan, Bernard J. F. *Method in Theology.* New York: Herder and Herder, 1972.

Luther, Martin. *The Theologia Germanica of Martin Luther.* Translated by Bengt Runo Hoffman. New York: Paulist Press, 1980.

MacDonald, George. *Unspoken Sermons, Series I, II, and*

III. Full text available at *http://www.online-literature.com/ george-macdonald/unspoken-sermons/*.

Magnus, Albertus, and Saint Thomas Aquinas. *Albert and Thomas: Selected Writings.* Translated and edited by Simon Tugwell. New York: Paulist Press, 1988.

Maloney, George A. *The Mystic of Fire and Light: St. Symeon the New Theologian.* Denville, NJ: Dimension Books, 1975.

Martensen, Hans Lassen, and T. Rhys Evans. *Jacob Boehme: His Life and Teaching or Studies in Theosophy.* London: Hodder and Stoughton, 1885. *https://archive.org/details/ jacobboehmehisli00mart*.

The Martyrology of Oengus the Culdee. Edited and translated by Whitley Stokes. London: Henry Bradshaw Society, 1905.

Matarasso, Pauline Maud. *The Cistercian World: Monastic Writings of the Twelfth Century.* New York: Penguin Books, 1993.

Maximus the Confessor. *On the Cosmic Mystery of Jesus Christ: Selected Writings from St. Maximus the Confessor.* Translated by Paul M. Blowers and Robert Louis Wilken. Crestwood, NY: St. Vladimir's Seminary Press, 2003.

May, Gerald G. *Will and Spirit: A Contemplative Psychology.* San Francisco: Harper & Row, 1983.

McGinn, Bernard. *The Essential Writings of Christian Mysticism.* New York: Modern Library, 2006.

McNamara, William. *Earthy Mysticism: Contemplation and the Life of Passionate Presence.* New York: Crossroad, 1983.

Mechthild of Magdeburg. *Mechthild of Magdeburg: The Flowing Light of the Godhead.* Edited by Frank J. Tobin. New York: Paulist Press, 1998.

Merton, Thomas. *The Asian Journal of Thomas Merton.* New York: New Directions Publishing, 1975.

———. *A Thomas Merton Reader.* Edited by Thomas P. McDonnell. Garden City, NY: Image Books, 1974.

Newell, J. Philip. *Listening for the Heartbeat of God: A Celtic Spirituality.* New York: Paulist Press, 1997.

Nicholas of Cusa. *Nicholas of Cusa: Selected Spiritual Writings.* Translated by H. Lawrence Bond. New York: Paulist Press, 2005.

Nicodemus of the Holy Mountain. *Nicodemus of the Holy Mountain: A Handbook of Spiritual Counsel.* Edited by Peter A. Chamberas. New York: Paulist Press, 1989.

O'Donohue, John. *Anam Ċara: A Book of Celtic Wisdom.* New York: Cliff Street Books, 1997.

Origen. *On First Principles.* Translated by G. W. Butterworth. Notre Dame, IN: Ave Maria Press, 2013.

Origen: Spirit and Fire—A Thematic Anthology of His Writings. Translated by Robert J. Daly. Edited by Hans Urs von Balthasar. Washington: Catholic University of America Press, 1984.

The Oxford Dictionary of the Christian Church. Edited by F. L. Cross and Elizabeth A. Livingstone. New York: Oxford University Press, 1974.

Palamas, Gregory. *The Triads.* Edited by John Meyendorff. New York: Paulist Press, 1983.

Panikkar, Raimon. *Christophany: The Fullness of Man.* Maryknoll, NY: Orbis Books, 2004.

Pascal, Blaise, and Honor Levi. *Pensées and Other Writings.* New York: Oxford University Press, 2008.

Patmore, Coventry. *The Poems of Coventry Patmore.* Edited by Frederick Page. London: Oxford Editions of Standard Authors, 1949.

———. *The Rod, the Root, and the Flower.* Freeport, NY: Books for Libraries Press, 1968.

Porete, Marguerite. *The Mirror of Simple Souls.* Edited by Ellen L. Babinsky. New York: Paulist Press, 1993.

Pseudo-Dionysius. *The Divine Names and The Mystical Theology.* Translated by John D. Jones. Milwaukee, WI: Marquette University Press, 1980.

Rahner, Karl. *Concern for the Church.* New York: Crossroad, 1981.

———. *The Mystical Way in Everyday Life.* Maryknoll, NY: Orbis Books, 2010.

———. *Theological Investigations*. Baltimore, MD: Helicon Press, 1961.

Richard of St. Victor. *Richard of St. Victor, The Twelve Patriarchs, The Mystical Arks, Book Three of the Trinity*. Translated by Grover A. Zinn. New York: Paulist Press, 1979.

Ridler, Anne, and Thomas Traherne. *Poems, Centuries and Three Thanksgivings*. New York: Oxford University Press, 1966.

Rohr, Richard. *The Naked Now: Learning to See As the Mystics See*. New York: Crossroad, 2009.

Ross, Maggie. *Silence: A User's Guide*. Eugene, OR: Cascade Books, 2014.

Ruusbroec, John. *John Ruusbroec: The Spiritual Espousals and Other Works*. Translated by James A. Wiseman. New York: Paulist Press, 1986.

Silesius, Angelus. *The Cherubinic Wanderer*. Translated by Maria Shrady. Edited by Josef Schmidt. New York: Paulist Press, 1986.

Stein, Edith. *The Science of the Cross*. Translated by Josephine Koeppel. Washington, DC: ICS Publications, 2002.

St. Francis de Sales. *On the Love of God*. Translated by John K. Ryan. 2 volumes. Garden City, NY: Image Books, 1963.

St-Thierry, William. *The Works of William of St-Thierry, Volume 1: On Contemplating God, Prayer, Meditations*. Kalamazoo, MI: Cistercian Publications, 1977.

Suso, Henry. *Henry Suso: The Exemplar, with Two German Sermons*. Translated by Frank Tobin. New York: Paulist Press, 1989.

Symeon the New Theologian. *The Discourses*. New York: Paulist Press, 1980.

———. *Divine Eros: Hymns of St. Symeon the New Theologian*. Translated by Daniel K. Griggs. Crestwood, NY: St. Vladimir's Seminary Press, 2010.

Tauler, Johannes. *Johannes Tauler: Sermons*. Translated by Maria Shrady. New York: Paulist Press, 1985.

Teasdale, Wayne. *The Mystic Heart: Discovering a Universal*

Spirituality in the World's Religions. Novato, CA: New World Library, 1999.

Teilhard de Chardin, Pierre. *Hymn of the Universe.* New York: Harper & Row, 1965.

Teresa of Ávila. *The Life of Teresa of Jesus: The Autobiography of Teresa of Ávila.* Translated and edited by E. Allison Peers. New York: Image Books, 2004.

Teresa of Calcutta. *Mother Teresa: Come Be My Light: The Private Writings of the Saint of Calcutta.* Edited by Brian Kolodiejchuk. New York: Doubleday, 2007.

Thérèse of Lisieux. *Story of a Soul: The Autobiography of Saint Thérèse of Lisieux.* Translated by John Clarke. Washington, DC: ICS Publications, 1996.

Thornton, Martin. *English Spirituality: An Outline of Ascetical Theology According to the English Pastoral Tradition.* Cambridge, MA: Cowley, 1986.

Thurman, Howard. *Mysticism and the Experience of Love.* Wallingford, PA: Pendle Hill, 1961.

———. *A Strange Freedom: The Best of Howard Thurman on Religious Experience and Public Life.* Edited by Walter Earl Fluker and Catherine Tumber. Boston: Beacon Press, 1998.

Traherne, Thomas. *Centuries.* Wilton, CT: Morehouse-Barlow, 1986.

Underhill, Evelyn. *Immanence: A Book of Verses.* London: J. M. Dent & Sons Ltd., 1912.

———. *Jacopone da Todi: Poet and Mystic.* London: J. M. Dent & Sons Ltd., 1919.

———. *Mysticism: The Nature and Development of Spiritual Consciousness.* New York: Oneworld Publishing, 1993.

———. *The Mystics of the Church.* Cambridge, England: James Clarke, 1975.

———. *Practical Mysticism.* New York: E. P. Dutton, 1960.

The Way of a Pilgrim and The Pilgrim Continues His Way. Translated by Helen Bacovcin. New York: Image Books, 2003.

von Hügel, Friedrich. *Spiritual Counsel and Letters.* Edited by Douglas V. Steere. New York: Harper & Row, 1964.

von Speyr, Adrienne. *The Boundless God.* San Francisco: Ignatius Press, 2004.

Weil, Simone. *Gravity and Grace.* New York: Routledge, 2002.

———. *Simone Weil.* Edited by Eric O. Springsted. Maryknoll, NY: Orbis Books, 1998.

———. *Waiting for God.* New York: Perennial, 2000.

Wesley, John. *John and Charles Wesley: Selected Prayers, Hymns, Journal Notes, Sermons, Letters and Treatises.* Edited by Frank Whaling. New York: Paulist Press, 1981.

Wheatley, Richard. *The Life and Letters of Mrs. Phoebe Palmer.* New York: Garland, 1984.

ABOUT THE AUTHOR

Carl McColman is a contemplative writer, speaker, retreat leader and spiritual companion. He is the author of *Answering the Contemplative Call*, *The Big Book of Christian Mysticism* and *Befriending Silence*.

McColman is a life-professed Lay Cistercian (a layperson under formal spiritual guidance of Cistercian monks) affiliated with the Trappist Monastery of the Holy Spirit in Conyers, Georgia, USA. He first received formation in the practice of Christian spirituality and contemplative leadership through the Shalem Institute for Spiritual Formation and learned the art of spiritual direction through the Institute of Pastoral Studies.

www.carlmccolman.net

Notes

Notes

HAY HOUSE
Look within

Join the conversation about latest products, events, exclusive offers and more.

 Hay House UK

 @HayHouseUK

 @hayhouseuk

 healyourlife.com

We'd love to hear from you!